DATE DUE

DEMCO 38-296

The Distorted Past

A Reinterpretation of Europe

THE MAKING OF EUROPE
Series Editor: Jacques Le Goff

The Making of Europe series is published jointly by five European publishers - Beck in Germany, Blackwell in Great Britain and the United States, Crítica in Spain, Laterza in Italy and Le Seuil in France. Each book is published in all five languages. Its aim is to publish informed, readable and provocative accounts of the central themes in the history of the European peoples, nations and cultures within a wide international context. The authors are distinguished scholars drawn from all over the world.

Published

The European City
Leonardo Benevolo

The Search for the Perfect Language
Umberto Eco

The Distorted Past
A Reinterpretation of Europe
Josep Fontana

The Enlightenment
Ulrich Im Hof

Europe and the Sea
Michel Mollat du Jourdin

The Culture of Food
Massimo Montanari

The Peasantry of Europe
Werner Rösener

The European Revolutions 1492–1992
Charles Tilly

In preparation

Democracy in European History
Maurice Agulhon

Migration and Culture
Klaus Bade

Women in European History
Gisela Bok

Divergent Christendoms
Peter Brown

The European Renaissance
Peter Burke

Europe and Islam
Franco Cardini

Literacy in European History
Roger Chartier

Nature and Culture
Robert Delort

The Origins of European Individualism
Aaron Gurevitch

The Law in European History
Peter Landau

The University in European History
Jacques Le Goff

The First European Revolution, 900–1200
R. I. Moore

The Frontier in European History
Krzysztof Pomian

The Birth of Modern Science
Paolo Rossi

State and Nation
Hagen Schulze

The Distorted Past

A Reinterpretation of Europe

Josep Fontana

Translated by Colin Smith

BLACKWELL
Oxford UK & Cambridge USA

Copyright © Josep Fontana 1995
English translation © Basil Blackwell Ltd 1995

First published in 1995 by Blackwell Publishers and by four other
publishers: © 1995 Beck, Munich (German); © 1994 Crítica, Barcelona
(Spanish); © 1995 Éditions du Seuil, Paris (French); © 1995 Laterza,
Rome and Bari (Italian).

publishing imprint of
well Ltd
y Road
1JF, UK

vell Inc.
Street
asetts 02142, USA

British Library Cataloguing in Publication Data
A CIP catalogue record for this book is available from the British Library.

Library of Congress Cataloging-in-Publication Data

Fontana i Làzaro, Josep.
The distorted past / Josep Fontana ; translated by
Colin Smith.
p.   cm. – (The making of Europe)
Includes bibliographical references (p.) and index.
ISBN 0–631–17622–5 (acid-free paper)
1. Europe – Historiography.   I. Title.   II. Series.
D13.5.E85F66   1995
940'.072 – d20   94–39077
CIP

Typeset in 11½ on 13 pt Sabon Symposia by Apex Products, Singapore
Printed in Great Britain by T. J. Press Ltd. Padstow, Cornwall

This book is printed on acid-free paper.

Contents

Series Editor's Preface   vi

1.   The Barbarian Mirror   1
2.   The Christian Mirror   20
3.   The Feudal Mirror   35
4.   The Devil's Mirror   54
5.   The Rural Mirror   74
6.   The Courtly Mirror   93
7.   The Savage Mirror   112
8.   The Mirror of Progress   128
9.   The Mirror of the Mob   145
10. Outside the Hall of Mirrors   161

Annotated Bibliography of Essential References   171

Index   208

Series Editor's Preface

Europe is in the making. This is both a great challenge and one that can be met only by taking the past into account – a Europe without history would be orphaned and unhappy. Yesterday conditions today; today's actions will be felt tomorrow. The memory of the past should not paralyse the present: when based on understanding it can help us to forge new friendships and guide us towards progress.

Europe is bordered by the Atlantic, Asia and Africa, its history and geography inextricably entwined, and its past comprehensible only within the context of the world at large. The territory retains the name given it by the ancient Greeks, and the roots of its heritage may be traced far into prehistory. It is on this foundation – rich and creative, united yet diverse – that Europe's future will be built.

The Making of Europe is the joint initiative of five publishers of different languages and nationalities: Beck in Munich; Blackwell in Oxford; Critica in Barcelona; Laterza in Rome; and le Seuil in Paris. Its aim is to describe the evolution of Europe, presenting the triumphs but not concealing the difficulties. In their efforts to achieve accord and unity the nations of Europe have faced discord, division and conflict. It is no purpose of this series to conceal these problems: those committed to the European enterprise will not succeed if their view of the future is unencumbered by an understanding of the past.

The title of the series is thus an active one: the time is yet to come when a synthetic history of Europe will be possible. The books we shall publish will be the work of leading historians, by no means all European. They will address crucial aspects of European history in every field – political, economic, social, religious and cultural. They will draw on that long historiographical tradition which stretches back to Herodotus, as well as on those conceptions and ideas which have transformed historical enquiry in the recent decades of the twentieth century. They will write readably for a wide public.

Our aim is to consider the key questions confronting those involved in Europe's making, and at the same time to satisfy the curiosity of the world at large: in short, who are the Europeans? where have they come from? whither are they bound?

Jacques Le Goff

1

The Barbarian Mirror

When was Europe born? The question is unclear, since it might refer without differentiation to the first settlement of humans upon the geographical space we now call Europe, to the appearance of distinctive cultural forms, or to the rise of a collective consciousness which eventually gave its present name to that space, to people living in it and to their culture.

This territory – a corner of the great continental mass dominated in size by Asia – cannot in itself serve as a characterizing element, since it has never had plain physical boundaries. The Greeks, as also the Egyptians or the Mesopotamians, believed that the Earth was a large island surrounded on all sides by 'the river of the Ocean' which 'barks around the globe'. Such is the image which Hephaestus (Vulcan) placed on Achilles' shield and which the first circular maps of the world reproduced.

As travellers' accounts added new details, this image of the world was enlarged and its limits moved further out, filling up with monsters and portents. The block of land was then divided into three parts: Europe, Asia, and Africa. The sea separated Europe and Africa, but the frontier with Asia – generally set along the Bosphorus and the course of the River Don – corresponded more to cultural than to geographical criteria.

Equally, there is nothing special or characteristic about the first European settlers. It is assumed than man reached these lands from Africa (perhaps also from Asia, as is suggested by the finding in Georgia of a hominid who lived more than 1,500,000 years ago), in a series of migrations. The last of these, the only one which has left descendants, was that of *Homo sapiens sapiens*, this taking place some 30,000 or 40,000 years ago. This means that although there were settlers at very much earlier dates – perhaps 650,000 years ago – the first Europeans we can consider as our certain biological ancestors are almost recent arrivals.

As for what we call our civilization, its origins spring from the group of advances made, between 8,000 and 7,000 years before our era, in the Near East, predicated upon an agriculture based on the domestication of certain plants and animals, and on the foundation of the first cities. The process of domestication went further than having merely economic consequences, since the adoption of more intensive techniques locked people into political and social structures on which they came to depend. Genetic evidence seems to show that agriculture spread very slowly from that first focus towards the west, moving at a speed of one kilometre a year (it took 4,000 years to reach the extreme west of Europe). The lands across which this new and more efficient form of food production advanced, bringing with it species unknown in the native fauna and flora, were already inhabited by a population of hunters and gatherers who depended above all on woodland. It was a population which first lived beside the farmers (the Basque language might have proceeded from that of the last Mesolithic hunters) and which eventually joined the old ways of assuring subsistence to the new ones in order to make a synthesis of the two.

The evidence for a cross-bred genesis contrasts with the traditional view of our history, which has striven to isolate from its context what was genuinely European in order to explain the whole of its later development in terms of unique and superior origins – origins, so the story goes, that eventually imposed themselves after a struggle against the retrograde threats posed by the various Asiatic and African invaders.

This view originated in the image which the Greeks elaborated about themselves, as they peered into the distorting mirror held up by the Asiatic barbarian – a counter-figure expressly invented so that it could serve as a contrast – at the same time as they constructed a history which legitimized their identity. Europeans of the late eighteenth and early nineteenth centuries, keen to define themselves in contrast to the 'primitive' and the 'savage', took the image up again. In Prussia and Great Britain it was then resolved to base education on the study of classical Antiquity and to justify the mass of cultural and social values of the established order by presenting them as the legacy of an idealized Greece.

At the heart of the Greek myth are the wars of the Medes. It has been said that 'faced with the Persian menace, Greece discovered its identity'. The Greeks were not integrated into a common space and did not obey a common ruler. There was little other than the language to unite them, and even this presented notable dialectal differences; for this reason it was not sufficient to nurture that sense of community which is expressed by *hellenikón* ('the Greeks' collectively), since this included a community spread beyond present-day geographical Greece into European lands and along the coasts of Asia.

It was this same difficulty about definition which was to push them into inventing, as a mirror in which to view themselves in order to distinguish themselves from others, the concept of 'barbarian'. Thucydides points out that Homer does not use a collective noun for the group of Greek peoples who went to the Trojan War, 'and neither does he speak of barbarians, for the Greeks, in my opinion, were still not designated by a single name contrasting with the name of the barbarians'.* It is plain that the concept 'Greek' was constructed at the same time as that of 'barbarian'.

---

*Sources for all quotations and for points of substance made in the text may be easily identified in the Annotated Bibliography of Essential References on pp. 171–207 below.

The word 'barbarian' originally designated the individual who was incapable of expressing himself fluently in
Greek: the word was simply an onomatopoeic formation
to echo the articulatory difficulties of a person who cannot
speak well and stammers (a common element in the xenophobic myths of all races). It was the struggle against the
Persian Empire that gave the word overtones of a political
and moral kind.

Herodotus presents this war as the confrontation between Greek liberty and the despotism of the Asian peoples,
'a thing as unrighteous and bloodthirsty as aught on this
earth'. In contrast to this image there is elaborated the
image of a free Hellenic collectivity, in which the citizens
share political rights, this explaining the triumph of the
Greeks: since 'it is obvious, as a general rule, that the
equality of political rights is a precious asset' which makes
men strive to preserve it and gives them the courage needed
to defeat the armies of tyrants.

The diffusion of this concept of 'barbarian' was owed
above all to the theatre. Nearly half of the Athenian tragedies of the fifth century BC that are extant portray barbarian personages: a chamber of horrors of the most diverse
kinds – incests, crimes, human sacrifices – characterizes
them and differentiates them from the Greeks. In Euripides'
The Bacchae a background of mysteries and excesses accompanies Dionysus on his way from Asia, and the play
ends with the lamentations of Cadmus and his daughter
on being forced into exile: 'Wretch that I am, having at
my age to go and live among barbarians!' To interpret
differentness as inferiority served, furthermore, to justify
slavery. For Aristotle slaves, who by definition were not
Greeks, differed from their masters 'as widely as the soul
differs from the body and the human being differs from
the lower animal'; the best thing for them was to live 'ruled
by a master'.

Yet this contrast between Greek liberty and Asiatic despotism was in large measure illusory. As Momigliano has
said: 'For the Greeks in general liberty was never joined
to a respect for other people's liberty.' The overworked

image of a Greek polis inhabited by free citizens who collectively participated in government is a mirage. It hides the burden of slavery, the relegation of the peasant to a marginal existence (masked by a false opposition between the 'cultured' city and the 'backward' countryside), the subordination of women (considered inferior to the point that Aristotle, convinced that they had fewer teeth than men, assigned them a purely passive role in conception as incubators for the reproductive power of men), and marked divisions between rich and poor citizens.

Athenian democracy never claimed to be egalitarian. Solon had been concerned to 'leave, as before, all the magistracies in the hands of the wealthy', and did not grant the people any more power than the minimum that was strictly necessary. The democracy for which the Athenians strove signified little more than the privilege which allowed a small group with full political rights – perhaps a tenth part of the Attic population – 'to debate matters of state in their assembly and to choose the magistrates by lot, with the aim that each one should have, at the proper time, a share in power'. (Herodotus himself was a foreigner in Athens and had no such rights.) Words such as 'liberty' and 'democracy' did not have the same meaning for the Greeks as they have for us.

Even this limited democratic programme lost its force when the economic problems of the fourth century plunged Greece into a crisis which threatened to cause a serious social confrontation. The Greeks found themselves divided. The traditionalist proposal of Demosthenes advocated striving to rebuild their union based around the hegemony of Athens – when general conditions were very different from those of a century before, and the state of society did not allow any persistence of the illusion that 'the people controlled those in power and checked all forms of wealth'. There was an opposing temptation to join the Macedonian empire, to participate in a great military enterprise which might open new markets and relieve social tensions, since a good part of the common folk would be recruited into the army.

They ended up accepting the tyranny of Philip of Macedon and of Alexander. Alexander realized the great dream of conquering the Persian Empire, but at the cost of the Greek cities renouncing their independence. Democracy was gradually destroyed by the alliance of the higher Greek classes, first with the Macedonians and later with the Romans, to the point when the very concept 'had been transformed into a chimaera that was vaguely remembered and later happily exterminated, but which, all the same, sent shivers down the spine of any wealthy man'. As Momigliano declared in 1934 – at a time when many intellectuals were bowing before fascism – this failure was linked to its own limitations:

> Nothing causes us to reflect more on the logic of the step from liberty which refuses to acknowledge the liberty of others to despotism, than the realization that the way in which the Greeks, in their toilsome struggle to attain the former, managed only (perhaps inadvertently) to call into being and prepare the way for despotism.

Neither is it clear that there was widespread participation in the higher levels of learning and of art which might have distinguished the Greeks from the barbarians. The culture of the classical world was fundamentally oral: writing was an accessory to recitation. There has been much discussion of the degree of literacy among the Athenians but the Spartans, prohibited by Licurgus from writing their laws down or putting names on tombs, were mostly illiterate. If we distinguish the person who is capable of spelling and writing out a few words from one who fully participates in written culture, it must be recognized that in the classical world readers were few.

The earliest written texts must have been laws, cut on hard materials in order to prevent their being altered. The book – in the form of a roll – was uncommon until the middle of the fifth century BC, and even after that its use was far from widespread. Its emergence may be linked to the development of prose and to the need to preserve complex kinds of philosophical or scientific knowledge, such as medical manuals, prepared for a small nucleus of readers. One of the first libraries to be mentioned is Aristotle's, the purpose of which was to ensure the preservation of the master's thought for his followers. Public libraries arose later in the capital cities of the Hellenistic kingdoms, and especially in Alexandria, built where the Nile enters the Mediterranean. Here it was intended to collect all the learning of the world in a vast store of 400,000 volumes whose twin aims were to preserve the culture of the rulers and to put at their disposal, in translations into Greek, the culture of the ruled. These libraries were first and foremost instruments for political control, created for use by a minority of Greek-speaking experts.

If the portrait which the Greeks drew of themselves, and which we have hung in the gallery dedicated to our ancestors, is fallacious, so is the history which accompanies it. The Greek-barbarian opposition has served to mask the reality of cross-bred origins, yet these are indicated by the myths of the very Greeks themselves. These myths (not without reason) made Europa the daughter of a king of Phoenicia who, ravished away from her native land by Zeus-the-bull – 'with her garments floating behind her in the wind' – settled in Crete and conceived Minos, king of Crete and '*dux Europaeus*'. Greek religion lost all notion of its origins on the northern steppes in order to absorb a whole range of new myths. It is possible to describe it as a syncretism between Mediterranean and Indo-European elements. One can see this, for example, in the figure of Zeus himself: he has an Indo-European name (from a root which means 'to shine', as in Latin *deus* and *dies*) but also a history that has him born in Crete and which suggests an association of the god of the conquerors with the cults of the conquered.

The flowering of Minoan Crete, 'Europe's earliest cradle of civilization', may be explained by the privileged position of the island in a part of the Mediterranean where not only the seaborne trade routes but also influences from the great cultures of the Near East, Anatolia, and the Balkans converged. In Crete, from the third millennium BC, there were formed the essential elements of a culture which, although interrupted by invasions, earthquakes, and the great explosion of the Thera volcano about 1470 BC, built great temple-palaces and created a writing system (linear A, still undeciphered) for a language that was close to that of the Hittites. Eventually, after the burning of the Knossos labyrinth in 1380 BC, it declined and disappeared, probably as a result of a Mycenaean invasion.

Minoan culture passed to the new settlers on Greek soil, the Mycenaeans, who adapted Cretan writing for their Greek language. They built great citadels and are taken to be the Achaeans who conquered Troy. The Mycenaeans in turn saw their history interrupted by a new invasion, within the so-called 'crisis of the twelfth century BC'. The notion of 'crisis' has been used in attempts to explain – in terms of invasions and of the military defeat of the war-chariots of the old kingdoms by armies of barbarian infantry – the coincidence in time of the collapse of the Hittite empire, the attack on Egypt by the 'peoples of the sea', the invasion of Canaan by the Philistines, and the start of the so-called dark age of Greek history. This crisis is viewed today less as a catastrophe – though there really were invasions and destructions – than in terms of its eventual outcome in the establishment of the Greek polis and the revitalization of Mediterranean trade.

However, it serves no purpose to demythologize the Greek miracle in order to replace it by other myths: Indo-European, Egyptian, Phoenician, or Minoan. What we must do is replace the notion of a single creative people by an idea of a broad framework of encounters involving all these peoples – as well as the Carthaginians, Etruscans, Celts, etc. – which made possible the evolution, based on the whole mass of their contributions, of a culture which embraced many shared elements.

A good example of what I mean is provided by the phenomenon of writing. It appears that we should seek its origins in the little pieces of Mesopotamian clay that were enclosed in hollow earthenware balls on whose outer surface marks and seals were incised. This system was simplified when the balls were replaced by solid tablets with incised signs. At first these were strictly pictographic and limited to representing numerals and objects. Then in about 3200 BC there appeared the first truly written texts, when the phonetic values of the pictograms were used in combination to represent concepts that could not be readily depicted, such as verbs. By about 2600 BC a cuneiform script had been consolidated, which allowed complicated texts to be set down. This was adopted by neighbouring peoples, at the same time as the Babylonian language was becoming an international one for culture and for relations between different cultures.

The system first invented by the Sumerians served as a model for a great number of later scripts, adapted to other languages, in an area which extends from Crete to the Indus and from the Black Sea to Arabia. But it was to be in Phoenicia, a crossroads through which all the commercial and cultural currents passed – and where the most diverse kinds of script were known – that the decisive invention would take place. This was a new method, adapted to the Semitic speech of its settlers, in which each sign represented a single consonantal sound, and, furthermore, which used linear strokes that were more suitable for writing on papyrus than the cuneiform signs employed on clay. In about 800 BC Greeks, who in the catastrophe which ruined Mycenaean culture had lost the knowledge of writing (so-called linear B), adopted the brief and practical alphabet of the Phoenicians. With it, they took both the name 'alphabet' and the word which designates the papyrus sheet, *byblos*, from which derives a good part of the terminology we still use about books. In their turn they improved the system with signs which represented vowels, a very important step for adaptation of the system to languages other than the Semitic (which, like Arabic and Hebrew, still today use writing systems based on representing the consonants). This alphabet re-elaborated by the Greeks served as a basis for Etruscan, which in turn may have been the model for runic writing, maintained in Scandinavia into the Middle Ages, as well as for Latin, the modern European alphabet, and for Slav Cyrillic. The alphabet was born, then, out of a series of cultural interactions in regions of contact in the eastern Mediterranean.

What has been said about writing is surely true also of many other areas – geometry, astronomy, or medicine, for example. The Greeks should not be considered either as inventors or as mere translators in these, but as the protagonists in a phase of perfecting the development of scientific activities which others had begun, and which others would go on developing later.

The combination of losses by destruction in the past and lack of interest among modern researchers has led to us knowing well only that form of cross-bred culture which displayed itself in Greece, and later in Rome. It has led also to our neglect of the part played in its elaboration by other peoples, such as the Etruscans, a people of pre-Indo-European speech who spread their products throughout the continent, gave life to a now-lost literature and drama, and, above all, created 'the first expression of a higher urban organization on strictly European soil'. The Etruscans influenced the origins of Celtic art and bequeathed to peoples of Latin speech such fundamental words as *littera*, *mundus*, *populus*, *publicus*, and *persona*.

On the other shore of the Mediterranean, something rather similar happens to the Carthaginians. It seems that literacy was more widespread among them than among the Greeks – even the peasants and fishermen were able to read and write – but of their culture, summed up in the Punic books, we know little, because Rome strove to erase memory of it by making presents of the libraries of Carthage to petty African kings. There were exceptions to this cultural genocide, however. Mago's great agricultural encyclopedia, whose twenty-eight volumes were deposited next to the Sibylline books in the temple of Apollo in Rome, were translated into Latin and propagated in numerous summarized versions, still influential on medieval Arab agronomy.

From Alexander onward, the Greek myth changed character and took on a new dimension. Political needs inseparable from the founding of an empire made it necessary to give a strictly cultural dimension to 'the Hellenic', in order to incorporate the barbarian who wished to become part of it. Plutarch relates that Aristotle advised Alexander to treat the Greeks as friends and the barbarians 'as if they were plants and animals'. However, Alexander did not follow this advice: instead, he tried to present himself 'as a mediator for the whole world', and eased the assimilation of leading native groups which he needed to administer so vast an empire.

The superficial adoption of Greek language and culture by the Hellenistic kingdoms was little more than a modernizing disguise. Under the outward show of the democratic institutions of the polis, the states which arose after Alexander's death maintained the old eastern political forms, translated into Greek and adapted to a period of mercantile prosperity. The cities of the Near East hellenized themselves with public buildings such as theatres and gymnasia (even the Jewish priests attended the Jerusalem one); but the agora, for example, had now no political function – it was simply a commercial centre surrounded by stores, banks, and shopping arcades.

Rome, which became master of the Hellenistic world by force of arms, proclaimed itself the continuer of that world, with arguments which included the affirmation that Latin was a Greek dialect, fitting Aeneas into Romulus' genealogy, and taking over the Homeric tradition, suitably adapted by Virgil, as its own history. Yet what really continued was Alexander's imperial programme, and, if Rome assimilated Greek language and culture, it was above all in order to manage the administration of that with its own hellenized cadres, topping off the making of a legalized authoritarian society with the ancient rhetoric of Athenian democracy. For empire and democracy were incompatible terms. A century and a half after Alexander's death Polybius, a Greek taken to Rome as a hostage, expressed his admiration for the Romans' form of government, for their 'mixed constitution', which bore no resemblance to the 'equality of political rights' proclaimed by Herodotus as characteristic of Hellenic civilization.

In imperial Rome there was no participatory democratic system. Formally it was an odd mixture of the apparent continuity of the Republic (in Rome the emperor governed, theoretically at least, together with the senate) and the direct control of the rest of the Empire, a system in which the ruler's personal decisions – made generally in response to the petitions of the provincials – were considered to have the force of laws. The ruling classes did not maintain social order in the city by force, but thanks to popular consensus based on gifts from the *princeps*, a system which has been called 'evergetism', including the bread dole, the circus, and religious sacrifices.

All this explains why, unlike the Greeks, the Romans did not limit access to citizenship, for this did not imply any real political rights. Instead, they showed themselves willing to concede citizenship to provincial notables, with the aim of drawing to themselves the ruling groups of other peoples, until the *Constitutio Antoniniana*, promulgated by Caracalla in AD 212, extended it to practically all the inhabitants of the Empire.

It has been said that the Roman Empire was 'a collection of settlements hardly integrated among themselves'. Indeed 'the common description of what we refer to as "the empire" is "the peoples subject to Roman rule". The empire is not thought of as a territorial entity.' There were no frontiers marked by some sign, among other reasons because the Romans lacked accurate maps which would have allowed them to define borders correctly (there were indeed frontiers, on the other hand, to separate provinces and delimit the governors' spheres of action). What kept these peoples united was not the efficiency of the administration, nor the might of the army, but the community of ideas and interests which existed between the Roman aristocrats and the local notables, by the mediation of whom the provinces were governed. The central government practised 'an immense delegation of administration',

since it could control the provinces only through a network of municipalities and, in general, of local authorities
which enjoyed considerable autonomy. This included the
client kings integrated into the Empire, such as Herod of
Judaea and his successors, and autonomous cities such as
Tyre.

Nor was there a widely shared culture. Unlike what
happened in Greece, where the oral diffusion of literature
shows that the language was accessible to the public at
large, we reasonably doubt whether the Latin of high literature was fully understood by the Roman people – and
still less by the inhabitants of the provinces. This might
explain the importance accorded to propaganda by image:
visual narratives conveyed by sculpture on triumphal arches,
thousands of statues of the emperor set up all over the Empire (in the city of Rome alone there were hundreds of
statues of Augustus, among them eighty silver ones) and
so on.

In the field of religion we know that 'nobody has been
able to count up the number of deities worshipped in the
Empire,' since all local religions were respected on the
basis of assimilating their gods to their supposed Roman
equivalents (in conquered Carthage, for example, the shrines
of Baal-Hammon were converted into temples of Saturn).
There was just one common element, the function of the
emperor as 'sacrificer' which made him an intermediary
between terrestrial society and the divine powers, in so ge-
neric a way that it could become acceptable for the faithful
(with the exception of the Jews) of any of the numerous
provincial religions.

Yet Rome was not able to assimilate the culture of the
peoples which made up that peculiar form of association
that the Empire was. If we exclude the case of the oriental
cults and mysteries, left over from the empire of Alexander
or imported by slaves, though rapidly romanized – as is
shown by the evolution which transformed the Iranian
Mithras into the Helios-Mithras of the emperor Julian –
the Romans took little interest in the culture of the peoples
that surrounded them, Greek culture always being excepted.

Shut in on themselves, they came to believe that the world was reduced to two parts: the Empire and the barbarians. This dichotomy was reflected in their geographical panorama. If the Greeks had divided the world into three parts, Pliny said that there were only two, since Europe was the best of them and the region which was 'nurse of the race that has conquered all the nations', for which reason many maintain 'that Europe is not a third but half of the world'. This is the same myopia as that shown by Ovid who, banished to the shores of the Black Sea, exclaims 'I have been abandoned on the sands of the end of the world': that is, on a frontier beyond which there is nothing but barbarism, cold, and horror. The habit of viewing humanity in the distorting surface of the barbarian mirror prevented the Romans from observing that out there beyond the *limes* there were other worlds, other cultures, and even science and technology superior to their own.

Seen in contrast to the ideal portrait of the Roman, the barbarians presented a stereotyped image, as can be observed in the terrifying depiction of the Huns which Ammianus Marcellinus has left us, as full of horrors as it is of inaccuracies. The very barbarian peoples themselves were in a way invented by the Romans, who credited them with characteristics of ethnic unity and territorial settlement which they did not really possess: Caesar's Gaul and Tacitus' Germania were the products of their authors' imagination ('not until the eleventh century or thereabouts did the people whom others called Germans feel the need to apply to themselves one collective name'). It was contact with the furthest military settlements of the Empire that, when barbarian incomers were attracted and settled nearby, helped to facilitate their unification and to make them group themselves in confederations. The possibilities for trade and for service in the Roman army, and later, the need to organize the share-out of subventions received from the Empire, consolidated these confederations and made them long-lasting. In this way the Romans helped to make the phantasms they had dreamed up into realities.

The first European barbarians the Romans knew were the Celts, a name by which they referred to a broad grouping of peoples, from the Gauls in the extreme west of Europe – such as those who, in the early fourth century BC, invaded Italy and wandered about in the deserted streets of Rome, 'terrified by their very loneliness' – to the Galatians of Asia Minor, who were soldiers and bandits. It is hard to determine to what degree the cultural similarities between them – the only decisive one would be the relationship of their languages – represent a reality or are owed to Roman prejudice, given the differences that there are, for example, between those Celts of northern Italy who lived, Polybius tells us, in unwalled settlements and 'slept on piles of leaves', and the builders of the great fortified *oppida* which stood all the way from Gaul to the Danube valley.

The second great group of European barbarians was that of the Germans. In Roman eyes they were all the same and were considered 'a pure race'. For Tacitus: 'In all of them physical appearance is the same: hard blue eyes, reddish hair, tall stature, strong only in rushing attack (they do not have the same energies for work and toil).' Four hundred and fifty years later, Procopius says something similar about the Goths: 'No differences can be found among them: they all have white skin, fair hair, great height, and good build. They obey the same laws, have identical religious beliefs, and speak one and the same language.' All this is no more than a reflection of the usual myopia when faced with the stranger: to a European, not much accustomed to seeing them, black people or Chinese may seem to be all alike.

There was, certainly, a Gothic people, which according to Cassiodorus originated in Scandinavia, in those lands which were 'like a factory of peoples or like a womb from which nations emerged'. There was also a Gothic language, which survived in the Balkans until the early Middle Ages. But the groups which intervene in the history of the Empire and which we usually call Goths were in fact an aggregate of peoples – Alans and Huns among them, for example – in which the Goths formed a dominant class. They had their own language, a common religion (which was not Arianism, as is usually said, but something intermediate between this and Catholicism) and laws and customs which had been defined before the arrival of the Huns (precisely because their contact with the Romans had helped to fix them) and which allowed them to preserve their cultural personality while they were associated with Rome.

These Gothic people did not, however, have the political unity which the histories of great leaders, dynasties, and barbarian kingdoms seem to indicate. In Attila's army which fought in the battle of the Catalaunian Fields the Huns were a minority within an aggregate of 'many peoples and diverse nations', united in a very loose association. After Attila's death this association rapidly broke up and the Huns themselves ended up by merging with other Germanic or Slavic peoples, and disappeared from history. Nor did the Ostrogoths and Visigoths, who formed longer-lasting political entities, seem to have been anything more than aggregates of tribes and warrior groups each with its own chief – what would be defined later as a Gothic aristocracy – and which had confederated, without merging, to form larger units which would seem like monarchies to the Romans.

On the other hand, it is hard to sustain the old cliché which presents the conquest of the western Empire by the barbarians as marking a decisive break. It must be recalled that relations between the barbarians and the Empire were not always those of confrontation, since they manifested themselves in a wide range of tints from trading to extortion, and from payment for services to collecting subventions for not attacking the Empire, and among these it is not always easy to identify differences.

Most of the barbarians who crossed the frontiers did so not as invaders, but as immigrants who settled on imperial territory with due authorization, as soldiers in the emperor's service (fitted at first into the Roman army, and later, as independent groups who obeyed their own leaders). Not only did they not seek to destroy the existing political-administrative structures, they had an interest in preserving these, since the structures were useful to them in collecting the taxes gathered for the maintenance of the army.

That the Goths (who in large numbers had crossed the Danube in 376) should rebel was owed to the behaviour of the Roman officials who restricted them to the most unproductive areas in the hope that hunger would make them knuckle under. But neither after their victory at Adrianopolis in 378 – where they started by holding back the Roman attack with a circle of carts, and finished by shattering the imperial army with their cavalry – nor after the capture of Rome by Alaric in 410, did the victors seek to go further than getting recognition of their position within the Empire. A recent book on the western Roman world maintains that the only thing that happened in the fifth century was that the Roman administration was replaced by that of certain barbarian peoples who had settled on those lands by more or less lawful means, and that this, far from signifying the end of the Empire, meant only its transformation. It has been said that it is doubtful whether the deposing of Romulus Augustulus in 476 changed anything in the lives of people living in Italy.

This system of relationships eventually failed in the western Empire (in the eastern part it kept going and the Empire survived there for another thousand years). Pressure from the barbarians increased at the same time as the Roman economy declined and fell back on itself, and the will to go on sustaining the growing costs of a system which was of little use to them decayed among the inhabitants, especially when the divisions at the very heart of imperial society became more grave than the conflict which on all fronts set that society against the mass of those external enemies.

In order to understand the collapse of the western Empire we do well to note the signs of paralysis in the central administrative structure, and the social fractures which were weakening it long before the barbarians took control over it. The centuries of 'decadence' – a term which expresses a distorted view of a complex process of evolution and change – witnessed progressive changes: privatization of public functions, an increase in economic inequalities, and, in consequence, the consolidation of a class of magnates who owned great properties and had them cultivated by settlers fleeing from indebtedness (caused above all by taxes) who placed themselves under the protection of a landlord. This started a process of subjection to the land which would bring in its train the decline of slavery, this being less profitable for the large landowner.

Who, then, were the barbarians assumed to have destroyed the Empire? The Russian historian Rostovtseff – obsessed by the Soviet revolution, which forced him to leave his country – tells us that Rome fell because, incapable of civilizing the rural masses, she had to watch while the culture of the upper echelons gave way before that of the peasants. At first 'the barbarism of the countryside began to submerge the cities' populations'; later, these populations 'were completely overwhelmed by the arrival of barbarian elements coming in from outside, partly by penetration and partly by conquest'.

It is plain from this analysis that the enemies who destroyed the Empire were as much internal – peasants who remained unromanized – as external. We have found too that the designation of 'barbarian' has been used not only to refer to invaders from beyond the frontiers, but to all those who for one reason or another did not accept the imperial social order and were consequently not disposed to defend it. The term refers chiefly to those peasants whom Latin culture did not integrate into itself and who were the cause of what Rostovtseff considers the essential feature of Roman decadence: 'the gradual absorption of the cultured classes by the masses'.

All this tells us much, not only about the ambiguity of the concept 'barbarian', but also about the reasons for the success achieved by the clichéd view of the fall of the Empire. The traditional image of a Rome which collapsed because of the failure of its governing classes, unable to hold back the onrush of barbarians, has had, and still has today, an exceptionally useful moralizing function. To many intellectuals and politicians today, our society is faced with the threat from other barbarians, that is the masses, who have to be held off in order to prevent their destroying civilization. Unwilling to face up to the real problems of our own world, it is easier for them to set up again the old scarecrow of the decline of Rome than to analyse internal factors causing divisiveness, such as the widening gap between rich and poor or limitations on freedom.

When certain modern historians tell us that what really became corrupted in the late Empire was the political process, when private interests were privileged over collective ones, it is in no way unexpected that their conclusions should cause others to have reservations, since we may be tempted to draw uncomfortable comparisons with present-day circumstances. An interpretation which emphasizes the internal problems of Roman society would have no need to bring in the barbarians in order to explain the crisis of the Empire, and those who wish to maintain the traditional view would find themselves in a situation in which we might apply to them lines from a Kavafis poem spoken by the emperor and the senators: they have waited in vain for the arrival of the barbarians, but depart in distress on hearing that there is no sign of them from any direction:

What will become of us now, bereft of barbarians?
It has to be recognized that those fellows were the
solution to a problem.

2

The Christian Mirror

In the traditional historical panorama the second element that characterizes that which is European, together with the heritage of classical culture, is Christianity, presented as a doctrine defined from its very origins, and diffused throughout the Mediterranean world until it became the religion of the Empire in the fourth century (when it was the Empire which changed, with the conversion of Constantine, while Christianity went on unchanged).

However, between original Christianity and that of Constantine's time there occurred a long and complicated evolution which had at least three important phases. In the first, the phase of the 'historical Jesus', it was a matter of one of the movements of religious renewal which shook Palestine at the start of our era. This was an essentially rural movement which was opposed to 'the city', this city consisting of both the religious hierarchy of the Temple, against which the movement proposed a direct relationship of man with the divinity without intermediaries, and the imperial administrators, which explains why these two powers joined to combat it.

In its second phase Christianity abandoned the Aramaic language for Greek, and spread out of rural Palestine into the Hellenistic cities. This transference implied a change in its adherents, who were no longer the poor and marginalized followers of Jesus but well-off citizens who joined Paul's groups, in which women had a notable place. The

pluralistic nature of this initial phase in the development
of Christianity reflects the diverse origins of the groups
of believers: circumcised Christians who went on being
strongly linked to Judaism, converts coming from groups
that were being persecuted in Palestine – Hellenists hostile
to the Temple, followers of John the Baptist who had em-
igrated after his execution – and finally, converts from
paganism who had not passed through Judaism. Paul, who
found himself obliged to take account of the confrontations
between the various tendencies, thought it natural that
among Christians there should be differences of opinion,
and he even thought it proper that there should be heretics.

It has been said that true Christianity 'included a great
variety of voices, an extraordinary range of points of
view'. In Syria and Egypt we find a first phase in which
Christianity lives beside various Jewish sects. This phase
is followed by another dominated by Gnosticism, in which
doctrine is impregnated with features of oriental thought
and of Graeco-Roman paganism. When we consider the
history of these early times, to speak of Gnosticism, Montanism, or Arianism as heresies is correct in terms of the
original meaning of the word *airesis*, which in classical
writers had the sense of 'choice', 'opinion', or 'school of
thought'; but it is not correct in the meaning 'sect' or
'faction' which it later acquired. In fact these schools coexisted without too many conflicts until Constantine associated Christianity with the Empire and created a Church
with a centralized authority empowered to fix the accepted
truths.

It is understandable, moreover, that doctrinal divergences did not seem important to groups who shared the
belief that the end of the world was nigh, like those Christians in Pontus who, convinced that the Last Judgement
was going to take place within a year, abandoned their
fields and their work and sold all their goods. This es-
chatological component, inherited from the apocalyptic
tradition which flourished in Palestine in the time of Christ,
was one of the features which the pagans criticized in
Christians: 'But what can one say about their belief that

the whole globe and the firmament itself with all its stars are threatened with fire and ruin, as if the eternal order established by divine laws were destined to suffer a cataclysm?', asks the pagan interlocutor in a controversial dialogue by Minucius Felix.

Only communities preparing themselves for the imminent end of time could, sustained by such tension, accept the renunciation of all goods and of all pleasures. But about the year 200, seeing that the moment so much desired did not come, the Christians of Pontus who had given everything up returned to ordinary life: 'The young girls got married; the men went back to the fields.' From that time extreme positions with regard to asceticism and the renunciation of sex were maintained only among the most radical groups of oriental Christianity. In orthodox Christianity the norm of absolute chastity was left to the desert fathers – the Egyptian ascetics or the hermits of Syria and Cappadocia – from whom the monks took it, and only gradually did it spread among the secular clergy, while for the mass of the lay community there was created a morality which limited itself to banning adultery and fixing rules to distinguish matrimony from the lusts of the flesh.

The third phase in this early history of Christianity concerns its association with the political power of the Empire, which transformed it into 'an ecclesiastical government in parallel with the secular one', with which it collaborated in order that imperial decrees should be carried out. One proof of the radical nature of this transformation may be provided by the fact that in 314 a synod fixed the penalty of excommunication for those Christian soldiers who left military service, contradicting the stance of the martyrs who had chosen death rather than go into the army, on the plea, like Maximilian's, that it was forbidden for a Christian to do harm.

The pluralistic and community character then disappears. Christian belief becomes Christianity, which considers itself, from the moment of its official recognition, to be a unified and hierarchical community which aspires to embrace all mankind in its bosom and extend its control to

all mankind's activities. It should be remembered that
Christianity is the only one of the great religions which is
subject to the control of a hierarchically organized clergy.

I have spoken of the political association between Christianity and the Empire and not of the conversion of Constantine. In fact the emperor, who had his vision of the
Cross only two years after another in which Apollo had
appeared to him, did not stop carrying out his duties as
religious leader of his pagan subjects, building temples for
the old gods in his new capital in the East. It seems that
his personal life was not changed either, if we recall that
he was obliged to accept responsibility for the violent
deaths of his father-in-law, three brothers-in-law, his first-
born child, and his wife.

What is not in doubt is the political sense which Constantine gave from the start to that recognition, within
what Santo Mazzarino has described as the emperor's revolutionary programme. Together with a greater political
centralization, an economy based on a gold coinage, and
a division of society between the possessors of wealth and
the *humiliores* who were ever more oppressed, being forced
to pay by their toil for the greater part of the maintenance
costs of the Empire, there was created, as an essential part
of the programme, a single universal Christian Church recognized by the state. Its clergy were provided not only
with wealth (Constantine's gifts have been reckoned at
about 1,100 kg in gold and 5,300 kg in silver), but also
with a series of privileges – tax exemptions, the granting
to the churches of the ability to inherit, and so on – which
would allow them to increase their wealth considerably.

In order to understand this alliance it helps to remember
that in the social structures of the Christian communities
the poor did not dominate, as has sometimes been said
(echoing in this their pagan detractors, who declared that
their members were recruited 'from among the lowest of
the low'). The communities consisted rather of a representative selection of the urban population of the Graeco-
Roman world, having leaders who came from its most
educated and prosperous sectors (in Hispania, for example,

christianization began primarily among the upper classes, which explains why the bishops were often aristocrats).

The Church thus became one of the principal pillars of that new Christian Empire which was to survive in the East until the fifteenth century. In the West, where the imperial structure collapsed much earlier, it was precisely the Church that tried to re-establish it by crowning Charlemagne in Rome (taking advantage of the vacancy on the imperial throne which had occurred in Byzantium when Constantine VI was deposed; his mother had him blinded). Similar in effect was what has been called 'the imperial papacy', which would lead the popes to try to unite in their persons both political power and priestly functions, basing this on their assumed status as heirs to the Empire, in accordance with the so-called *Donation of Constantine*, a ninth-century forgery which implied recognition of a continuity and of a legitimacy not interrupted by the barbarian invasions. All of this explains how Hobbes could declare in the middle of the seventeenth century: 'The papacy is no other than the Ghost of the deceased Romane Empire, sitting crowned upon the grave thereof.'

In the new situation created by political recognition, peaceful coexistence between the various Christian tendencies could not continue. The dissenters – heretics and schismatics – had to be marginalized and could be (and ought to be) punished. Indeed, the first dissenters to be persecuted, the Donatists of north Africa, did not differ in doctrine, but were opposed to the alliance of Christianity with political power, this leading them to consider themselves, with good reason, as the true continuers of the Church in its early phase of persecution and martyrdom. It led them also to declare that those who, having allied themselves to the Empire, aided it and at the same time made use of it to be heavy-handed with divergences among Christians, were traitors.

Some of the faithful chose individual solutions which did not imply any threat to the hierarchical Church and which the latter was able to accept, as happened with the anchorites who went off into the desert to withdraw from the world, or with the coenobites who shut themselves away in monasteries in order to live communally. These ascetics who preserved the virtues of the earliest times, but who did not seek to make of those virtues a norm for the whole of Christianity, found themselves harassed by pilgrims who came to visit them on account of their saintly reputation, and adopted all manner of ways to be free of them, as did Simeon, who sat himself atop ever taller columns till he reached some twenty metres above the ground, living there for more than forty years until his death in 459.

Once its authority was established, the Church of Christianity found itself forced to construct a new view of the origins of the faith in which all traces of pluralism would be eliminated, these being silenced or retrospectively condemned as unlawful. At the same time the Church associated its history with that of Rome: Jesus was born at the moment when Augustus was founding the Empire and establishing the *pax romana*. 'Triumphant orthodoxy proclaimed a monopoly and rewrote its own history', it has been said. This rewriting allowed the construction of a negative image which drew together and personalized all the features of early Christianity, which it was hoped to banish and which received the name 'heresy', now given a new meaning. The face of orthodoxy defined itself in this distorting mirror, contrasting itself to certain faces which, although bearing different names, generally had some features in common: an oriental origin, elements of dualism (that is, of the recognition of the existence of a principle of evil together with the principle of the good, represented by God), immorality, and witchcraft. So efficacious did this model prove that the Church was to employ it for many centuries, using it to identify dissenters, and we find it still used in the condemnations of the Templars and the Cathars.

The origin of the various elements which make up this stereotype is easy to establish. The oriental origin attributed to most of the heresies has to do with the pluralistic nature of Christianity in those regions and with Roman fear of Manichaeism as a doctrine owed to Persian enemies, but this was coloured also by remains of the Greek prejudice against 'the Asiatic'. It is not hard to find dualistic features in any heresy, since these are present, for a start, in the New Testament and the apocalyptic writings, being 'one of the perennial beliefs of mankind'. As for the supposition about immorality, understood almost always as promiscuity, this generally has a lot to do with the greater participation by women in the heretical churches, following the model of the communities which adopted Pauline Christianity (it is revealing that this accusation was made against groups which for the most part condemned sexuality and advocated an ascetic life).

The political nature of the association of the new Christian Catholic (that is, 'one and universal') Church and the Empire is reflected in the designation of the 'bishop of those outside', that is, of the lay people, adopted by Constantine in order to legitimize his intervention in support of directives about doctrine and clerical discipline, even when these went against his personal beliefs. For this reason the emperor approved the condemnation of Arianism at the Council of Nicaea, despite his leaning towards that doctrine, to the point that a little before his death he chose to receive baptism from the hands of an Arian bishop. This is not really at all surprising when we remember that Constantinople went on being a predominantly Arian city until the end of the fourth century, long after the death of its founder.

The 'officialization' of Christianity should not however be confused with the christianization of the Empire, which took place over a long period and in a series of phases. The fourth century was, until its last decade, an epoch of peaceful coexistence in which the old traditional religion went on opening temples, receiving state subsidies, and marking the passing of time with its festivities.

After the brief restorative interlude of the reign of Julian, for whom the re-establishment of paganism – restructured around the worship of Sol-Mithras – was associated with an attempt to introduce moral reform into the administration, the army, and the court (in Constantinople Julian found a palace with a thousand cooks, innumerable barbers, eunuchs, spies, and hangers-on of every hue), things began to change, especially under Theodosius I, who adopted a policy of imposing religious unity by force. He condemned heresies in a law of August 379, ordered the inhabitants of Constantinople to follow the Nicaean doctrine, closed pagan temples and banned sacrifices, classing these as acts of high treason which would be punished by death and the confiscation of property.

This was no easy task. In Constantinople, where people were passionately devoted to theological disputation, the Arians predominated, divided in their turn into various tendencies, and there were in addition Apollinarians (who maintained that in Christ there was a human body and a divine soul), Novatians, and others. Gregory Nazianzen, chosen by the emperor as the restorer of orthodoxy, was on occasions stoned by the populace and needed all the imperial support there was to keep going. Yet if expelling Arian clergy from the churches was not hard when force was available, the task of converting their parishioners certainly was.

The same happened with the pagans. Despite the repressive measures taken in the next few years, the only thing achieved was that sacrifices had to be held in private, or at least clandestinely, and they were still being so held in Justinian's time, thus defying repeated bans and the severity of the punishments. Persecutions and military campaigns – now it was the pagans who were thrown to the lions or burned by the Christians – were needed to finish off the last pagan communities, but this did not happen until the ninth century. The leaders of these campaigns were the bishops, who, as 'protectors of the poor', not only had great influence on the urban masses, but also controlled groups of men – gravediggers, orderlies, and so on – who acted as real militias at their orders.

We know, for example, about the complicated situation in Alexandria where, in Julian's time, the pagans had killed the bishop and certain Christian dignitaries who had been harassing them. When Christianity was again officially approved it brought about the destruction of the Serapeion in 389, at the instigation of Bishop Theophilus, and the start of a reign of persecution which his nephew and successor, Cyril, who instigated the murder of Hypatia, made still worse. Hypatia, an elderly pagan lady, a philosopher respected for her learning, was stoned and quartered in front of a church by mobs urged on by the bishop's orderlies.

Hounded by the patriarch's thugs, the last pagan philosophers of Alexandria were forced to flee from the city. Some went to Syria, avoiding the christianized cities and seeking refuge in the countryside, where they continued to worship the local gods; or they set off for Mesopotamia. There were, then, small groups of intellectuals who preserved ancient philosophy from the persecution of Christian barbarism: these included the group which at Harran, on the border between the Roman Empire and Persia, founded a Neo-Platonic school which survived up to the eleventh century and played a notable part in the transmission of Greek learning to the Islamic world.

In this same period in Gaul, Martin, Bishop of Tours, although facing opposition from local people, devoted himself to burning temples, chopping down sacred trees, smashing idols, and violently confronting those pagan priests who wished to go on celebrating their traditional feasts as they had done from time immemorial.

In order to understand the change which the inhabitants of the Empire experienced with the official adoption and gradual imposition of Christianity, it is well to remember that the ancient pagan religion was not, as beliefs go, much more than a syncretism which integrated local deities into a common pantheon of Graeco-Roman origin (it appears that Alexander Severus even wished to erect a temple in honour of Christ and include him among the gods). The fundamental element which held this 'mosaic of religions linked to the established order' together was a civic-religious ritual designed to reinforce political unity, to give the emperor a religious dimension, as heir to the priestly functions of magistrates and senators. For this reason the religion of the Empire did not have a Church or a real sacerdotal caste which were differentiated from the public powers. It was the senate and the emperor who had to watch over religion, and the persecutions of those who, like the Christians, sought to remain outside the system were based on political motives.

The Constantinian revolution meant the beginning of the end of the old system, eclectic and tolerant in doctrinal matters, and it gave way to a religious centralization which would not now be limited to ritual, but would extend also to the domain of personal conduct and beliefs. What happened in consequence was not so much the confrontation between two religions as the confrontation between two political-religious systems. This explains why conflicts manifested themselves especially among the ruling urban groups, while the countryside, in which the greater part of the Empire's population lived, went on being pagan, in the sense of preserving local religious beliefs, for a long time.

The mutation of early Christian faith into official Christianity – there has been mention of the end of an 'old Christianity', which suffered an identity crisis between 380 and 430 – brought numerous changes with it. When a persecuted faith was transformed into a stable Church, what was intended was not only that it should have a presence in society, but that it should control society. For this to happen imperial public order had to be christianized and people's habits and customs had to be changed (the people went on celebrating the traditional feasts, such as that of 1 January, and remained passionately keen on games in the circus).

It was necessary to create a new sense of time and of history, embracing as an essential daily element a new calendar, including the Paschal cycle; this depended on complicated calculations, but was needed in order to regulate the series of new religious feasts which were to reinforce the solidarity of the faithful. Later came the reckoning of years according to the Christian era, which was worked

out in the sixth century but did not become general until
the eighth.

A new concept of space appeared. The geography of
classical culture, realistic if imprecise, was replaced by maps
of the world which put Jerusalem at the centre and mingled
the real with the symbolic. This concept was reflected still
in the great *mapamundi* of the Ebstorf monastery made
in the thirteenth century, in which the cardinal points were
identified with the body of Christ – his head, feet, and two
hands – which in Christian terms represented the identi-
fication of the world's macrocosm with man's microcosm.

A re-ordering of the city occurred too, since the churches,
linked nearly always to tombs of martyrs and to relics,
were transformed into essential elements of population
groups whose structure was irregular and whose growth
was spontaneous, in open contrast to Roman urban models
whose grid pattern was intended to reflect the nature of
the political structure, the latter serving to integrate local
societies into the broad unity of the Empire.

It was necessary furthermore to modify a whole series
of rules for life, such as those concerned with sexuality,
in the search for a middle way between pagan morality and
the extreme asceticism of certain groups of early Christians
who condemned all sexual activity, including that occurring
within marriage. The new christianizing norm arose from
the great enterprise of theological systematization undertaken by the Fathers of the Church in the fourth and fifth
centuries. Spouses were urged to limit sex to the minimum
required for reproduction, and not to seek pleasure in the
act. Coitus was banned on the wedding-night, during Lent,
on the eves of liturgical feasts, on Sundays, during men-
struation and pregnancy, and always when a person was
doing penance for some sin, these penances sometimes
lasting from five to ten years.

We have already said that the Church of the new Christianity strove to eliminate those dissenting tendencies which
tried to preserve elements of early Christianity that were
not tolerated in orthodox doctrine and practice. Harassed
by a clergy which had the armed force of law on its side,

the dissident oriental groups followed the route taken earlier by the pagan philosophers towards Mesopotamia, Persia and central Asia, where some of these 'outer churches', such as Nestorianism, would have a long and brilliant future, as we shall see in due course.

People who found themselves more remote from a welcoming frontier had to learn, from the example of Priscillian, Bishop of Avila, that the fate which awaited them was persecution and even death. From what we know of Priscillianism it embraced principles recalling those of early Christianity: the expectation of an early end of time, asceticism, celibacy, vegetarianism, a moderate use of numerology and astrology, an esteem for the apocryphal Gospels from the Gnostic tradition. However, it is always hard to discover the truth about ideas held by condemned persons when these are buried under the heap of aberrations attributed to them by their persecutors, these being usually the only ones who have been able to make their voices heard to us. But the fundamental factor seems to have been the question of discipline – that is, of fear in the face of certain ascetic tendencies that tried to keep going outside the bishops' jurisdiction – and not of dogma. A religiosity which involved more active participation by lay people – women included – in ecclesiastical life threatened the bishops' monopoly of power and provoked a reaction from them.

As could have been foreseen, the Priscillianists were accused of Manichaeism (which generally included presumptions of immorality and witchcraft) by a bishop about whom we are told that he was a stupid, devious man 'without the least sign of saintliness'. The execution of Priscillian and several of his followers in Trier in 385 had a plain political overtone. Among the Priscillianists there figured notable members of the senatorial nobility whom the usurper Magnus Maximus considered to be potential enemies, and it was he who condemned them and hastened to confiscate their property in order to use the profits for the campaign by which he hoped to become master of the Empire.

For many years the Church in Galicia venerated the Trier martyrs as saints, this being possible because the barbarian invasion put the Galicians beyond the reach of Rome. It has been suspected that the cathedral of Santiago de Compostela was erected atop a sanctuary built earlier to house Priscillian's tomb, and if this is true it would endow the pilgrimages made over the centuries to this place, the supposed tomb of St James, with the character of some sort of reparation.

For some, this second phase of the Christian history of western Europe – the patristic epoch or Church of late Antiquity – ended when the process of fixing Catholic doctrine in the West was completed and a start was made on the great task of converting the barbarian world. In this new phase, the dialogue with the Germans and with the Celts of the British Isles served to enrich European culture, creating a synthesis which would give colour to the originality of medieval Christianity. Such a view reduces the making of medieval Europe to the integration of new peoples into the ambit of a common Christian culture, and identifies the expansion of Europe with missionary preaching. However, matters are not so simple.

In the first place, what we habitually call conversion to Christianity was in many parts limited to the ruling urban classes (which provided members of the new clergy, as earlier they had provided members of the pre-Christian priesthood). In the countryside what the Church called paganism survived, but this was rather a form of syncretism between ancient autochthonous beliefs – many of which are alive today as superstitions or folklore – and elements drawn from the religion of the Empire, to which Christian features had been gradually added later. The canons of the Council of Elvira, in the early fourth century, reveal a Hispanic society in which Christian landowners have to compromise with popular paganism, in which Judaism coexists with Christianity (the Council forbids rabbis to bless the fields, since this would cancel the effects of the blessing given by a bishop), and in which magical practices are mingled with Christian rites, as in the celebration of Masses for the Dead on behalf of some living person whose death it is hoped to encompass by this means. When Martin of Braga composed his sermon *De correctione rusticorum* about 572, the beliefs of the Galician peasants he denounced in it had nothing to do with the subtleties of Priscillianism, still alive in that region, but rather involved autochthonous superstitions:

> lighting candles next to rocks, trees, springs, and at crossroads; ... acts of divination and auguries; ... being careful about which foot is put forward, scattering grain and wine in a fire made on a treetrunk, and placing bread in springs; ... uttering incantations over herbs to be used in spells ....

In Gaul in the early sixth century the ancient customs, such as those involving dancing by men disguised as wild animals, were still alive among people who, according to St Caesarius of Arles, 'go to church as Christians but come away from it pagans'. There seem to have been pagan origins also in the cult of St Guinefort, the 'holy dog' unjustly sacrificed by his master; mothers took their sick children to his tomb so that he could heal them, in a tradition which, despite the Church's condemnation, survived into the nineteenth century.

It has been proposed that we should enrich our panorama of a Christianity which replaces ancient autochthonous beliefs, by superimposing upon it the idea of a horizontal expansion which came about as Christianity associated itself with the non-Christian spiritual world and assimilated numerous elements taken from it. We know that popular culture in medieval Europe went on being characterized for a long time, even in regions that were early christianized, by a certain religious syncretism. But this is merely a facet of something more widespread and profound. Aron Gurevich has pointed out that beside the theologians' systematically elaborated symbolism, there existed numerous symbolic rites and formulas which reflected 'a stratum of the medieval consciousness which lay deeper than Christianity' and which took from it no more than a certain colouring. This leads him to maintain that 'The symbolic consciousness of the Middle Ages was not born out of Christianity, but is rather a variation of the archaic "primitive" consciousness.'

To simplify the historical interpretation of such a complex process as the formation of society and culture in medieval Europe by juggling with all too general concepts, such as 'Christianity', 'paganism', or 'heresy', is to adopt the impoverished and equivocal language of the repressive people who watched over the purity of the faith, that is, over their monopoly as interpreters of that faith; but it does not help us to understand the real situation. Christianity was, above all, an effort to prolong the life of the Empire in order to preserve a threatened social order.

In those same years in which Constantinople was on the point of falling to the Turks, the Byzantine philosopher Georgius Gemistus, known as Pletho, called upon the 'gods who are arbiters of reason', whoever they might be 'and whatever your number might be', proposing to abandon Christianity and return to the pagan gods in what was really a programme for deism. It was not a question of returning to the ancient beliefs, but of re-establishing society on new religious and philosophical bases. The crisis in the Empire demanded the rethinking of the Constantinian system. Significantly, the man who cast Pletho's book into the flames, scandalized by its impiety, was the same who hastened to accept nomination as Patriarch of Constantinople from the hand of the sultan who had conquered it.

3

The Feudal Mirror

After the fall of the Roman Empire, there followed according to traditional history the Dark Ages: an intermediate period of stagnation, even of regression, between the splendours of classical Antiquity and its recovery by the Renaissance. Later this thousand-year period was shortened and a whole series of key points was proposed: of renaissances, the Carolingian one, that of the twelfth century, that of the thirteenth century; or revolutions, that of the year 1000, or the birth of feudalism, the commercial revolution of the Middle Ages, of technology, and so on.

There is much that is dubious about this image which combines a great break with the past – the fall of the Roman Empire – with a recovery. Gregory of Tours, who wrote his histories at the end of the sixth century, did not mention the fall of the Empire, and did not even seem to think that an ancient world different from his own had ever existed. For those who lived in those times it was not obvious that the Roman Empire belonged to the past because, among other reasons, the successors of Augustus and Constantine were still ruling in the East.

The crisis in the western Empire did not mean the end of relations between barbarians and Romans, but merely a gradual transformation of these. The first great wave of invasions – the one that was assumed to have been the most destructive – was absorbed in some parts within a continuity that showed no great changes. The cities did not disappear; what changed at times was the nature of their inhabitants, and more and more, the nature of their relations with the countryside which surrounded them. There were industries and commercial activities which went on being managed by Germans. It has been said about the water-mills of the Frankish kingdom 'how little the collapse of Roman authority had affected everyday activities such as corn milling'.

The weakening of relations between the barbarian world and the Mediterranean favoured the development of interchanges among the barbarians and the search for new routes for trade towards the East. There was formed a cultural region of the North Sea which stretched from the Rhine valley to Britain, where the departure of the Romans had left a confused situation. There arose, first, a sub-Roman kingdom, the legendary Arthur's – 'the only one of the Roman race who has survived the catastrophe' – with fortresses inhabited by a war-like aristocracy. In later Anglo-Saxon times there were periods of marked progress, especially in Northumbria during the age of Bede and in the south during and following the reign of Alfred: towns and settlements grew as centres of craft production and as active urban markets. An abundant and well-regulated coinage indicates that considerable international trade existed: and it was from the surplus generated by their trade with north-west Europe that the English were able to pay the huge Danegeld sums in silver demanded by the Viking invaders.

Trade among the Scandinavian peoples was not interrupted either. In the tombs of Helgö and Birka, two Swedish trading towns which had a period of splendour between 400 and 1000, Arab, Frankish, and Anglo-Saxon coins, and luxury products from China, India, and Egypt have been found. These coins, more than 250,000 of them, and the precious objects accompanying them cannot have come from booty or from tribute alone, as supposed by the clichéd view of the Vikings according to which it was all a matter of piracy and looting. It was not the quest for booty which led them to colonize Iceland and Greenland, where they devoted themselves to stock-raising and hunting, nor to undertake the American adventure in Vinland in search of lands to occupy. Study of their activities in the British Isles has revealed that, following a phase of looting, the Scandinavians began another in which they came to settle. In Ireland it was they who founded the first towns and made Dublin into a great trading and craft centre.

The coins of the Caliphate which reached Scandinavia about the year 800 resulted from trade in which the Vikings carried skins, swords, amber, honey, walrus ivory (elephant ivory was very scarce then), falcons, and slaves across Russian lands as far as Byzantium, or, crossing the territory of the Khazars, on towards the Caspian and to Baghdad. Ibn Fadlan, who met these Rus traders on the banks of the Volga, describes them as fair-haired, big-bodied and well-built, covered in tattoos, dirty and evil-smelling, 'the filthiest of God's creatures'.

It was during periods when this trade slackened – as a result of the crisis in the Caliphate – that the Vikings devoted themselves to looting and piracy. Trade with the East started up again with a new objective – the coin came now not from Baghdad but from Bukhara and Samarkand – and this, together with the development of the Scandinavian economy, lessened the importance of their aggressive activities. From the eighth century they used part of the cash they acquired as a means of payment in their internal market, and from the ninth and tenth centuries they minted their own coins, which have been found in such distant places as Poland and Russia.

As can be seen, there was more adaptation than clean break. What was new did not arise out of any catastrophe, but out of the slow maturing of the early medieval centuries. The barbarian kingdoms did not seek to found new nations, but tried to preserve what they could from an Empire on which they based their own legitimacy. Clovis accepted the title of consul which Emperor Anastasius granted him, and made use of it to crown himself with a diadem in St Martin's in Tours, adopting, equivocally, the titles of 'Consul' and 'Augustus'. In Iceland Snorri

Sturluson married the history of the Vikings to that of the classical world, making Odin a descendant of King Priam of Troy (rather as the French had done centuries before, seeking their founding monarchs among those who fled from Troy).

However, this will to preserve what had been Roman could not amount to a restoration, since it was impossible to turn around a decadence which had ended with the disintegration of the old system. Charlemagne's attempt to have himself crowned emperor of a restored Rome was not viable and it failed. Contemporary chroniclers show his successors in a constant struggle against the barbarians: now the Franks have become 'the Romans' faced with other barbarians. Their gloomy pages show us prodigies of nature – earthquakes, comets that stain the night skies red, 'thick showers of tiny fireballs like arrows' – and seem to reflect the powerlessness of the new Caesars, unable even to prevent the Vikings reaching Paris or burning the church of St Martin in Tours. The project of re-establishing the Empire was a regressive one, doomed to fail when faced with the resistance of the European peoples. Europe was not made on the basis of the Carolingian empire, but in opposition to it. One of the most important features of the new European reality being forged in these centuries is indeed that the consolidation of new universal empires against the political diversity of its peoples and nations proved to be impossible.

Preservation of the ancient was, on the other hand, most effectively carried out on the terrain of lettered culture (which it is important not to confuse, as often happens, with the whole of culture). The Church managed to impose the exclusive use of Latin, access to the knowledge of which was denied except through education which that same Church controlled, in order to maintain its cultural hegemony and make the collaboration of the clergy indispensable in administration and politics. The Church combatted vernacular languages too, since they were the vehicle for the transmission of pagan cultures. In England most of the monarchs before the year 1000 (with a major

exception in Alfred) could not read, and when in France
there was one, Chilperic, who could, and even wrote Latin
verses, Gregory of Tours disqualified him on the grounds
that 'he did not follow the accepted rules of prosody'.
Charlemagne himself struggled to learn to write, 'but he
started on it too late and the results were mediocre'. What
the emperor really liked were 'the very ancient barbaric
songs' in his Germanic language.

The importance which legal texts in Latin seemed then to
acquire and the greater abundance of writings should not
mislead us about literacy in the Carolingian world. Many
legal decisions were transmitted orally – the written text
serving a double function as memorandum and as guar-
antee of elevated status – and many of those who went
to a notary to fix an act in writing, or to take part as
witnesses of the act, had only a passive kind of literacy.
Not even the lower clergy was literate. For parish priests
it was enough if they could spell out and memorize a few
formulas, and they did not always do this correctly, as
St Boniface discovered when he heard one priest baptiz-
ing 'In nomine Patria et Filia et Spiritu Sancta'. Graphic
representations, especially the paintings which adorned
churches in accordance with instructional iconographic
programmes, provided the 'books' by which the illiterate
faithful were educated.

A literate culture based on memory and not on the document considered learning as something outside time, something in which past and present mingled without a clear
distinction between them. When we speak of medieval renaissances, implying a certain sense of renewal, we distance
ourselves from the thought of the period, which did not go
beyond pure and simple *restitutio*, the recovery of the past.

It was indeed the Carolingian renaissance which consolidated the separation of old-style written Latin, understood only by the learned, from the vernacular languages.
Up to that time men such as Gregory of Tours or Bede had
written a *sermo humilis* closer to the speech of the people.
Their successors converted Latin into 'a purely artificial
language, written according to ancient models, and often

degenerating into a kind of pedantic puzzle', a language which produced only dead poetry, while out of the vernacular oral tradition there would later emerge the epics. Whoever insists on going in search of renaissances needs to be reminded that what is really valuable about the Middle Ages is not what it preserved but what it created. Also that those who did preserve the wealth of classical culture were in any case the Byzantines.

Furthermore, the culture of the Church cannot be properly understood if it is detached from the political dimension of its activity. When one speaks of the christianization of pagan peoples, the conversion – that is the public acceptance of religion by a ruler – is often confused with the propagation of the new faith among the people, which is a much slower process. Conversion to Christianity was, just as with the adoption of Islam, a political option. To join one or other Church involved integrating oneself in a system of relationships and alliances, and it had further important internal consequences.

Those Churches which preached that all power proceeds from God legitimized monarchical authority against the aspirations of the aristocracy, and offered the monarchy, besides, the help of people trained to handle the written word and organize the administration. Following his conversion, the ruler ceased to be first among equals and became a sovereign by divine right. If the Visigothic kings proclaimed themselves 'chosen by God', Otto III – son of a Saxon emperor and a Byzantine princess – was portrayed on his throne enveloped in the mandorla which usually surrounds Christ, while the hand of God the Father places the crown on his head.

Since law and religion were closely intertwined, religious unity was a necessary condition for legal uniformity. Recared's conversion to Catholicism eased the juridical unification of Germanic invaders and established inhabitants in the Iberian Peninsula. In Iceland the parliament decided that it was unhelpful for there to be two different lawcodes, and so encouraged the pagans to convert, for eminently practical reasons.

All this explains why rulers, once they were converted, were those most strongly concerned to win recruits for the new faith, by whatever means. In Denmark the runic monument set up at Jeling states that King Harald 'made the Danes Christian', while a Scandinavian poem says that King Olaf of Norway 'has made five lands Christian', since 'the king will always redden his shield and punish the wicked heathen practices'. We do not know what Clovis's religion was originally, but when he was converted he carried with him the greater part of his Frankish soldiers.

For the great Christian powers – Byzantium, the papacy, and the Carolingian Empire – acting as intermediaries in the conversion of a people meant taking it over politically: nominating its bishops and forging links of ecclesiastical dependence. This is why confrontations and disputes occurred. When, about the year 860, Prince Rostislav of Moravia asked for missionaries to come from Byzantium, the brothers Methodius and Constantine (he later became a monk with the name Cyril) were sent to him. These two selected a Slav language, devised an alphabet for it – Glagolitic, out of which would come the one we still call, in their honour, Cyrillic – and translated several holy texts. However, the attempt failed owing to political pressures from the Franks.

Pope Hadrian II called the two brothers to Rome, approved the liturgy in the local language, and sent Methodius as legate to the Slavs, hoping to secure the allegiance of new peoples. It was a time of strong rivalry with the Church in Constantinople and with that of the Franks: the latter did not hesitate to cast Methodius into prison so as to stop him disputing territory with their own missionaries, and they banned the use of the vernacular liturgy. After Methodius' death, Frankish pressures and disappointment at the small results obtained up to that time led the popes to abandon the priests Methodius had trained, these being imprisoned or sold as slaves. The popes further condemned the Slav liturgy, though the Church in Constantinople went on accepting it, on the grounds that the holy word could be translated only into the three languages that figured on the placard above Christ's Cross: Latin, Greek, and Hebrew.

The outcome of this struggle was a Slav Europe still divided today by religious-cultural frontiers that separate Croats and Poles, with their Catholic religion and Latin writing, from Serbs, Bulgarians, and Russians, with their Greek religion and Cyrillic writing. This has meant that each group shares much more than a choice of religion: each has a distinct model of thought and expression.

When it was impossible to convert pagan peoples by peaceful means, there remained the option of catechizing them by holy war. Charlemagne, troubled by the hostility of the Saxons, resolved to bring them to heel and converted them by such apostolic methods as chopping off 4,500 heads at a time, or issuing a law which threatened with death all who refused baptism. This method would be imitated later, thanks to the attractions offered by the chance to remain master of a good part of the lands of those who converted. The Slavs around the Baltic, who had built well-organized and prosperous societies, were an appetizing objective for this kind of conversion, in the same way as later, further to the east, were Prussians, Lithuanians, and Letts. In the Baltic, evangelizing activity began as an enterprise of Saxon knights who invaded Slav lands by force of arms, taking with them peasants to plough the fields and priests to pacify the dispossessed. The campaign was renewed later on a larger scale with the pope's approval. A whole series of northern crusades, begun in 1147 by Saxons and Danes, and continued later by the knights of the Teutonic Order, led to 'the defeat, baptism, military occupation, and at times the despoiling and extermination' of the Baltic peoples, subjected thereafter to the conquerors in body and soul.

Comparing the differing religious evolution of three peoples of similar ethnic and cultural origin may teach us something about this political dimension of conversion. The Bulgars were divided into two groups: one that founded a khanate close to the Danube, and another which settled around the confluence of the Volga and the Kama. Between these, on the shores of the Black Sea, their kinsfolk the Khazars had established themselves.

In 863 Boris, ruler of Danubian Bulgaria, decided to convert to Christianity. Franks and Romans hastened to send him bishops and missionaries, but the Byzantines persuaded him, using the powerful argument of a military expedition, to choose the eastern form of Christianity, which he did, adopting at the same time the writing system and the Slav language and the liturgy devised by Cyril and Methodius. Adoption of the language eased the fusion of the Roman and Slav settlers with the small ruling group of Bulgars who spoke a tongue related to Turkish, this group having until then communicated with the rest in Greek; while Christianity helped the ruler to strengthen his authority over the Boyars.

Half a century later the ruler of the Volga Bulgaria, seeking to draw a population of very diverse origins together, and needing help to resist the pressure of the Khazars, converted to Islam and made an alliance with the Baghdad Caliphate, which, thanks to its geographical situation, was the sole power from which help could reasonably be expected. A traveller from Granada, Abu Hamid, who crossed these lands in the middle of the twelfth century, picked up an old tradition according to which, when the Khazars began to attack the recently islamized Bulgars, 'certain huge men, riding whitish horses' fought at their side and assured their victory: these were 'God's troops'.

Meanwhile the Khazars had created a rich and powerful state between the Don and Volga basins, with cities devoted to trade in which people of all races and cultures could be found. Their prosperity was owed to their control of the routes used to exchange silver from the Caliphate for goods brought by the Rus from the far north. The need for the motley populations of their mercantile cities to live together in peace explains the tolerance shown by the Khazar rulers, who practised the Jewish religion but respected the faiths of their subjects, to the extent that they appointed seven judges so that they could give verdicts in accordance with the religious traditions of each group.

Here, then, there was no conversion in the sense of the official adoption of a particular religion.

On the other hand, the elements on the basis of which the medieval synthesis was built cannot be reduced to the sum and fusion of contributions from Roman, Germanic, and Christian cultures, as usually happens. Such a view neglects the significance of the reappearance of ethnic substrates – the legacy of preclassical cultures. It also omits the productive exchanges between the various European cultures, such as that between Vikings and Celts, and everything that we received from Asian science and technology, transmitted especially through the Islamic world, of whose cultural importance in the Middle Ages we get some idea from the fact that: 'Until the Renaissance and the Reformation, that is, until the period when the great wave of translations from scriptures and classics began in the West, Arabic was probably the most widely translated language in the world.'

Eurocentric prejudice, which reduces Islamic science to a mere translation of ancient Greek learning, forgets that Hellenistic culture was originally cross-bred, mingling Greek and oriental elements, and that the Arabs shared in this from very early times. It was in the Near East – where pagan sciences proscribed by orthodox Christianity were preserved, and 'kept going in secret until Islam arrived', as al-Farabi said – and in the period from the eighth to tenth centuries, that a start was made on the systematic translation of Greek works, especially by Nestorian Christians of Syriac speech. They made their Arabic versions from Greek originals and from the abundant Syriac versions then extant, the fruits of earlier symbiosis between these cultures.

There were also many other contributions that have nothing to do with Greece or with Hellenistic culture and which reached us through the Muslims: new crops, better irrigation methods, paper (cheaper than papyrus and parchment, which promoted the diffusion of texts), and a whole range of technical and scientific knowledge. In this the Indian numerical system which we still use should be emphasized, described by a modern scientist as 'the most successful intellectual innovation ever made on our planet'. This system and the numbers used in it – those we still call 'Arabic numerals' – came to us through the western Muslims, by the mediation of Catalonian monasteries in the tenth century, in one of which Gerbert d'Aurillac learned them. Had they not been adopted, the development of modern science would have been much more difficult.

A Europe open to all cultural breezes was ideal soil on which new things might grow. The failure of attempts to rebuild the Empire – from the east, by Justinian, or from the west, by Charlemagne – and the failure of the Church of Rome to impose rigid norms on thought and conduct, favoured the appearance of a space for communication and exchange, of goods, men, and ideas, where a culture rooted in the autochthonous substrate matured, with a large capacity to assimilate and integrate contributions from outside: a culture that was not Greek or Roman, but truly European.

This was no dark age locked in immobility. The notion of medieval stagnation does not fit the evidence that, in the course of 1,000 years, the continent's population doubled or tripled, cultivation conquered lands to the north of the Alps, and towns proliferated upon them. The increase in population and in agricultural production was accompanied by a boom in trade. This commercial revolution of the Middle Ages was a sufficiently new and surprising phenomenon to lead one author to speak of 'the explosive nature of the economic change which took place in the eleventh century'. Associated with the increase in trade was the industrial revolution which affected especially the weaving of wool, with the application of the waterwheel to the fulling-mill (from at least the tenth century), the adoption of the horizontal loom, and the spread of the spinning-wheel, which seems to have enabled production per hour and per person to quadruple in these activities. The enrichment of the producers led them to organize themselves (the guilds of the various crafts involved in textiles appeared in the twelfth and thirteenth centuries), and furthermore it led to the spread of work for wages.

It is agreed also that this was a period of cultural renewal, out of which there arose 'a more rationalist view of the way in which God acted on nature'. To this was joined 'the birth of the arithmetic mentality', with the abacus being used from the tenth century, and the spread of Arabic numerals from the middle of the twelfth century. There was also 'the invention of invention': a new attitude to technology which would lead, for the first time in history, to invention being no longer an isolated event but one transformed into 'a coherent project'.

Why did this sequence of inventions take place? At its origin lay, obviously, the progress in agricultural production which allowed the growth in population. But what were its causes? Conditioned by the nature of their written documentation, which reflects above all the interests of lords and landowners, historians have busied themselves especially with the institutional framework within which agricultural advances took place. It is impossible to synthesize here the various proposals made to explain these advances, complicated as they are by the fact that none seems to be valid for the whole of western Europe. The reasoning has to be varied for each regional model: from Galicia to the Rhône the initiative came mostly from the small peasants, moved by the struggle for survival and a hope of freedom; in other parts, within the bipartite system which combined the exploitation of the seigneurial demesne with the work of the peasants on lands granted to them, the lords took the decisions in their castles.

About the year 1000 – the supposed terrors of which seem to have existed only in the fantasies of those writing centuries later – the effects of this progress began to be fully visible. There was then in European society a fundamental mutation: the emergence of feudalism. This system legitimized itself by adopting the formal scheme of a society divided into three 'orders' or 'estates': that of the people who pray, that of those who bear arms, and, the largest, that of those who work to maintain the rest.

Each of these discharged a different and necessary function. Another view, more realistic and directed to an aristocratic public, compared society to a set of chessmen, in which the pieces are simply divided into two: nobles and pawns.

One recent piece of research maintains that what happened around the year 1000 was a revolution: a general break with the past which took place over only a few years and which has to be reckoned a European fact. Its results were the establishment of new modes of exploitation within the framework of the fief, new forms of political control based on personal bonds, a division of work between countryside and town which gave an impetus to the economy, and, in response to the rise of violence in the knightly class, the intervention of the Church and its movement in favour of the 'Peace of God'. 'There were thirty or forty years of convulsions; such was the price to be paid for the "birth of feudal society".'

When we speak of feudalism and of chivalry we refer to a complex which includes many very varied aspects. The word 'feudalism', says Duby, embraces two fundamental aspects: a political one, springing from the dissolution of sovereignty, and a territorial one, which creates a network of dependencies involving 'all lands, and, through them, those who occupy them'.

The power of chivalry grew out of its military capacity, which was closely linked to techniques of armament and of war. At an early stage, the efficacy of the mounted warrior faced with a fighter on foot explains the social rise of the former and the fact that he should be granted lands on which to subsist and to maintain his horses. Later the castle became the highest expression of feudalism, with its double intention so perfectly expressed by a twelfth-century historian who said 'there were many castles all over England, all defending their own districts, or rather plundering them'.

The growing use of bowmen in warfare – the Church in Councils of 1139 and 1215 tried to ban those arms being used against Christians – forced the knights to strengthen their defensive clothing more and more, passing

from chainmail to thicker and heavier armour between
1250 and 1350. But the proliferation of castles – which
transformed warfare into 'perhaps one per cent battles and
ninety-nine per cent sieges' – diminished the mounted
knight's importance (this passed to the castellan), and personal firearms made them virtually useless. When their
decadence began, the knights reinforced their legitimacy
by building an ideology which placed their social function
before their military usefulness. In this way the myth of
chivalry was created, with its mixture of aristocratic and
ecclesiastical values, and later European society preserved
it, since it offered the ideal model of how a superior
minority had managed to dominate the masses.

The second aspect of feudalism, that concerning the way
it brought lands and those who tilled them under control,
is harder to explain. What had been the old Roman lati-
fundium and the slavery system had given way in some
fashion to freedom and to the small peasant holding. How
and why was there now a return to this new form of subjection which we call serfdom? The answer to this question
leads us to note the existence of various strategies, adapted
to diverse social realities, which were applied in long and
complicated processes. There were no revolutions obeying
a single model of the sort that can be completed in a few
years.

A careful analysis shows how some of these changes
occurred over the eleventh and twelfth centuries in a place
in Catalonia. Where earlier free peasants had held their
property in allodium, there now began a period of domination by a family which accumulated lands, bought the
count's rights over the vill, established itself in a castle
and 'distinguished itself clearly from everybody else by
specializing in warfare and by its lifestyle'. This same
family founded a monastery to which it ceded some of its
rights. The monastery for its part increased its properties
gradually thanks to donations, but also by purchases from
peasants who were overwhelmed by financial problems
aggravated in their turn by the arbitrary impositions of
the lords in their castle. There then appeared a type of

personal seigneurial relationship which led to new forms of serfdom, at the same time as the monastery was strengthening its hold over people by new funerary customs which demanded larger offerings. In this way we can see how, in a rural spot remote from great centres of power, peasant freedom disappeared and a new society arose in which the emergence of the three orders reveals a simpler reality: the division into the rich and powerful on one side, and the poor and powerless on the other. Explanations of this kind – which can be reduced to a unitary model only when we have at our disposal a broad range of cases for comparison – bring us closer to the reality of the matter than simplistic models.

This great plan for the domination of European rural society could not have been carried out, however, without the aid of the Church. This is the period of the so-called Gregorian reform which takes its name from Gregory VII, pope from 1073 to 1085. The reform began inside the Church itself, with action involving the clergy. This included condemning the simoniac priests (those who had purchased their ordination or their posts; in reality, what mattered was preventing the lords and princes from awarding these offices), and trying to impose celibacy (the children of clergymen had to be stopped from inheriting ecclesiastical property, and even their fathers' churches), but the Paris synod of 1074 opposed the measure, holding that celibacy was contrary to human nature.

These measures of control over the clergy were complemented by the strengthening of the power of the Roman pontiff in the Church, by the creation of the college of cardinals and the holding of councils which met with the pope in order to take decisions which would be universally binding upon all the faithful. In the *Dictatus Papae* it was declared that the pontiff was above all synods, that he could personally depose bishops, and that there was no jurisdiction capable of judging him. Not for nothing has this period been described as that of 'papal monarchy'.

However, the most important aspects of the reform were perhaps those aimed at 'clericalizing' the Church, reducing the part played in it by laymen, and controlling the daily lives of the faithful through the parish, which sought to become the centre of Christian life and which strengthened its role by overseeing the setting up of guilds. This Church, ever more institutionalized and ever more enmeshed in the affairs 'of the world', caused in many Christians disillusion and unease, and in these lies the origin of future heresies.

Control over the faithful was reinforced also by new and much more restrictive rules concerning marriage and sexuality. These included greater limitations on marriage between relatives, and were accompanied by a serious effort to eliminate polygamy in aristocratic circles, where it was customary to repudiate spouses and contract new unions to suit one's convenience.

The relationship of the Church with the secular powers was a complex one. The Church at first tried to impose its primacy – maintaining that political power came from the pope as intermediary, not directly from God – but it ran up against the resistance of rulers and magnates. And when, in a period of confusion and insecurity, it tried to ally itself with the lower classes in the 'Peace of God' in order to defend itself from the violence of the nobles, the ever more resolute and independent actions of the peasants frightened the churchmen and led them to patch up their alliance with the aristocracy. The Church then sanctified the gentleman's knighting and encouraged the creation of military orders parallel to the ecclesiastical ones.

What has been described so far is, however, only the history of how there was established the rule of lay powers, dispersed along an interconnected chain of sovereigns and lords and of ecclesiastical powers over Christian Europe. The impulse towards growth in the Middle Ages had little to do with this. For a start, it seems that it is in the early centuries of this period – the darkest ones, in the traditional view – where we should seek the deeper reasons for the expansion. Recent findings of archaeology provide us with an innovative image of the phase which lasted from 600 to 1000, with agrarian growth beginning in the seventh century before the appearance of feudalism.

To explain this, the traditional view, preoccupied above all with the ownership of land and the appropriation of surpluses, should be complemented by another from below, one closer to the work of people. From this perspective we see that at the base of medieval agrarian growth lay the introduction of new methods of cultivation collectively organized by the peasants: the division of the lands into sections, allowing the fields to be left open once the crop had been gathered, so that livestock could graze on the stubble. This system represented an advance when compared with methods of cultivation by the individual, and it made it possible to develop more intensive methods of tilling which allowed the area under crops to be extended to the maximum (and to pass from a system of sowing every two years to sowing twice every three, that is where the climate allowed this). At the same time common grazing land was maintained to feed the small herd belonging to each peasant, thanks to which there was manure available for the crops, wool for the textile industry, and cattle which provided the pulling power that was needed for the heavier ploughs, required when ploughing most European land north of the Alps. (In a second phase, as trade in agricultural products developed, oxen tended to be replaced by horses.)

This growth took place in the context of a Europe that was changing in many ways. From 700 to 1000, in a broad region extending from Dublin to Kiev, there were many towns in which commercial and industrial activities linked to long-distance trade were carried on. Archaeologists have concerned themselves especially with the relationship existing between this trade and the acquisition of prestige goods by the ruling classes: these show the emergence of social distinctions and a hierarchy of power and wealth which announce the evolution of the tribe into the state. But the acquisition of these luxury goods presupposes that the societies receiving them had other goods to offer in exchange. This implies the existence of internal markets and, in consequence, of a complementary relationship among the kinds of work performed by the inhabitants.

If we place the European cities around the year 1000 on a map, we find that the greatest density of important nuclei occurred in France and Italy, as could be foreseen; but also in frontier lands such as Germany, Bulgaria, the Iberian Peninsula, and Russia. Most of them are grouped in regions presided over by a major nucleus, devoted usually to long-distance trade (which was generally the seat of political power, since trade was a good source of income from taxes), and surrounded by a series of settlements of the second, third, and fourth rank which together with the capital made up a coherent unit. Europe about 1300 was divided into a grouping of regions which prefigure the later division into national states.

What characterizes these structures, and makes them all too permanent – unlike older kingdoms, based on subjection to a central political power, and disappearing without leaving much trace except for ruins of palaces and fortresses – is the interconnection of activities in each one of those spaces. This forges links of solidarity among the inhabitants, on which a community of culture and language can be built. Medieval Europe had no large metropolis equivalent to those of the Roman Empire in its greatest moments – Augustus' Rome may have had more than a million inhabitants – nor in their time like those in the Islamic world, China, or south-east Asia, which got a good part of the food they consumed from international trade (about 1550 the nearly 200,000 people of Malaka, in Malaysia, depended for their subsistence on rice received by sea from Siam, Pegu, and Java). But European towns, unlike those of Asian empires, were solidly rooted in their surroundings and provided a stimulus for their growth.

Interconnection meant interdependence: a relationship between towns which establish themselves in a particular regional space (the relationship is between long-distance trade and craft production), but also between country-side and town. Urban growth and agricultural progress go hand in hand and allow first for a development of internal markets which not only assure the continuity of the economic boom, but also create protonational solidarity among people.

All this has to be explained as the result of an evolution which was not at any time interrupted. In place of 'the revolution of the year 1000' we would then have a long-lasting medieval mutation. The great social changes could be not the cause of growth in the economy, but the consequence of it: the strategy employed by the lords (and by the Church, whose interests were the same as theirs) in order to control a peasantry ever more emancipated and prosperous, with the aim of subjecting it to a new kind of control and profiting from its greater productive capacity. The very fact that the way of ensuring this was different in each area – according to the circumstances under which each situation unfolded – shows that the development of feudalism was in the nature of a response. Rather than a revolution, it was a reaction.

The explanation for the progress achieved then has to be sought at other deeper levels, concerning the collective activities of people, those that are less visible in written documents. These levels are those we can reach only with the aid of archaeology and of what some choose to call historical anthropology, which should help us construct a truer panorama of the history of medieval European man. In this instance the distorting mirror, the feudal mirror of chivalry, has been used to hide the role of the masses – that of ordinary men and women – from us.

4

The Devil's Mirror

When there is talk of the great awakening of the year 1000, it is often forgotten that the period was also one of social and religious conflict, this leading to the fixing of new frontiers: external frontiers which would separate Europe from the Muslims and from eastern Christianity, but also other internal frontiers, which would mark off a part of society itself. This falling back of Europe upon itself was supported by the making of a new image of 'the other', to be excluded and combatted. This 'other' was now not the barbarian or the pagan, but the heretic and the infidel, two names for the same face, this face being that of the devil who stands behind the two manifestations. The struggle against the devil's followers was carried on by means of crusade and Inquisition, with the systematic use of torture and the imposition of rules to segregate minority groups.

It was not only the Church that directed and inspired the crusade, for there was an alliance between the aristocracy and the clergy, a 'convergence of spiritual and material interests', which allowed the acquisition of immense wealth 'both temporal and eternal' as Baldwin of Flanders said.

The first enemy against whom the crusade was preached was Islam. The relationship between Christians and Muslims, which had not always been wholly confrontational, was from this time presented as a warlike epic that was to give a new sense to the whole history of medieval Europe (at the cost of glorifying trivial incidents such as the so-called battle of Poitiers in 732, which appears to have been little more than the elimination of a band of marauders).

This myth-making perception of the collision between Christians and Muslims did not correspond to perceptions in the Muslim world, which functioned with other sets of values (the world's most powerful ruler was the Caliph; the Emperor of Byzantium came in fifth place, and the kingdoms of the West figured nowhere in their reckoning), and it had a relatively tolerant attitude towards the 'religions of the Book' (Christians and Jews, but also Mazdeists), always provided their followers did not try to proselytize among Muslims. While Christianity denounced Islam as a 'false religion', and Muhammad as the devil's agent, the Koran speaks with respect of 'the prophet Jesus', accepts that he was conceived by Mary, a virgin, and agrees that the 'peoples of the Book' should be tolerated provided they pay tribute and maintain obedience.

For Europeans, the East was a land of marvels and uncounted riches, while in contrast, the Muslims saw little to admire in Christian Europe, considering this, not without reason, half-civilized. Ibn Jubayr found Messina 'full of stinks and filth', and Ibn Batuta thought no better of Constantinople, whose markets were 'piled high with rubbish' and many of whose churches 'are also filthy, and there is nothing goodly in them'. It was not only cities that seemed dirty to them, but European people too, for as a traveller reported 'they do not wash or bathe more than once or twice a year' and 'they do not wash their clothing every so often, but wear it until it falls apart'. Christians, for their part, were aware of their inferiority. In the *Histoire anonyme de la Première Croisade*, the author draws a revealing self-portrait when imagining the 'Emir of Babylonia' desperate with shame on having been defeated by the Christians, 'beggarly, unarmed, and wretched' people.

The Islamic world's superiority was based on an agricultural revolution which allowed the area under cultivation to extend and production to be intensified. This made it possible for a rich web of cities to be created, among them Baghdad and Cordova, the two greatest cities of their time. It was also a textile civilization, which promoted wool production in the Iberian Peninsula with the merino sheep, introduced cotton into the Mediterranean world, and propagated silk. The first eggs of the silkworm were brought from central Asia to Syria in the sixth century by a Nestorian monk and Syrians established in Andalusia acclimatized the silkworm in the West. Islam spread across an interconnected space from the Indian subcontinent to the Iberian Peninsula, a space in which people and ideas circulated freely and in which a brilliant syncretic culture was created, able to engender truly universal views of history, such as that of al-Tabari, or four centuries later that of Ibn Khaldun, who thought that 'history has as its objective the study of human society, that is, of world civilization'.

One consequence of this cultural superiority was its capacity for assimilation. We cannot overlook the ease with which Islam managed to transform a great part of the old Graeco-Roman and Christian world, in contrast to the unwillingness of Muslims to accept Christian culture. In the middle of the eighth century only ten per cent of the inhabitants of this immense empire had adopted Islam, but after two more centuries the greater part of the population had accepted it and a unified culture had been created, with a universally understood language.

Against the prejudiced view that conversions were effected at knifepoint, what characterizes the diffusion of Islam above all else was its ability to engender a feeling of collectivity and to cement together tribal groups and 'peoples otherwise living in highly factionalized or fragmented societies' into proto-state communities. If the ease with which they conquered huge areas of the old Mediterranean world, where they seem to have been welcomed as liberators, is impressive, the speed with which the assimilation of the conquered took place is more impressive still, since it did away with the effects of a 1,000 years of

Graeco-Roman civilization and several centuries of christianization. At the moment of the conquest of Egypt
(639–41) it was a matter of the entry of only a handful
of invaders, but by the tenth century Arabic was spoken
almost exclusively, and when Ibn Jubayr passed through
these lands in the twelfth century the country was pro-
foundly islamized, especially in urban areas of Hellenic
origin. The same happened in that great melting-pot of
peoples and cultures in the region extending from Syria
to the Persian Gulf, and in north Africa, the homeland of
St Augustine, where Christianity and Latin disappeared
early and the persistent substratum of autochthonous culture reappeared (while Judiasm, practised by a minority,
resisted without giving any ground).

The most spectacular instance is doubtless that of Asia
Minor. The land in which the Trojan War had been fought,
the land in which Herodotus, Anaxagoras, and Heraclitus
were born, and which is linked to Christian history by
such names as those of Antioch, Tarsus, and Nicaea, lost
both cultural legacies in little more than three centuries.
The long process of the Islamic conquest of Anatolia, with
its advances and withdrawals, destroyed the old structure
of the Christian churches, the sole cohesive force which
might have maintained the unity of the conquered. In their
place there began to arise mosques, schools, hospitals,
and Islamic charitable institutions which built an alternative social pattern and provided for the inhabitants aid
and social services of kinds which they had earlier received
from Christian institutions. Although there were some excesses, forced conversions, and a martyr or two, the reasons why in the early sixteenth century there were recorded
ninety-two per cent of Muslim homes in Anatolia have
more to do with assimilation than with the use of force.

Many things prove that the confrontation between Muslims and Christians was neither natural nor inevitable. Relations between Christian Europe and the Islamic 'Levant'
were frequent and very important for both, since the integration of a large part of Asia into Islam transformed
the Levantine harbours into ideal places for interchange

between East and West. Neither papal bans nor crusades put these relations in jeopardy. The trading peoples of the Christian Mediterranean – Genoese, Venetians, and Catalans – went on buying and selling in Muslim harbours, and were well received there as suppliers of wood and iron, little attention being paid to what the pope might think.

Although it cannot be said that the crusaders undertook their adventure with material gains in mind, it is certain that, once they had them in their grasp, they did not scorn them and kept up commercial activities which were vital for the survival of the Latin states in the East. In his travels through these lands Ibn Jubayr was amazed to see war and business existing side by side: 'At times the two armies face up to each other and form up in battle order; but caravans of Muslims and Christians come and go among them without being stopped.'

The crusading spirit has distorted our view not only of Islam, but of eastern Christianity too, and has led us to exclude Byzantium from the history of Europe (we see Byzantium as a decadent civilization, with oriental features – *Byzantinus est, non legitur*), and to exclude Russia born of the amazing fusion of Scandinavians, Slavs, and Mongols, and, worse, to exclude Asiatic Christianity. What we call 'the Byzantine Empire' never existed. The Byzantines called their state 'the Roman Empire' as they had every right to do, since imperial history there suffered no break with the past. In Byzantium people went on studying and glossing Homer's poems at times when in the European West ignorance of classical culture was such that somebody thought Venus a man, and François Villon included Alcibiades among the 'women of yesteryear'. Byzantium kept a notable interest in scientific knowledge going too – Alexius I frightened off the Scythians by knowing beforehand that an eclipse of the sun was going to occur.

The fact that the Byzantines were Romans and Christians was not enough to persuade western Christians to give them any help. First there was the Fourth Crusade, which captured Constantinople in 1204 and shared its wealth and lands out among those taking part. The crusaders, said

Condorcet, 'amused themselves by taking Constantinople and sacking it, as they were allowed to do, since its inhabitants did not believe in the pope's infallibility'. Later when the final campaign by the Turks began, and even though the Churches of East and West were reconciled by then, Latin Christianity had no qualms about accepting that an Ottoman sultan could become legitimate heir to the imperial throne of Constantine – as it showed by hastening to appoint a new patriarch of the Church in the East. The price paid for this was that 'Europe lived under fear of the Turk' for the next two and a half centuries.

Furthermore we have forgotten even the memory of that Asiatic Christianity which in the thirteenth century extended from Egypt as far as the China Sea, with ancient and well-rooted nuclei in Mesopotamia, Armenia, the Caucasus and Syria, and with more recent converts in central Asia among Turkic and Mongol peoples. To attribute the disappearance of these Christian communities to the triumph of Islam is to confuse the result with the cause. The religious situation of central Asia went on being unstable up the fourteenth century at least. The nomadic Asian peoples were tolerant or indifferent in religious matters and distrusted both the Chinese Empire and the expansionist tendencies of Islam, which led them to consider Christianity as a religion that helped them to civilize themselves without expecting them to renounce their own personalities.

The first Christian expansion into Asia was carried out by the Manichaeans, reaching its most brilliant point with the conversion of the Uighur people. These established an empire, maintained active trade with China, and had their capital at Karabalghasun with its twelve iron gates and a large royal palace.

The Uighur people collapsed in the middle of the ninth century, but Manichaeism survived: in the tenth century there was still a Manichaean monastery in Samarkand, and the faith seems to have survived into the thirteenth century in some of the small Turkic states. Rather than being a Christian heresy, however, Manichaeism was a kind of syncretism which united Christian, Judaic, Mazdeist, and Buddhist elements. Mani (216–76), who belonged to a Judaizing Christian sect, tried to forge a religious synthesis that should be valid for East and West at the same time, but although its missionaries, the chosen, carried his word from north Africa to China, they did not manage to create a stable ecclesiastical structure or to identify themselves with any of the peoples to whom they preached.

The important form of Asiatic Christianity was the Nestorian Church. Its origin lay in the Persian Church, which broke away from the Church of the West in 424 and sixty years later adopted Nestorius' duophycism – the belief that there are two distinct natures in Christ – thereby breaking the last links with Byzantium. Its religious leader, the 'Catholikos', resided in Ctesiphon, but their missionary activities followed the caravan routes and allowed them to set up Christian communities over a large area which extended from Sumatra to Azerbaijan. They also helped to transmit Hellenic culture to Persia, creating a great teaching centre at Khundishapur, and they were outstanding in the practice of medicine. The Muslim invasion did not interrupt their activities: most of the doctors in Baghdad were Nestorians, and one of them, Hunayn ibn Ishaq, figured among the organizers of the House of Learning in which the task of translating scientific and philosophical works from Greek was systematically carried out.

In 1009 the Keraits, the largest and most cultured of the Mongol people of central Asia, converted to Nestorian Christianity, at almost the same time as the Turkic Ongut people, descendants of the Huns. The Kerait state fell before the irresistible onslaught of Temuchin, who took the name Genghis Khan. This man maintained his relations with heaven on a personal basis, without mediation by priests (the *Secret History of the Mongols* narrates his religious practice as follows: 'He beat his chest with his hand and, kneeling nine times to the sun, gave offerings and prayers'). He respected the religions of the peoples he had drawn into his empire, while among his successors there were several who nurtured sympathies for the Christians.

It was at the urging of Kublai Khan that the Polo brothers asked the pope to send to him 'sages learned in the Christian faith and in all seven arts', and that they undertook their second journey to China, in the company of the young Marco (but without the sages, since the friars chosen for this mission by the pope had second thoughts along the way and 'went off with the Master of the Templars').

The Mongols were the incarnation of those hopes which Christianity had placed in the legendary Prester John. In 1258 they dispatched an Asiatic crusade which captured Baghdad, Aleppo, and Damascus, which the victorious troops entered in 1260 under the command of a Nestorian general, accompanied by an Armenian prince and a crusader. There too the Christians were able to recover a mosque for their worship, and to hold public processions. But the Franks from the Kingdom of Jerusalem, more intent on looting than on the crusade, chose to ally themselves to the Mamelukes and allow the latter to defeat the Mongol general, an action by which they sealed their own fate and ruined the possibility of an eastern Christianity extending from Mongolia to Palestine.

The blame did not rest with the petty crusading commanders alone. When the Ilkhan Abagha, protector of the Iranian Christians, sent an embassy to the pope in 1285 to ask him to organize a joint crusade against Islam, western Christianity refused the alliance. It preferred the annihilation of traitorous Christian heretics – every person who would not bow to papal authority was an enemy – to a joint triumph over the Muslims. At the time the head of the Church of Rome was busy organizing a crusade against Christian Catalonia in order to strengthen his political interests. He could not hope, on the contrary, for any benefit if Jerusalem were to be kept, since the crusaders had not accepted his claims to sovereignty. The Nestorian prelate Rabban Çauma was sent to the west again in 1287 in order to propose an alliance that might reconquer Jerusalem, which in the interim had returned to Muslim rule. He administered communion to the King of England and celebrated Mass in Rome itself, but nobody paid him any heed. The same happened with later embassies from the Mongols.

Little by little the last remnants of the crusader states fell, and although Nestorianism survived for a while in the monasteries of Uighuria the fate of oriental Christianity was sealed. Central Asia was wholly absorbed by Islam, and Roman Christianity was to fail when it tried on its own account to penetrate China and Japan. The Roman Church had lost its ability to assimilate other cultures and in future would manage no expansion worthy of the name other than the conversion – preceded and accompanied by harsh political action, conquest and domination – of the indigenous American peoples.

The closing-off of European society happened inwardly too, inspired by the actions of the Church, which isolated and repressed dissenters: the heretics. From Gregory VII onward papal control was consolidated – the *Unam sanctam* bull of 1302 declared that people could save themselves only if they remained obedient to the Roman pontiff – and the principle that the definition of doctrine was the business of the topmost hierarchy of the Church was established. These norms were implanted with the help of another of the new creations of these renovating centuries, the Inquisition, strengthened when ordinary means proved insufficient by recourse to a domestic crusade against men and women who had been baptized as Catholics.

The heresies now being persecuted had little to do with those of the first centuries of Christianity, held to have disappeared ('Either there are now no heretics or they don't dare to show themselves', said a Bishop of Norwich about 1100). What was now being called heresy was something less well organized and closer to the mass of the people, among whom, quite apart from doctrinal matters condemned by Rome (these being what stand out in the verdicts, in order to legitimize them) we find a substratum of popular beliefs which antedate Christianity, together with criticism and rejection of corruption in the established Church.

It is hard to know the true nature of these movements. The judges who condemned them have left us a biased view of them, one shared by many historians. They prefer to accept that a handful of fanatics, poisoned by the notions of a Bulgarian cleric, seduced the masses over half Europe, rather than wondering whether these masses might have been able to think for themselves and to mobilize when faced with problems that affected them.

We can now perceive the existence of two separate cultures: clerical culture and a folkloric tradition which 'burst out into western culture from the eleventh century, in parallel to the great heretical movements'. But we do not know what element of the living and productive there was in that alternative culture, beyond the treasure of traditions from which myths and representations have been taken. 'All that we know about the vast majority of the laity in the tenth century', says a German historian, 'is what clerics thought worth knowing. Modern historians must deal with a "silent majority", for their tenth-century counterparts rarely drew attention to the lower orders of society.'

When we start to dig around beneath the platitudes we realize that these people's ideas were more complicated than is generally thought. In the substratum shared by most of these movements we find elements of critical Christian thought (the demand for a return to brotherhood among the faithful, for a return to poverty and to the purity of customs which were assumed to have been typical of the early Christians). Such demands were reinforced in many cases by the feeling that the start of the third age was approaching, of that millennium of peace and happiness announced in the prophecies, and were reinforced too by a series of criticisms of a corrupt Church which was making common cause with the beneficiaries of an unjust social order. The Gregorian reform, while condemning simoniacs and postulating a return to the innocence of the early Church, caused some clerics, on seeing that this return was not happening, to join in criticism of a hierarchy which was incapable of carrying its own programme out. Ramirdus was burned at Cambrai in 1077 for having asserted that people should not receive the sacraments from clergy who were simoniacs or married or living in concubinage: that is, he maintained what the popes were preaching.

Priests and religious who desired a purer and poorer Church, peasants who resisted new ecclesiastical imposts – or who expressed their unease and their opposition to the new forms of feudal exploitation which were being laid upon them – and townspeople who condemned the alliance between the higher clergy and the aristocratic urban oligarchies, can all be found mingling in the common stock of heresy. One of the features that appears on occasion, and the one the Church seemed to fear most, was the emergence of women with an active role. Robert d'Arbrissel was followed by men and women who lived together. He founded Fontevraud, where the women lived the enclosed life, the clergy conducted services, and the laymen worked (the Waldensians seem to have arisen from the same context, since their founder had placed his daughters in Fontevraud before devoting himself to preaching). In some instances, the Church strove to integrate some of these ideas into its programme for reform, thus neutralizing them and even benefitting from them, but when it could not do this and deemed them likely to disturb the social order, it stigmatized and persecuted them.

The new heresies appeared precisely when the Church was no longer successful in imposing its authority, and it was the challenge to its power that provoked condemnation rather than the nature of the doctrines being preached. We can see this in the case of millenarianism, so deep-rooted in Christianity, which re-emerged through the agency of Joachim de Fiore (c.1135–1202). He enunciated a prophetic message based on the study of biblical texts and on a reinterpretation of history, which gave his doctrine intellectual prestige and assured its persistence in culturally lettered circles for some centuries. After his death his ideas found an enthusiastic welcome among the spiritual Franciscans who preached the imminent beginning of the 'reign of the Holy Spirit', an age in which men would live in accordance with the laws of love, without need of the sacraments. The Church, alarmed by the resonance these prophecies were obtaining, hastened to bring the Franciscans to book and condemned those who applied the Joachimite message to their own times, but without censuring the works of Joachim himself. One of these Franciscans, Gherard, who declared that Alfonso X the Learned of Castile was the Antichrist, was sentenced to live the eighteen years that still lay before him on bread and water. 'Had he not been a Franciscan', says Lea, 'he would have been burned.'

All these are ideas which were wholly or in part accepted by the Church and were condemned only when the groups proposing them escaped from the Church's control. When they did, the Inquisition garnished them with a sprig or two of sexual orgies and a few appearances of the devil, and sent the millenarianists off to prison or to the stake. This is what happened to Fra Dolcino, who announced that the third age had already passed and that a fourth one had begun, which would be characterized by the destruction of the fleshly Church (this losing its power and its wealth), domination by laymen, and a return to the apostolic model of absolute poverty. Dolcino and his followers were shown no consideration: an official crusade was organized against them and the 'apostle' and his woman companion were cruelly put to death.

An example of the ambiguity concealed behind the definition of heresy is provided by the *humiliati* of Lombardy. These were groups of laymen who lived on what they earned by manual labour, mostly in the wool industry, and they based their lifestyle on rules of biblical purity. They were officially condemned in Verona in 1184 by Pope Alexander III to perpetual anathema, but went on preaching and spreading and, surprisingly, they managed to get their case reconsidered by Innocent III in 1201: he let them become an accepted religious order, even allowing preaching by their 'tertiaries', mostly married laymen who went on living in their homes. Yet the most notable aspect of this case is that it becomes hard to distinguish their orthodoxy from that of other similar groups which were condemned, such as the Waldensians. Today, now that we know their early history better, we can note that such groups, persecuted above all for their criticisms of the clergy, began to drift away from orthodoxy only *after* having been separated from the Church.

A heresy is, in the last analysis, that which the ecclesiastical hierarchy finds unacceptable, for whatever reason (not always doctrinal) it might be. There are 'political heresies', cases in which the pressure for condemnation may have come from a monarch fearful of powers competing with his own, or keen to get his hands on others' property; the Church then provides the ruler with a suitable complement of aberrations, which it was not difficult to base on some confession extracted under torture. Guibert of Nogent, for example, speaking of certain heretics, assures us that

> They have their meetings in underground vaults or secret cobwebby places, without distinction of sex. After they have lighted candles, some loose woman lies down for all to watch, and, so it is said, uncovers her buttocks, and they present their candles at her from behind; and as soon as the candles are put out, they shout "Chaos" from all sides, and everyone fornicates with whatever woman comes first to hand.

If from these encounters any child was born, they burned it at a collective ceremony and made a loaf out of its ashes, handing this round to be eaten in a kind of sacrament. How is it possible that a clergyman who showed himself reasonably sceptical in the matter of the cult of relics should be able to believe tales like this?

The profitable piece of business which the trial of the Templars represented for the French monarchy at the start of the fourteenth century – they being probably innocent of many of the horrors attributed to them, though they were guilty of being too wealthy – was almost on the verge of being repeated a few years later when a plot by the lepers was invented, it being said that they planned to poison and infect all Christians, and that for this purpose they had allied themselves to the Moorish King of Granada. Behind this crazy fantasy, which led to a great number of lepers being tortured and burned alive, there lay one of those irrational panics which can come over a population, but also, doubtless, an intention to take over the rich financial resources of the leper houses.

One of the most monstrous examples of the political use of theological condemnation is that of the Cathars, whom, in order to ensure their punishment, the Church identified with the Bogomils. The latter had in their turn been helpfully described as Manichaeans, since this guaranteed that the death sentence would be applied to them: 'The accusation of Manichaeism', it has been said, 'was the ultimate political weapon in theological controversies.'

The Bogomils had emerged in Bulgaria in the tenth century, when there were still pagan Slavs and when in lands adjacent to the Byzantine Empire there were groups of exiled Armenians who professed Paulicianism, a form of Christianity which included dualist elements. The Bogomils' teaching, which included dualist features in moderation, proposed a return to the simplicity of early Christianity. The 'perfect ones' practised celibacy, lived in poverty, and ate only vegetables and fish; all rejected the liturgy, the sacraments, and images, and attacked the established social order, inciting serfs and slaves to give up working for their masters. It was not surprising that the movement spread through the Byzantine Empire, in which the peasants felt the increasing burden of their dependence on their lords, to whom the state had granted both lands and those that worked them. To the extent that they were proposing a return to the purity of the Gospels, they emphasized also the links between the official Church and the Empire, and thus became politically dangerous, since 'to challenge ecclesiastical dogma was equivalent to challenging the political ideology of the State'. What made them even more dangerous was the fact that they drew together the anti-feudal aspirations of the peasants: 'By slandering the wealthy, they taught their followers to stop knuckling under to their lords', said the priest Cosmas, author of a treatise against them. Although persecuted, they lasted until the Turkish conquest.

It seems clear that the dualist groups in the Balkans – Bogomils and Paulicians – influenced the rise of Catharism in Italy and Occitania. Yet the broad and enthusiastic welcome for these doctrines would be inexplicable if we were to reduce it all to merely passive acceptance. For a start, we have to distinguish the small group of those who followed the strict teachings of a Cathar Church (it seems that there were only about 1,500 to 2,000 perfect ones in Occitania) from the larger number of Christians who sympathized with men who preached a simple working life, took up beliefs closer to the common heritage of popular culture than to an imported theology, and used a few simple prayers, these not requiring any glossing by Church councils to define the sense of each word. What mattered above all was that in Occitania the Cathars, like the Bogomils in Bulgaria and in the Byzantine Empire, responded to the aspirations of the people much better than did the respective official Churches.

The danger for the Churches lay, then, not so much in the theologians' lucubrations as in that simple faith of the lower classes which resisted the efforts of the preachers. These preachers, speaking as they did in the name of a hierarchy given to accumulating wealth – drawn in good measure from tithes paid by the peasants – and allied to the feudal political order, could not enjoy among the masses the credibility of those who maintained that the authority of some men over others came not from God, as the Churches maintained, but from the devil. He had promised his followers that 'he would give some of them lordship over others, and that among them there would be kings and counts and emperors'.

Arnaud Gélis, a former servant of a canon and assistant sacristan, was among those arrested and interrogated by the Inquisitor Jacques Fournier, a century after the crusade against the Cathars. On occasions the dead appear to Arnaud, as to so many other peasants, and speak to him. In principle this is tolerated by the Church. What the Church cannot accept is that these dead persons should come to confirm the popular view of the other world, the one which holds that punishment, penance, and salvation of souls are matters to be resolved without the mediation of the clergy. After death, most souls must do penance while wandering about in this world, until the moment comes for them to withdraw to Holy Rest, a sort of earthly paradise, awaiting the day of the Last Judgement on which, says Arnaud: 'I believe that no soul of a person who has been baptized will be damned, but rather Christ, at Judgement, will in his piety and pity save all Christians, however evil they have been.'

How can one be surprised that confronted with such a faith, which allows itself to do without the Church, the latter should have insisted in imposing its view of Purgatory as a place of suffering and not of rest, a place in which to shut away once and for all those *revenants* who communicate directly with the living? Also that it should have imposed mediation by a clergyman, he being the only person who can negotiate for the relief or shortening of the torments of the dead by means of Masses, alms and indulgences? In these ways control over the faithful was secured and the foundations of a profitable business were laid. The business concerned the legacies which Christians made in their wills so that clergymen should pray for their souls, thus shortening their punishment, which helps us to understand the growing numbers of pictorial representations of Purgatory (with a collecting-box nearby for 'alms for people's souls') which are now being discreetly put aside.

There was a world of difference between this Church and that of the Cathars: a Church which does not demand tribute, does not excommunicate, or imprison, or kill; which is not in league with feudal lords, but instead casts doubt on the legitimacy of their power; a Church into whose doctrine the peasant's world of ancestral beliefs fits perfectly and whose conduct approaches the ideals of evangelical poverty. We must not fall into simplistic interpretations which identify religious dissidence with anti-feudal resistance; yet there is no doubt that the alliance between the city aristocracy of Toulouse, the weavers, and the peasants, fomented by shared opposition to the established Church, was perceived as a threat by the privileged class of feudal society in the north. The threat had to be removed; even the very seed of heresy had to be killed off, and a climate of terror created which would facilitate the reconquest of the faithful by orthodox preachers. The poor Franciscans seem to have carried out this mission better than the Dominicans who had lit the fires on which to burn heretics (although, in the end, it was only a question of a proper division of labour).

This sufficed to justify a crusade which jointly subjected the guilty – of thinking and believing differently – and the innocent to a fierce and excessive repression (one man was burned because he resisted the orders of the inquisitors to kill a hen which, in his opinion, had committed no crime for which she deserved to die). There are few horror stories more shocking than the song of the Albigensian crusade which describes the massacre of young and old, women and children:

> Flesh, blood, brains, and entrails,
> Limbs torn off and bodies disembowelled,
> Livers, hearts crushed and broken
> Dotting the public squares as if it had rained.

With this triumph of orthodoxy the expansion of the kingdom of France towards the south was assured, feudalism was saved and the rule of the Church of Rome was strengthened. The Church went on using the Inquisition's arm to liquidate not only heresy but also 'the disaffection of Occitania for the Church'.

However, the extirpation was not so complete as had been assumed, for it left a legacy of non-belief and anti-clericalism. A few years later the troubadour Peire Cardenal denounced the Church's lust for power – the lordship over the world was now being exercised by 'the clergy, who obtained it by robbery and treachery'. Peire addressed a *sirventés* to God in which, after complaining that 'this evil century has tormented my whole life', he denied it the right to condemn people after death, since it had allowed the devils to operate freely: 'If down here I suffer evil, and evil awaits me in hell also, by my faith it will be an injustice and a crime.' The old beliefs, coloured in the case of Cardenal with Catharism, refused to die.

A century after the crusade Jacques Fournier's interrogations show that popular religiosity had changed very little in a hundred years of repression and indoctrination. It was a less intense religiosity than is generally believed, and had a strong dose of scepticism, like that of the priest of Montaillou who did not believe it was God who made the seed germinate, for, if he did, seeds would produce flowers as much on stone as on the earth, 'it being the case that this happens on account of the fertility of the soil, and God doesn't come into it at all'. So we go on finding a mixture of old beliefs and Christian elements. Each person builds his own view of the world and orders his life, doing without greedy priests who demand new taxes – such as the first-fruits on the products of livestock which Fournier imposed by dint of official condemnations – and priests who threaten excommunication if he refuses to pay up. There are peasants too like Jean Joufre from Tignac, who attacks the clergy that excommunicate parishioners when they refuse to pay the new tithes, since he has not found in the Scriptures any mention of God excommunicating anybody or this being done to anybody. Furthermore he dares to criticize certain bishops who surround themselves with armed knights: 'I wish they were as keen to go off and fight the Saracens, conquer their land and avenge the death of Christ, as they are to demand their tithes and their first-fruits on meat.' All this led to him being walled up and dying.

Perhaps the most revealing example of the consequences of these domestic crusades, of this segregation of minorities, is the persecution of the Jews. They had been living on European soil for many centuries before the Slavs, Bulgars, and Magyars: why do we persist in considering them a foreign community when they are founding members of what we understand today as Europe? They were not a different people but a collectivity with its own cultural tints, one which shared in the making of European culture, not only as the principal channel of contact between East and West, but with their own contributions too.

Up to the eleventh century the Jews lived fully integrated: 'They were free men who spoke the same language as the local population, wore the same clothing, were authorized to move about on horseback with weapons, and to take oaths in the lawcourts.' The Sephardim, for example, showed pride in their status of having been born in Spain, went on doing so after their expulsion, and have preserved the Spanish language as their own up to the present, which shows up to what point they felt themselves to be integrated into the local community in which they lived. It was the Church, unable to accept the existence of a culture outside its control, which undertook the task of marginalizing them – from the Fourth Lateran Council in 1215 it never stopped demanding that they should dress distinctively and carry identifying marks – and it strove to prevent any contact and familiarity between Jews and Christians.

The persecutions of the Jews are often presented as a consequence of hatred based on irrational prejudices among the masses. But it is forgotten that that hatred and those prejudices, apparently unknown before the eleventh century, were fed by the Church, which created the myth of the internal enemy which it could blame for any collective misfortune. 'Let the Jews and the Moors live apart, not among Christians ... Let them be shut off behind a wall, for we have no greater enemies.' These words were uttered not by some ignorant fanatic, but by a prestigious clergyman whom the Church later canonized.

Is it any wonder, then, that the First Crusade was preceded and accompanied by persecutions and massacres of

Jews? The fact that the wealth of some – and their closeness to monarchs, which made them seem responsible for the rise in taxes – should have prepared the ground ought not to allow us to forget who sowed the seed. In this way there was eventually forged the stereotypical image of the Jew, easily recognized in pictorial representations. Practices such as usury, which were habitual among Christians, were condemned in them – in the courts of medieval Murcia there were cases brought by Jews against usurious loans made to them by Christians. Even a way of life which seems closer to our own than does that of late medieval Christianity was condensed, since they were reproached for cooking with oil instead of with animal fats, and for washing their hands before eating. Such prejudices might make us smile, were it not that they were the culture-medium which nourished legends about ritual crimes, such as that of the young martyr Simon in Trent in 1475, on whose account nine Jews were sentenced to be burned at the stake, or that of the Holy Child of La Guardia in Castile, which cost five persons their lives in 1491, even though nobody had missed a child at all and none had been reported found dead. But not as much as that was needed to prove the guilt of Jews who were now perceived in accordance with the devilish image reflected in the new distorting mirror.

5

The Rural Mirror

The later European Middle Ages are often divided into two phases: one of ascent and growth lasting until the middle of the fourteenth century, the second of crisis and decline lasting well into the fifteenth century. Estimates of the population of the continent pass from 79,000,000 in 1340 to as low as 55,000,000 in the year 1400 (implying an unprecedented catastrophe), the number climbing again to 75 million about 1500, a return to the figure of 200 years earlier.

The origin of this crisis lay in the very growth shown in the previous phase. Excessive expansion of the European population after the year 1000 forced people to till marginal, less fertile lands, in order to ensure food supplies, but this left subsistence generally dependent on a fragile balance which any climatic accident could upset. 'The happy times of high productivity were followed by bitter times in which marginal land, no longer newly tilled, punished those who cultivated them with repeated floods, droughts, and dust-storms', one historian has written. But the poet Ausiàs March expressed it better in the fifteenth century, writing of 'the rough peasant who casts good seed onto bad land, hoping to win a fine crop from that wretched field which will leave the granaries empty'.

A Europe biologically weakened by hunger was easy prey for the plague, with which the Mongols infected the Genoese at the siege of Kaffa in the Crimea. The Mongol khan who was besieging the place ordered the bodies of those who had died of the plague to be catapulted into the town, following a practice common at the time. The siege failed, but the plague, carried by twelve Genoese ships, reached Messina in 1347, and in the space of the three years following spread throughout most of Europe. It was a disease that was endemic in central Asia, which caught a European population defenceless and destroyed much of it.

The plague infected towns especially and in a few days killed half the inhabitants. Whole families disappeared, houses were left empty, and in the surrounding area fields were left untilled. It killed rich and poor: the King of Castile died, as did Giovanni Villani, a businessman and exact chronicler who left among his papers the words 'the epidemic ended in … ', and was unable to fill the gap by writing the date, while Petrarch lost 'the double treasure' of his patron, Cardinal Colonna, and his beloved Laura. 'Rotta è l'alta colonna è'l verde lauro', he wrote in a poem (Laura was by then a lady of mature years who had produced eleven children, probably fathered by Hugues de Sade, which makes her an ancestor of the 'divine Marquis'). The chronicler Froissart said that the plague had carried off 'a third part of the world'.

The medical world's remedies were useless: at the University of Montpellier, which had one of the best medical schools of the continent, all the doctors on the staff died. Equally ineffective were repeated acts of devotion (solemn processions and preaching campaigns in which it was taken for granted that the plague was a punishment for collective sins). The same was true of the bloody remedy of exterminating the poisoners supposed to be responsible for spreading the sickness (on this occasion, the Jews; in Milan in 1630 those thought to have smeared infectious materials, and in nineteenth-century epidemics friars or doctors, depending on the region).

The catastrophe begun by the Black Death explains the abandonment of ancient settlements and changes in agricultural production, with a decline in corn-growing, which needs a lot of human labour, and an expansion of pastoral farming which needs little. It left a deep mark too on people's minds. A frightening picture of the plague in Florence figures in the opening pages of the *Decameron*. Petrarch wrote in a letter: 'Will posterity believe such things, when we ourselves, who have seen them all, can hardly credit them?' Moreover the plague in Italy and central Europe was accompanied by great earthquakes and fearful portents. Villani said: 'These are miracles and signs such as those in Christ's preaching to his disciples, that are to appear at the end of the world.' It is logical enough to complete this sequence with a picture of profound social change into which can be fitted the frequency of commotions in the towns and the great peasant revolts, together with the rise of millenarianist sects. The Flagellants, for instance, started as a pietistic movement and ended up preaching the extermination of the clergy and the suppression of differences between rich and poor. It is hardly surprising that this impressionistic portrayal, in which phenomena of a social nature appear as repercussions of the natural catastrophe, should long have satisfied historians. However, several of the pieces in this portrayal are dubious, and the logic of the linkage between them is debatable.

The hypothesis concerning exhaustion of the soil is uncertain. Why should lands which in 1300 could not sustain 79,000,000 Europeans be able to feed them in 1500, when in the intervening years there were no changes from which we might expect an increase in productivity? The ruin of the once prosperous Italian cities and of their bankers was due especially to the bankruptcy of European rulers to whom they had made huge loans that could not be repaid. Villani, involved in the crisis as a partner in the ruined Bonaccorsi company, exclaimed that it was all a just punishment for the vice of some citizens who 'in their greed to make money out of the lords, entrust their own money and that of others to their power and dominion'. As for the social consequences – revolts in town and countryside, messianic movements, and so on – it seems plain that their origins must be sought in times before the plague, in the contest between those of middling status and the great to win power in the cities of France, Flanders, Italy, and the Empire, which had been going on for a long time.

Rather than persisting in seeing the plague as the cause of everything, we do better to place the facts in the context of the evolution of medieval society. In the upward-movement phase of this evolution there was agricultural advance, an improvement in town industries and a great increase in the interchanges between countryside and town. This situation benefitted small and middling peasants who sold their surpluses in town markets. It also led feudal land-owners to use personal services less and less (the peasant forced to work in this way ate more than he produced) and to commute those services for payments in cash, needed to meet the costs of tillage by wage-earners and to sustain the seigneurial family. In the towns enrichment created prosperous new groups which banded together to safeguard their interests and secure their rights against the opposition of ruling oligarchies. In Italian towns in the thirteenth century 'political conflict derived from the determination of the powerful to remain so and the growing desire of the new men to have a voice in the decisions that affected the entire community'.

While the economic improvement lasted and the connection between rural prosperity and urban boom went on, these conflicts were resolved by negotiation and compromise. Italian society then appears relatively open and mobile, and city government evolved gradually from aristocratic despotism towards republican liberty. In the countryside too the retreat of feudal domination took place at the same time as the economy of the great fiefs tilled directly by the lords was on the wane.

The signs of variability in economic advance were already present at the start of the fourteenth century, but there is no doubt that the plague accelerated and aggravated them. For the peasants the weakness of town markets meant the end of their prosperity. One might think that the natural effect of this would be to turn back along the chosen course, with a return to production for one's own consumption. But the changes were irreversible. The countryfolk needed money to pay the feudal dues that had been commuted and to meet growing tax demands. In a situation of falling agricultural prices, many peasants found themselves forced to give up farming, and not a few tried to defend their livelihood by revolting.

Pressures towards social transformation were irreversible too. Yearnings for freedom which had stamped themselves upon men's minds were not going to disappear because the economic situation had changed. The *popolo minuto* went on struggling to have its say in urban government; the serfs, for their freedom; the peasants, for the abolition of feudal abuses. With the economic crisis, the resistance of the upper class hardened, which stopped the functioning of the combination of violence and compromise that had characterized Italian society. After the Black Death the social structure of the great Italian cities petrified: social mobility diminished and the polarization of rich and poor increased. The outcome of this was ever-increasing violence in society.

This can be seen in the revolt of the Florentine craftsmen and wool workers. Machiavelli tells us how as the conflict went on the very fear of repression drove the lowest group, that of the wage-earners, to make more extreme demands, feeding a social consciousness which led them to discover that society was not based on reason but on force: 'God and Nature have placed the fortunes of all men among them, being exposed more to robbery than to industry, more to evil arts than to goodly ones; hence it comes about that men gobble one another up, and that the least powerful among them always comes off worst.' These radical declarations from the wage-earners did not now suit their former allies, the craftsmen in their guilds, who ended up by reaching an agreement with the oligarchy and helping to put the rebels down in bloody fashion.

What came out of these confrontations in Italy was an oligarchic régime able to restore peace in the small states, handing the legislative function to the *pars valentior*, to those who are stronger. These were republics in which power was in the hands of a small group of citizens – generally around one or two per cent of the inhabitants, that is some 200 to 600 persons in cities such as Florence and Venice – who were qualified to be elected to a state office, all this creating a sharp distinction between these *statuali* and the great mass of the common people.

This class was able to overcome threats such as that posed by Savonarola's plans for democracy. He maintained that it was 'necessary to resolve that the authority to distribute offices and honours resides in the whole people', and had the great Hall of the Five Hundred built in the Palazzo Vecchio for the Great Council of the People for that purpose. They also managed to maintain social cohesion by various means. They provided the common people with plenty of work building and decorating churches and palaces: it has been reckoned that a quarter of the guild craftsmen belonged to the building trades. At the same time they provided a chance of rising in society to those who showed talent for art: Fra Filippo Lippi was a butcher's son; Botticelli was the son of a tanner, Andrea del Sarto a tailor's and Pollaiolo a poulterer's. With good reason this sumptuary spending has been described as 'a process of redistribution of wealth'. The ruling class was also able to draw the people to itself in more subtle ways, through the support given to some lower-class city groups such as the *potenze* in the various quarters of Florence: these, having started as charitable brotherhoods, took on a decisive role in organizing public festivities, which gave them a presence and a representative function.

Italy led the rest of Europe in discovering forms of social integration which allow us to explain why, after the violence of the thirteenth century and the great conflicts of the fourteenth, on the whole it stood aside from the European crisis of the fifteenth and sixteenth centuries. But this very fact, which rendered unnecessary the formation of one of the great absolutist states there, left Italy in an inferior position when faced with the military power of the great European monarchies, who invaded her soil from

1494 and for three centuries turned the peninsula into the object and the victim of conflicts having nothing to do with it.

Italy was an exception. We must look at other European scenarios. In England, for example, we must distinguish the effects of the long-term crisis, to which people adapted themselves, from the unforeseen blow of the plague which, by suddenly worsening the situation, made the pressure of the lords upon the peasants and the continuous tax demands of the state intolerable. The response of rural society was the great rebellion of 1381. It all seems to have begun with the refusal of the peasants in Essex and Kent to pay their taxes, this leading, at the end of May and beginning of June 1381, to an open confrontation with the commissioners sent to enforce collection. Out of these early skirmishes there emerged a broad movement headed by Wat Tyler, in which craftsmen and clergy participated, among them John Ball, he who put the question 'When Adam delved and Eve span, who was then the gentleman?'.

This movement had two bases. The first was the peasants' opposition to seigneurial demands, customarily shown in refusal to pay and in various forms of attack, generally localized, upon seigneurial authority. The second was an anticlerical undercurrent among the people which enthusiastically welcomed the denunciation in *Piers Ploughman* of corruption and greed among the clergy, with the declaration that, if things did not change, 'the worst misery of man will mount up quickly'.

This time the revolt went further than local struggles against the lords and became a confrontation with the government and the social system as a whole, for it included as one of its demands freedom from all serfdom. Some of its leaders, such as John Ball, even spoke of setting up a society in which everything would be in common and there would be no differences between villein and knight.

Supported by the city's poor folk, the rebels entered London, and Wat Tyler presented the king with a petition whose principal point was that 'in future no man should remain a serf, and should not render any kind of homage or service to any lord, but should pay him instead a rent of four pennies for his land'. While forces were being prepared to suppress the rebels, the king accepted all the demands; then Tyler was assassinated by the Mayor of London – who was rewarded for this with a title of nobility – and the revolt was quickly crushed.

At this same time the heresy of the Lollards was growing in strength. It was inspired by John Wycliffe, an Oxford theologian who conceived Christianity as the communion of the chosen. He accepted the Bible as the sole undisputed reference text (and hence promoted its translation into English, in order that the faithful could read it), and criticized the corrupt hierarchical Church, proposing that its property should be taken from it so as to restore its purity. After being expelled from Oxford and having his doctrines condemned, Wycliffe spread his ideas through a group of poor parish priests who denounced the tyranny of the higher clergy and the hypocrisy of the friars. He explicitly condemned the rebels of 1381, but could not prevent the Lollards being blamed for spreading the kind of ideas that were causing the peasants no longer to respect property rights in woodland, parks, and seigneurial preserves. The Lollards were stigmatized as enemies of the social order, and with that behind them in 1401 the bishops secured a law which allowed them to burn the heretics.

Unrest did not disappear, however. In the middle of the fifteenth century the so-called rebellion of Jack Cade caused upheavals in the English countryside once more. In Sussex, peasants and craftsmen rebelled against the abuses they were suffering and especially against seigneurial exactions. Their purpose, according to evidence from the time, was to 'destroy the lords, both temporal and spiritual'. They first asked for a new king, and later, that twelve of their number should rule the land.

The social upheavals arising from confrontations had nothing to do with any demographic catastrophe; this is shown by the fact that one of the most important, the

Hussite revolution, happened in Bohemia, which had not suffered the consequences of the plague. It was precisely here, among the poor of Tabor and in the communities of Brethren, that the people's demands were expressed in their most radical form. This does not mean, however, that this movement was different in nature from the others, as is proved by the presence beside the Hussites of Waldensians, Picard heretics fleeing from France, and followers of Wycliffe such as the English Lollard Peter Payne, formerly a master at Oxford.

John Huss, educated in the midst of a local movement for reform of the Church and strengthened by reading Wycliffe, began to preach in 1410 in favour of rejecting the sale of indulgences (which the pope had sent to be sold in order to collect funds to finance his war against Naples), and began to write in Czech for a middle-class and lower-class public. Summoned to defend his ideas before the Council of Constance, which he attended with a safe-conduct from Emperor Segismund, he was imprisoned and died at the stake in 1415. Four hundred and fifty-two noblemen of Bohemia and Moravia signed a letter of protest, at the same time as the Hussite clergy began to give the laity communion under both species, as a protest against the privilege which kept this for the clergy. This converted the chalice into the symbol of a Church then called 'Utraquist', on account of the communion under both species, or 'Chalicist'. At this same time too an intense emotion tinged with nationalism affected Czech lands, with the result that what had begun as a demand that the papacy should accept a minimal programme of reform became a war of religion led by a national Church with the support of nobles and bourgeois.

The Hussite revolution shows us the complexity of motivations which might come into play in one of these great movements, and they allow various interpretations of it to be given, according to one's point of view. In this interpretation, reforming action supported by nobles and bourgeoisie, who aspired to little more than control of the Church and the secularization of its property, coexisted with the radicalism of the people's movement in Tabor. While in Prague they contented themselves with proclaiming the four articles – freedom to preach, communion under both species, poverty for the clergy, and social control of morality – in Tabor the faithful thought the end of the world was nigh and expected the coming of Christ. They exhorted Christians to abandon the cities and take refuge in the hills or in holy places. 'In this time there shall be no kingdom, no rule over others, no serfdom', they said, and all things shall be in common: 'Nobody should possess anything of his own, for he who has something for himself commits mortal sin.' The hour of vengeance had come, and the brethren of Tabor were 'God's representatives', sent to exterminate all evil people 'with arms and with fire'.

Six crusades sent against the Hussites failed to finish off the Chalicist Church, and if the radical wing of the movement was crushed by the moderate Hussites themselves, its ideas, especially criticism of a society graded into estates and the refusal to accept than men had the right to appropriate lands and subject others to serfdom, reappeared in the teaching of the Union of the Brethren. The first three priests, ordained in 1467, were a peasant, a miller, and a tailor, and the last bishop, as late as the seventeenth century, was the great philosopher Comenius.

It is not easy to clarify the deeper motivations of these movements. The task is made more difficult by the use of a religious language which was part of these people's culture, of men for whom the transformation of society was linked to their religious expectations. These expectations led them to hope, in accordance with promises in the Gospels, for 'new heavens and a new earth, wherein dwelleth righteousness'.

In Europe in the centuries from the fourteenth to the sixteenth these episodes tended to have increasing importance and to happen more often. No earlier peasant revolt had attained the dimensions of the Jacquerie or the English rising of 1381. There thus began an era of social conflicts which were to be linked almost without interruption to the German peasant wars, and which became a huge threat that gravely alarmed not only the privileged classes but also broad sections of the bourgeoisie.

The clergy itself was divided. Most of those who wanted to reform the Church had no intention of subverting society. Neither Wycliffe nor Huss wished to lead a rebellion of the people, but there were Lollard clergymen who followed Wat Tyler in his struggle to create an egalitarian world, and those who organized Tabor as a community in which private property had been abolished were priests.

Social agitation continued without pause up to the German peasant wars which inspired great fears. In 1476 the Virgin appeared to Hans Behem, shepherd and drummer of Niklashausen, urging him to preach a life of poverty and devotion. Since peasants were travelling many miles to hear him, the Church mobilized against the false prophet: he was accused of preaching against lords and clergy, arrested, charged with heresy, and burned alive. Movements such as that of poor Konrad and the rebellions of the Bundschuh, in 1517, link these episodes to that which broke out in 1524.

The great upheaval began in the spring of 1524 in the Black Forest, when the peasants refused to pay rents and feudal services to the abbey of St Blasien. It got worse in June, when a countess claimed that some of her peasants who should have been occupied getting the hay in were busy hunting for snails. Taking fire in countryside and towns, the revolt spread from Alsace to the Tyrol in the course of the two following years. What gives this movement special importance and distinguishes it from earlier peasant revolts is its extent and generalized nature, making this the greatest revolutionary movement that has ever occurred in Germany.

Although it is usually called 'the peasant war', the contemporary rural folk referred to were not only peasants but included lower-class townspeople too. Some idea of the complex motives for the revolt is conveyed by the various programmes of the leaders. They include demands about freedom for the serfs and the lords' abuses (appropriation of lands held as communal property, requirements of excessive services of work, and so on), together with other demands concerning municipal government and those about ecclesiastical matters, such as the community's right to choose and remove its pastor, the suppression of the monasteries, and other matters. Beneath these programmes lay grave peasant unrest, a tradition of anticlericalism, and the belief that these demands from the people were part of the movement to re-establish the law of God that was being set forth by the theologians of the Reformation. The Memmingen constitution, for example, ends by nominating a series of theologians – Luther, Melanchthon, Zwingli, and others – who are to 'determine the substance of the divine law'.

The movement began peacefully in many places, trying to force the lords to negotiate, with the certainty its members had in their conviction that they were asking only for what was right. Luther hastened to condemn them and to ask the princes to punish these 'peasant hordes of thieves and murderers', but the rebels had on their side theologians of the stature of Thomas Müntzer, who legitimized their actions by declaring that God had given the power of the sword and the power to pardon sins to the community of Christians. He ended by paying for this concession with his life, having his head cut off in Mülhausen.

After the defeat and bloody repression of the peasants – which inspired in Dürer, in 1525, the project for a monument to a dead countryman – the radical reform went on. Ten years later there was a further episode of the same struggle in Münster, from where it might have spread to Holland. But the attempt to instal the Kingdom of Christ in the city ended in a bloody massacre in which Catholics and Protestants collaborated to murder even Anabaptist women and children.

All the while their gaze took in only aspects of religious demands, the Christian humanists who were heirs to the *devotio moderna* took a kindly view of these mass movements. Erasmus himself was not too scandalized when he heard the first news of attacks on friaries, thinking that it was just a matter of protests against the friars. But when

social aspects began to appear – that is when a group
of Dutch craftsmen took part in the Kingdom of the New
Zion in Münster and tried to take over Amsterdam –
Erasmus, who was at death's door, could not conceal his
horror at the possibility that the lower orders should seek
to control society. One of his followers, the Valencian Luis
Vives, maintained in his book *De communione rerum* that
these communitarian ideals were not suited to Christianity,
which preaches only voluntary charity. He wrote that to
apply them would be impossible, since they shattered the
just social order and overlooked the fact that 'Christ's
law distinguishes between masters and servants, between
magnates and people of low estate.'

The radical groups were persecuted with equal enthusiasm by Catholics and Protestants: the tragic death of
Servet on the Calvinist bonfire shows that inquisitorial
horrors could occur in both camps. They managed to survive in the few refuges for religious freedom that remained
in Europe. The Anabaptists fled from Germany. Some set
themselves up in Moravia, where they found a climate of
tolerance that allowed them to live according to their
principles, living in communal houses and sharing work
and consumption. What awaited them if they fell into their
persecutors' hands was shown by the case of Jakob Hutter,
who was arrested in the Tyrol in 1536, subjected to torture
and burned alive: 'They sat him in freezing water and then
moved him immediately to a boiling bath, and they lashed
him; they opened his wounds, poured brandy into them
and set fire to him, leaving him to burn.'

All such cases of resistance to the established order –
on the political, economic, social, and religious planes –
are usually presented to us as anomalies in the normal
course of history. This is because we have built our explanation of the evolution of European society in such a
way that we are led to see everything that leads up to
our present time as normal, and to consider what departs
from this norm as aberrations or, for those who view them
sympathetically, as non-viable Utopias. Such a viewpoint
demands that we see these aberrations as concrete events

to be measured against the normality of their time, without seeking too many relationships between them – that could lead us to admit that there might have existed an evolutionary line distinct from the normal one, this having its own rationale and coherence.

However, if we examine European history in its passage from the Middle Ages to the modern period with eyes not clouded by mirages (such as that of attributing all economic, social, and even cultural changes to the plague, or that biased interpretation passed down to us by those who triumphed over people who tried to change the world), we discover that perhaps there was an alternative to the evolutionary path so far followed, a coherent programme for founding a more just and egalitarian society. Traces of this may be discerned in the complex of ideas forming what we are wont to call the 'popular culture' of the period, which it would be much better to call 'critical culture', since its characterization as 'popular' is a resort thought up in order to relegate it to a plane below that of the 'lettered culture' of the elites. This would allow us to set up a model which would bring the so-called anomalies together and point towards a global interpretation of the grave social crisis which shook the continent. We spoke earlier of the existence of a folkloric tradition which appeared from the eleventh century, at the same time as the great heretical movements, and which presented itself as in some sort an alternative to clerical culture. It is not a question of something merely rustic, as the modern sense of the term 'folklore' might suggest, but of a broad current of critical culture in which members of the literate population played a part.

In the margins of medieval manuscripts – missals, books of hours, courtly *romans* – there are burlesque drawings: a nun giving suck to a monkey as a parody of pictures of the Virgin, scenes of coition and of defecation, fantastic creatures and trees whose blossoms are phalluses. In churches and monasteries satirical and indecent images are common: prodigies of obscene wit can be found on the woodwork of choirstalls.

We find ourselves in a world of tales, images and representations which feed, on one side, on proverbs, myths
and popular beliefs, but which are also closely related to
an alternative culture of literate origin, coming together in
a symbiosis in which it is hard to separate out the con-
stituent elements. This is the world of the Goliards and
the *Carmina Burana*, of macaronic texts which parody the
Bible, of imitation liturgies which include grotesque prayers,
the *Gospels of the Distaff*, the erotic *fabliaux* and the
farces, such as that of 'Master Pierre Pathelin' in which a
shepherd from the countryside ends up deceiving a shyster
lawyer.

Chivalry as idealized in the epics is ferociously parodied
in works such as *Audigier*, the poem in which the scene
of the protagonist's knighting is ruined by an old woman
defecating in the middle of the ceremony, or in *Trubert*, in
which a clever peasant cuckolds a duke and deceives a
king in bed. Best of all, with its fully aware intentionality,
is *Aucassin et Nicolette*, in which the principals are a bun-
gling knight given to tearfulness and a heroine full of resolve and energy. It also has elements of 'the world upside-
down' as in the kingdom of Torelore, where the king keeps
to his bed for the birth of his son and the queen goes off
to a war in which the combatants are armed with fresh
cheeses, ripe fruit, and huge mushrooms, and in which the
king cools Aucassin's warlike enthusiasm by telling him
that 'it's not the custom for us to kill each other'.

The kinds of reversal and parody that were practised in
festivities form part of this culture. Festivities of religious
origin included that of the madmen, in which a choirboy
was named 'bishop' for Holy Innocents' Day and was
taken out in procession, while his canons generally ended
up disguised as women, burdened down with bottles of
wine and playing dice in the church. There was also the
Feast of the Donkey in which liturgical ceremony was
imitated inside the church. Especially there were lay festivities, such as Carnival – even though it took the religious
event of the start of Lent as its pretext – organized by
brotherhoods, guilds, and societies.

Bakhtin managed to interpret this collection of parodic manifestations in a global way, concluding that the essential function of grotesque realism was degradation, which allowed lofty things to be expressed in bodily form and vulgarized. He did not perceive, however, what this implied in the domain of social criticism. It is a question not only of ridiculing certain of the fundamentals of a society organized by estates – the liturgical forms of religion, the knighting of the gentleman – but of recalling the essential unity of mankind, by displaying kings and bishops performing the same physiological functions as their subjects and as their flocks.

If this cultural complex is to be understood there must be added to it, furthermore, the aspect of religion known as the 'popular' one: that particular and peculiar view of religious matters which is compatible with ridiculing ceremonies and official rules, that anticlericalism which demands a greater share for the laity in the religious sphere.

It is not a matter, as is often said, of an essentially peasant culture. The opposition between the poor townsman and the peasant is a false one. Countryside and town live in a much closer relationship than is usually supposed. Criticism is directed above all at the privileged groups who seek to rationalize their exploitation of others by using the theory of the three orders (or by the older version which compares society to the human body, reaching the same objectives of justifying the idea that certain limbs must work in order to sustain other nobler ones), and is extended to literate people who share this ideal about society. Ridiculing the peasant – which some attempted to justify on account of his stupidity, but was really directed at his lack of docility – comes from these circles, and is sustained by an unspoken fear of his rebellious nature. What is reflected in the episode of Lietard and the bear in the *Roman de Renart* is not contempt but hatred and fear, natural enough in a literate author who is on the lords' side and who advises them to be tough with the peasants, whose word is not to be trusted, 'and I speak from experience'.

To put aside the whole of this critical culture as 'popular', contrasted with 'literate culture', is to falsify reality, since many elements of it appear in the work of the literate of the period. The Machiavelli who wrote the discourses on Livy is the very man who wrote *La mandragola* and the *Canti carnascialeschi* and who deals in *Dell'asino d'oro* with the theme of the dispute between the animals and man about who is the more noble, concluding with the condemnation of man, the sole animal that 'kills, crucifies, and despoils' others of his own species:

> There can be no other animal that has
> A life more fragile, also more desire to live,
> More confused a fear, or greater rage.

The bias with which we have been taught to view these things, with an explicit scorn for the 'little tradition' of the illiterate, prevents us understanding fully today men like Machiavelli or Pieter Bruegel. Faced with the depictions so full of vitality and merriment in which Bruegel has reflected the peasants' world, viewers give us time and again the cliché that these are caricatures. In his engravings and pictures, it is said, the rustics 'have coarse features and empty faces', from which one deduces that 'it is possible he shared the traditional view about the peasant's stupidity'. This is a gratuitous affirmation. It is enough to see the *The Wedding Banquet* in the Vienna gallery to spot calm, intelligent faces, among which there figures the painter's own face, portraying himself at one of those popular festivities in which he did not disdain to join. Bruegel got the greater part of his income from the sale of engravings produced for a broad public, engravings nourished by elements drawn from popular culture and especially from the fables, proverbs and sayings of his country. (In just one of his works allusions to 118 different proverbs and sayings have been identified.) A viewer today sees invention and fantasy in things that were for the people of his time a shared language which everybody understood.

The most eloquent example of what could be achieved with the cross-breeding of the popular and the literate, joined in a single critical vision, is doubtless Rabelais's work. He had all the treasures accumulated by popular wisdom and at the same time had a solid scientific and humanistic training. He called Erasmus 'father', ridiculed arid traditional bookish learning in the prodigious catalogue of the library of Saint Victor, and celebrated the progress of the new learning – 'today all the disciplines are reborn' – in the letter in which Gargantua sets out an extraordinary programme for study by his son. He scorned 'those who build anew with dead stones' and set up his programme against them: 'I build only with living stones, that is to say men.' He did not hesitate to denounce, part-seriously and part-joking, the religious intolerance of both sides. This resulted in the censuring by the Sorbonne of his *Third Book*, 'full of various heresies', and in the condemnation and banning of the *Fourth Book*, which may have put him in jail and whose publication came only a short time before his death. The fact was that the journey through those wonderful islands which he proposed in the *Fourth Book* and which someone finished in the *Fifth* on the basis of his drafts was already an impossible one. The project set out in Gargantua's letter for the making of a world illuminated by science, in which tolerance and civility would rule, as in the Abbey of Thélème, could not be carried out. The *Fifth Book* was published at the time when Ronsard was writing his *Discours des misères de ce temps*, concerning the misfortunes of a country riven by the wars of religion, of a France 'which her own sons have imprisoned, stripped, and vilely beaten to the point of death'.

The great fear of social upheaval finished off any plan for a transformation which might have merged humanism's ideals of political and religious reform and the aspirations of European lower classes seeking a more egalitarian society into one sole undertaking. An undertaking close to the ideals of the Gospels, in which peasants would do no more than pay a proper rent to their lords (as the English rebels were demanding in 1381), towns would be governed by broadly representative councils (as Savonarola wished), and religion would not be controlled by a hierarchical Church but would actively involve the laity. Such a programme would have allowed the building of a society in which learning and thought were free, unburdened by censures or inquisitions, and in which men like Huss and Servet would not have had to pay with their lives for thinking differently.

By the middle of the sixteenth century such dreams had been practically extinguished. A new spectre had come to terrify Europeans: that of the coarse, stupid, and evil rustic who put the established order in peril. The image of the enemy to be combatted was now that of the rustic, coloured in all the possible shades of barbarousness, ignorance, and baseness that characterize the villein compared to the noble.

6

The Courtly Mirror

At the start of the sixteenth century the established order in Europe seemed to be threatened. The ancient pressure of the nobles and the new pressure from monarchs demanding more taxes and more soldiers weighed grievously on the lower orders, particularly on the peasants. Unrest among them was expressed in ever more frequent revolts. It has been reckoned that in the fourteenth century on Germanic soil there was generally a revolt in every generation (that is every twenty-five years) while at the start of the sixteenth century these had grown to eighteen in each generation (nearly one a year). These revolts were ever more self-aware and radical. They might start because of a specific outrage, but often set forth demands for social reform. It does not matter that they demanded an illusory 'moral economy' on the supposition that the lords had infringed this, nor that they invoked divine law and went in for egalitarian readings of the Gospels, thus giving a traditional colouring to their discourse. Behind these ways of stating demands there was generally hope for a new society in which men would have equal rights, authorities would be elected, and religion would not be an instrument of social control in the hands of the clergy.

From the end of the fifteenth century the *rustica seditio* caused terror 'in castles, monasteries, and bourgeois dwellings'. It was a terror which the war with the German peasants, and above all the Münster episode, greatly heightened and which was to last many years, since there was no falling-off of the revolts until the middle of the seventeenth century. How could the threat be contained? A canon of Zürich maintained that 'to cut down the peasants' presumption, which grows like weeds', their houses and property should be destroyed every fifty years. It would have been a costly solution, since the intending destroyers themselves had to live, in the last analysis, on the products of the toil of those to be destroyed.

It was not enough to crush each new movement by force, since what was needed was a recovery of control over the lower orders, and a moral reconquest which would bring about a new consensus. European history in the sixteenth and seventeenth centuries is marked by this effort towards internal reconquest, designed to create a homogenous society and to strengthen the hegemony of the ruling groups. Reformation and Counter-Reformation strove equally in the twin tasks of battling dissent – that is, against the warlock, the heretic, the unbeliever, anyone who infringed established morality, the Jew and others – and propagating an orthodox religiosity which would facilitate social control through the pastor or the parish priest.

Witchcraft was nothing new. What people in the Middle Ages called by such a name was a mixture of pagan elements, popular traditions, and lower magic, to which was added the notion of a pact with the devil in order to justify punishing the practice. Magic, defined by Bodin as 'the science of things divine and natural', must not be confused with witchcraft: 'The witch is a person who strives consciously to obtain something by diabolical means.' Witchcraft was customarily attributed to marginal social groups – Jews, heretics, and especially women – and, like heresy, was associated with lust: 'All witchcraft stems from carnal desire, which in women is insatiable.'

The first waves of persecution occurred in the Low Countries, Germany, and northern France in the fourteenth century, but these were unimportant compared to the witchhunts of the sixteenth and seventeenth centuries, in which there were thousands of trials and a large number of death-sentences, the latter reckoned between a minimum of 50,000 and a maximum of 200,000. Eighty per cent of those tried were women – it is said that on average two women a day were executed in some part of Europe or another – most of them over forty years of age. Executions went on into the eighteenth century: the last took place in Glaris (Switzerland) in 1782, but five years later, at the very time that the United States Constitution was being drawn up, the mob killed one witch more in Philadelphia.

What had originally been a rustic view of spells and curses changed when the initiative passed into the hands of the Church. In 1486 two German Dominicans published their *Malleus maleficarum*, in which witchcraft became 'a diabolical conspiracy organized to overthrow Christianity'. The Church took the chance to intervene in peasant society. The association of the witches' Sabbath with night-time was connected with the nocturnal activities (fights, amusements and courting) common in rural society. The blameworthiness of women had a lot to do with their role as transmitters of popular culture and their functions as quack doctors and midwives (the 'wise woman', expert in occult arts applied for the benefit of others, particularly against illnesses), leading such people to rival the parish priest in influence. The campaign against them was used also to demonize peasant sexuality, which seemed far too free.

To be understood properly the phenomenon has to be set in its particular historical context. In France the persecution of witches was begun as the persecution of heretics ended (but still in 1748 the Bishop of Nîmes urged a parish priest to preach 'against the warlocks, witches, casters of spells, and sooth-sayers of the village'). It has been said too that in general persecutions were most intense in places where weak rulers, feeling themselves insecure, resorted to identifying potential enemies as the devil's agents. In Holland, with its stable society, they were much less important.

Witchhunting hardly ever occurred in Spain, Portugal, and Italy, not because of any wisdom and firmness on the

Inquisition's part, as is usually said, but because this body was fully occupied in persecuting and burning Protestants, Moriscos, and Judaizers, in no less barbarous a fashion. (Father Garau described delightedly how a Judaizing Majorcan burst in the fire: 'He was as fat as a sucking-pig and his insides caught alight.')

In Spain it was the Moriscos first, then the Judaizers. The surrender terms agreed with the Muslims of Granada were not respected and they were forced to convert. This enraged them and led to a series of revolts, these ending with forced conversions, the enslavement of some 25,000 Granadine Moriscos, and the deportation of 80,000 others (of whom between twenty and thirty per cent died on the way). These were dispersed throughout the Peninsula and subjected to a real reign of terror, controlled by the Inquisition. I limit myself to mentioning just one ordinary and normal case which may reflect the climate of daily terror better than the more spectacular trials. In the auto-da-fé held in Majorca city in 1579 a Moorish slave woman of Granadine origin was condemned 'for having given herself the Moorish name Fatima, and not answering to the name Isabel but only to Fatima'. It was suspected that she had encouraged other Moriscos to 'live like Moors', and she had not been to confession in the seven years she had spent in slavery as a Christian. Since she was an old woman of more than seventy, and agreed to abjure all that was asked of her (even though no crime had been proved against her), she was punished 'only' by a degrading appearance in the auto-da-fé, one hundred lashes, and imprisonment for life.

Neither watchfuless nor repression sufficed. The Moriscos persisted in keeping to their own cultural models, behind which it was suspected that adherence to Islam continued. In 1609 the mass expulsion of these Muslim converts to Christianity was resolved, even though such converts might, in accordance with Islamic law, be sentenced to death as guilty of apostasy. It seems that some 300,000 were affected, not counting 10,000 or 12,000 more who died while resisting or from the hardships suffered when being transported to the harbours or being put on the ships.

It would have been hard for them to be assimilated by a society which hated them not only because it suspected they went on keeping up their religion in secret, but also because they were different: they worked hard, consumed little, and saved. It will not be necessary to call up evidence of fanatical incomprehension, which exists abundantly, since it suffices to let one of the greatest voices of Spanish literature in the Golden Age, that of Miguel de Cervantes, speak. He has left us a fierce portrait of the 'Moorish rabble', ending with this consoling reflection: 'Our State has most prudent guardians who, aware that Spain nurtures and keeps in her bosom these Moorish vipers, will with God's help find a sure, quick, and infallible remedy for this great hurt.' At the time when this text was published, the final solution to the Morisco problem had already been applied.

The main target of the Spanish Inquisition then became the Judaizers. Those Jews who had not converted were expelled from Spain in 1492, but this did not end the persecution, since there was still mistrust of them. (One functionary of the Aragonese Inquisition compiled a genealogy of converted families in order to prevent persons of untainted blood mingling it with that of new Christians.) In a period for which there are precise figures, from 1660 to 1720, we find that seventy-one per cent of cases brought to court concerned 'crypto-Judaism', that is, practising the Jewish religion in secret.

The second part of this programme, the imposition of orthodox religiosity and morality, demanded above all else control of popular religion, and the elimination from that of all aberrant practices, which were condemned as superstition. That the essential criterion for defining this was aberration – what occurred within the Church was not superstition – is shown by cases such as that of the orthodox exorcism which in the middle of the seventeenth century cast out from the body of a mayor of Madrid no fewer than fifteen million demons. The outcome was the 'confessionalization' of society: an acculturation which transformed the lives of the ruling groups and allowed them to fix norms for the whole of society, though with very different results depending on the area and the circumstances.

In Germany peasant society had to face up to a process of demographic growth, economic differentiation, and impoverishment. 'For the struggle to create social order in the midst of disorder, the attempt to impose social discipline and hierarchy, would inevitably become bound up with the search for political and religious order in the empire as a whole.' Princes, Protestant ministers, and peasant proprietors worked together to establish this new order which began by reinforcing the family, and paternal authority within the family, and by establishing a close relationship between family and land (in a process parallel to the establishment of property registers which facilitated tax-collecting). The destruction of the community was made easier by the emergence of a class of wealthy peasants, who took part beside the landowners and the pastors in this effort to establish a new social order.

In England acculturation was marked by the essentially political nature of the start of the Reformation under Henry VIII: between 1532 and 1540 a total of 883 people were tried, and more than 300 were executed, 63 of these for voicing opinions opposed to royal policy. During the temporary reaction against the Reformation in Mary's reign, there was more violence and there were more executions and martyrs. Repression assured the gradual spread of the Reformation, which was speedily welcomed in those parts which had lived through the experience of the Lollards. The monarchy was now able to control the whole of the religious machine, and the ecclesiastical courts, complemented by special commissions, served the Crown in their turn by ensuring that official religious policy was applied and by strengthening controls on moral and social conduct.

In France the situation was conditioned by the violence of the sixteenth-century wars of religion. It was a period dominated by misfortune and terror, characterized by omens, sinister prophecies (such as those of Nostradamus), bloody conflicts between Catholics and Protestants, and the gradual worsening of repression. Before 1510, for example, there were hardly any laws to silence blasphemy; from that date up to 1594 fourteen condemnatory edicts followed, and throughout the seventeenth century the penalties were ferociously applied. The complexity of the religious confrontations, which led to the most diverse alliances between classes, delayed the explosion of the social crisis until the end of the sixteenth century, but there was then a sequence which began with the revolt of the *croquants* and ended only well on in the reign of Louis XIV. Peasant revolts and witchhunts coincided in that time which was, in words of Robin Griggs, 'the period of the "great repression", during which the monarchy and the Church joined forces to impose order and obedience on the mass of the population'.

In some parts, such as Spain, the process occurred in a slow and imperceptible way, but was no less efficacious. Here the Church had to battle against the religious ignorance of the lower classes, especially that of the peasants who, according to the clergy, 'seemed like Indians'. When the Jesuits took up residence in Galicia in the middle of the sixteenth century they found a people with a slack Christianity, full of superstitions, and with the additional grave problem that they considered sexual relations between the unmarried to be no sin. The rural clergy were as befitted such a society: 'between 1561 and 1700 the Inquisition tried 161 parish priests for blaspheming, for using the confessional to court girls, or for defending from the pulpit the notion that "mere fornication" between the unmarried was no sin.'

In this area action was taken in the form of preaching, the formation of brotherhoods (especially those of the Rosary), and missions: religious 'shock' campaigns in which the whole life of a village was shaken up, to the point of creating in the faithful a climate of terror when faced with the pains of hell. All this was reinforced later by public ceremonies and ended with a more or less general confession, leaving in its wake people who were much easier to subject to parish control.

Soundings undertaken in various parts of the Peninsula show that the seventeenth century witnessed a slow but sustained increase in orthodox religiosity, one well under the Church's control. This succeeded in getting the ruling groups to accept the new culture of death – this having an essential role in imposing a belief in Purgatory and in the efficacy of the Church's mediation in the life to come – and to convert this into a generally accepted social norm. This is reflected both in the growing presence of death in religious matters, and in the increase of the income obtained from Masses for the soul which the faithful paid for in their wills. The aldermen of the city of Madrid in Philip II's time paid for a minimum of 1,000 Masses (one asked for 5,000 in 50 days, so as not to wait too long in Purgatory), and King Philip IV ordered 100,000.

In Catholic countries the control of private life could be efficiently exercised through confession. Jean Delumeau explains that the campaign for making the European West feel guilty began in the thirteenth century, following the decision of the Fourth Lateran Council to make annual auricular confession (that is, into the priest's ear) obligatory. However, in the peasant world it seems there was resistance, since the parish priests feared that exclusion from the community might prevent them being the repository of the personal secrets of the faithful.

The Council of Trent busied itself with regulating and extending the sacrament of penitence, but this extension, which the Jesuits effected while taking the drama out of it, ended up by provoking a conflict. In theological terms this is generally presented as a confrontation between the probabilism of the Jesuits and the Jansenism of Port-Royal, a Cistercian house which Abbess Angélique Arnauld, inspired by St Francis of Sales, reformed in a rigorist direction at the start of the seventeenth century and which later received the influence of her brother Antoine Arnauld and of Blaise Pascal. But behind this dispute there lay also the collision between a patrician rigorist ethic (Antoine Arnauld's most famous book was written because of a discussion between the Princesse de Guemené and the Marquise de Sablé about whether or not one could attend a ball the same day one had taken communion) and the need to make penitence easier of access for the greater part of the population and so reconquer the lower orders.

In his *Noticias singularísimas* published in 1676, the Franciscan José Gavarri – with eighteen years' experience behind him in missionary work and many thousands of confessions from the common people, especially peasants – tells us that ordinary folk, above all rustics and simple women, go fearfully to confession, since they are afraid to confess sins for whose absolution they would have to go to Rome, such absolution being reserved for the pope alone, or being in the competence of the Inquisition, with which they wish to have no dealings. The friar is convinced that 'out of three-quarters of the Catholics who are damned, at least one quarter is damned solely because they remain silent about mortal sins out of the mistrust and shame they feel when confessing'.

One of the fundamental aspects of this religious reconquest involved the regulation of sexuality, with the aim of strengthening the family as the basis of social organization (this was the moment when, for example, the face-to-face or so-called 'missionary' position was defined as the only lawful one in sexual relations between spouses). Religion and morality were associated, so that freedom of thought was identified with profligacy of customs (libertinage), and homosexuality was designated 'the philosophical sin'.

To understand the difficulty inherent in this task of reconquest it is best to rid ourselves of old illusions about the peasants' ingenuous purity, and about the degree to which they had internalized Christian moral norms. French peasants had a highly complicated erotic life, and the English, if what happened in Somerset was at all typical, frequently practised mutual heterosexual masturbation. Married women moreover were wont to keep up relationships outside marriage, often with their own servants, as happened too in south Germany, where the strongest brake on illegitimate births seems to have been not the clergy's preaching but control by the peasant community itself, in no way desirous of fathering bastards having no family to maintain them. In Sweden from 1635 to 1778, the date on which the last man condemned for bestiality was decapitated and burned, between 600 and 700 persons, mostly adolescents and youths were executed for this crime – together with the cows, mares, sows, ewes, and goats with which they had sinned – while a larger number were sentenced to lashes and forced labour. That bestiality should represent around one-third of all the executions in the country can be explained only by the importance which Church and State attached to the social control of the peasantry by watching over its morality.

In Spain Father Gavarri displays to us, from his wide experience in the confessional, a sexual life among the people, especially among the peasants, of an unsuspected complexity. Bestiality was common with 'ewes, bitches, goats, hens, turkeys, sows, mares, cows, mules, etc., and with other birds'. People talked with complete openness about sodomy, incest and men who masturbated two or three times a day. Female sexuality was no less important. Gavarri maintains that women tend to confess only about their thoughts, without mentioning that they had been engaged at the time in 'unchastely fondling' themselves. Penitent women subjected to sufficient questioning reveal that they masturbate with extraordinary frequency. Gavarri began by asking, in order to put them at ease: "Tell me, my daughter, these fondlings you speak of, have there been fifty every day?" And let no novice confessor be amazed at this, for many have come to my feet confessing forty a day, three said fifty a day, and one, sixty.'

The basically social nature of this campaign explains why it was undertaken equally in Catholic and Reformation Europe, why it enjoyed solid political support when harshly punishing deviations from the norm, and why, when the Churches' influence began to wane in the eighteenth century, medical science took on its role. (A good example of the repressive scientific methods used was the terror campaign launched against masturbation, which led to adolescents being tortured and even mutilated.)

How effective was this sexual restoration? Studies of the figures for illegitimate births show a fall in the seventeenth century, interrupted from the first half of the eighteenth, and rising thereafter in proportions never before known. Was it, then, a lost battle? On the contrary, it is clear that what mattered most was in fact achieved: officially to impose acceptance of the rules about sexuality and the family, on a basis of tolerating unauthorized sexuality in practice provided this was in private or was discreetly regulated. This happened with prostitution: in eighteenth-century Paris there were some 20,000 professionals controlled by the police, who used them as a source of information. Complete transformation of the habits of Christians was not achieved, but at least they were made to accept blame and a sort of schizophrenia which left the approved social order untouched.

Not everything lay in the religious sphere. The repression of the alternative culture could be seen also as a fight against rusticity. This fable was revived some decades ago by Norbert Elias, who claimed that at the same time as modern states were being constituted, there developed a civilizing process which led to the emergence of courtly society and changed people's manners, making these more similar to models we consider acceptable today. However, the concept of courtly culture appeared in Europe in the twelfth century when gentlemanly manners were being described: forms of dress, foods (there were 'noble foods' and 'peasant foods'), ways of behaving at table. The gentleman 'should not only be noble, handsome and skilled in arms, but should also have a mastery of the refined manners of the court, the rules of decorum and etiquette', which all sounds very similar to what Castiglione would expect of the courtier in the early sixteenth century.

What was new was the wish on the part of the cultivated to change attitudes and values in the rest of the population. What had earlier been typical of a small number of privileged people was now to become a rule of life for a broad segment of society. This explains why the

designation 'courtly culture' was abandoned and replaced
by 'civilization' or 'urbanity', two terms which are plainly
contrasted with 'rusticity', the new name for barbarousness. Voltaire maintained that European peasants, 'who
speak a jargon that cannot be understood in the cities, have
few ideas and, in consequence, few expressions', and that
they were inferior to African Kaffirs.

This reference to jargon is revealing, since one of the
ways in which rustic culture was marginalized was by the
appropriation of vernacular languages by the literate. The
language of culture up to the seventeenth century was
'learned' Latin, which was not medieval Latin in a more
or less developed form but a dead language rescued from
the texts of classical Antiquity. But the struggle against a
subordinate culture which, after using macaronic Latin,
had developed essentially in the vulgar tongues, meant that
the battle had to be fought out on the same ground, and
this, in countries where the Reformation had triumphed,
was reinforced by the need to translate holy books into
the vernacular. The result was that learned people decided
to appropriate the vulgar tongues and elevate them to
the level of learned languages – as Dante had proposed –
providing them with grammars corresponding to that of
Latin and deciding which usages were to be accepted and
which rejected.

In Castile the first grammar was published in 1492,
the year in which Granada, the last Muslim redoubt,
was captured, and the Jews were expelled. However, the
weakness of some learned groups who found themselves
on the defensive in the face of inquisitorial watchfulness
made this appropriation less effective. Juan de Valdés's
Diálogo de las lenguas, written in 1535, could not be
published for another two hundred years, and a literature that kept itself quite close to the popular wealth of
tales and proverbs was able to retain its vitality in the
seventeenth-century narrative genre, particularly in the
picaresque novel, and thus stay close to a lower-class
public. Latinizing *culteranismo* was invented precisely in
order to drive the lower orders away from culture, since

its essential principle was that 'one's discourse should not be that of common talk, which is vulgar baseness'.

The conflict between the two languages was resolved by the Royal Academy, founded by Philip V in 1713 to 'cleanse and fix' the language (that is, fossilizing it around sixteenth- and seventeenth-century models) and to establish a normative grammar which would shatter the illusion that the language 'could be perfectly well learned by use alone', subjecting it to rules from which 'nobody could depart without exposing himself to public scorn'. At the same time measures were taken against the other tongues of the Peninsula, particularly against Catalan.

In France, as in other European countries, 'grammatization' was started in the first half of the sixteenth century. About 1530 some began to demand the establishment of 'good usage' and the cleansing of 'corrupted French'. The grammarians proposed to embalm the language of Chrétien de Troyes and François Villon – in which Rabelais was just then writing his work with incomparable freshness and lexical richness – and to refashion it in the image of classical Greek and Latin. Malherbe proscribed the use of 'low and plebeian' words in the 'high style', and his heirs, who predominated in the Academy, completed the task of mummifying French, this in the eighteenth century having become a 'special jargon of diplomats, Jesuits, and Euclidian geometricians' kept going on the margins of the living language.

Students were shown as a model the insipid ode in which Malherbe boasted in 1610 of being one of the 'three or four' privileged persons able to write immortal verses. They were not told that in the same year there had been published a Rabelaisian book, in the noblest sense of the word – *Le Moyen de parvenir*, by Béroalde de Verville – which was to achieve at least thirty editions in the seventeenth and eighteenth centuries. It has been well described as 'a real workshop of language', but was excluded from respectable literature as being 'low' and 'plebeian' (and lukewarm and tolerant in religious matters). The aim of this regimentation of language and penalization of any departure from the grammatical and orthographic code was to control usage, condemn plebeian vocabulary as unfitting, and thereby weaken any capacity the lower orders had to express their ideas in ways corresponding to that vocabulary.

Brought up in a culture born out of that secular crusade, we have got used to accepting all its myths as truths. These are the myths which set modern Renaissance brilliance against medieval obscurantism, the religious Reformation (and the Counter-Reformation) against superstition and witchcraft, the rationality of science against the senselessness of magic and courtly refinement against rustic coarseness. Our image of the Renaissance was created in the nineteenth century so that it could be used as a precedent, either by progressive thought which valued its innovatory aspects, or by conservatism which presented it as 'a spiritual guide for our times'. This image has been enriched since then with new shades and hues, and we now appreciate on the one side the continuity of many medieval elements, and on the other all that there was in the ventures of the Italian humanists into a project for transformation, which was defeated at the end by the Church.

We have also constructed a history of science which goes in a straight line from Greek rationality up to the present, passing through the scientific revolution of the modern age, but leaving aside magic, astrology and alchemy. We cannot ignore, nevertheless, the contribution made to scientific renewal by natural magic and the hermetic philosophies. The Renaissance magi were 'men actually generations ahead of their times in learning and science', but who attempted to make 'a combination of the exact sciences with magical thought'. The illusion would still affect Newton, of whom it has been said that he was 'not the first of the age of reason; he was the last of the magicians': he was seriously interested in alchemy and in prophecies, to which he devoted a book that announced the imminent fall of the papacy and placed the end of the world at about 1867.

These were the men who brought in empiricism and observation, against the reasoners who thought that everything it was proper to know was already included in the summation of classical and Christian culture, that is in 'the great Thomist compromise' which had translated Christianity into Aristotelian terms. For Cornelius Agrippa natural magic was the study of the forces of nature, 'of all natural and celestial things', thanks to which 'natural miracles' could be worked. Astrology too sought to give material explanations for events, which shows why it maintained its influence in certain departments of science up to the end of the eighteenth century. (It should not be forgotten that magi, astrologers, and alchemists were appreciated by rulers. Philip II of Spain was interested in these disciplines, and Francis I de' Medici had a *studiolo* for his own alchemical work.)

The great enemy of scientific progress was not speculation and experiments in natural magic, but the old fossilized bookish learning. Galileo felt alienated from university culture and closer to learning derived from concrete experience as diffused through the streets, squares and shops of Florence. Reasoning was not enough for him: instead, he resorted to observation 'in order to take in with my own senses that which the intellect had no doubts about'. This scientific revolution based on experimentation and the use of mathematics was at first impregnated with a certain animism, with a pantheism which recalls its origins in magic. But the danger that the Church saw in it was not this, but the fact that science would dispute the validity and authority of a tradition which was the basis not only of its learning but also of society.

'These novelties', Campanella wrote to Galileo in 1632, 'about ancient truths, new worlds, new stars, new systems, etc., herald a new century.' The threat was plain. The Catholic Church faced up to it and thus prevented science continuing along this road: the condemnation put fear into Descartes, who thereupon resolved not to publish his studies on 'the world'. It was decided to maintain the old scholastic tradition in the universities, at the cost of holding back science. 'Those who claimed to be men of science preferred to subtilize, ergotize, and reason away without

pause, developing all the way to the infinite any principle
of Aristotle or St Thomas, rather than devote themselves
patiently to the observation of facts.'

In Protestant lands, on the other hand, there was an
effort to associate science and religion in order to provide
new foundations for society. Such was the task undertaken by the Newtonian system. The image of the correspondence between macrocosm and microcosm, between
the universe and mankind, traditional in magic, was now
transformed into an image which identified the cosmos
with human society. Isaac Barrow declared that the natural
world provides us with a model with which to understand the political world. His follower Newton developed
this cosmological-social model: 'The whole natural world,
which consists of the heavens and the earth, signifies the
whole political world, which consists of thrones and the
people.'

To confront the established version of history, even in
order to criticize it, is not enough to enable us to escape
from it altogether. Truth is not always a negation of falsity, but may be something altogether distinct, which we
have to rebuild by completely rethinking the way the data
hang together. The path that leads from the Renaissance
to the Age of Enlightenment does not pass through the
historical landscape we have explored, but is remote from
it. I shall limit myself to pointing out some milestones in
this alternative landscape, which should be associated with
other better-known ones concerning the hermetic tradition,
freethinking, and the continuity of the republican tradition
inspired by Machiavelli.

We talk of popular religion, but there are currents from
learned origins in this alternative culture. If we know little
about them it is because the authorities' watchfulness en-
forced dissimulation. There were not only literate people
who were dissident in a personal way, for beyond this
there existed a coherent alternative tradition, based on
communication between groups right across Europe. There
were English Lollards among the Czech Hussites, Hussites and Anabaptists with the Dutch Collegiants, and the

Socinian Church of Poland arose out of the thought of a Siennese humanist who had been influenced by Servet.

One of the areas where the most productive encounters took place was Holland. Their origin was among the Sephardim expelled from Spain and Portugal, who in the seventeenth century formed a community involved in the business world, their culture being often expressed in Spanish. This community, in common with the greater part of Judaism, was shaken in 1665 by the preaching of Sabatai Zevi, a Jew from Smyrna whose mental balance was precarious – he had had two unconsummated marriages, and a third one to a prostitute – and who was proclaimed the Messiah by the kabalist Nathan of Gaza. News of his coming raced around Europe, and it was only the difficulty of sailing through the Mediterranean at the height of the Anglo-Dutch war that prevented numerous groups of Jews from going off to the Holy Land. Sabatai abjured his religion in September 1666, when the Turks offered him the choice of conversion to Islam or death, which produced a huge disappointment (some of his followers, nevertheless, interpreted his apostasy as a mystery and remained faithful to him).

Sabateism coincided with a stance of millenarianist anticipation that flourished at the time among Christians too, encouraged by eclipses in 1652, a comet in 1653, and the kabalistic significance of the number 1666. In 1650 Menasseh ben Israel published his *Esperança de Israel*, in which he declared that in America were to be found, mingled with the natives, the lost tribes of Israel awaiting the moment when 'they shall become lords over all the earth, since it was theirs before', while the signs of the times showed that this moment was now imminent. In 1647 he had discussed these subjects with the Portuguese Jesuit António Vieira, who announced in his *Historia del futuro* that in 1666 there would begin the Fifth Empire prophesied in the Bible, and that under the world sovereignty of a Portuguese monarch the heretics, pagans, and Jews would convert and a thousand years of peace would be ushered in.

Disappointment with the failure of so many prophecies and the problems that the return to the older Jewish observance held for converts explain how it could happen that men emerged in the groups established in Holland who, although loyal to the Jewish community, found it difficult to accept their religion. They included deists such as Uriel da Costa (who ended up by killing himself as a result of his confrontation with the synagogue), possible atheists like Juan de Prado (who declared that 'the world was not created but has always existed in the same form and will continue to exist for ever', and who did not believe in the afterlife), and persons who cannot be classified. These included Isaac de La Peyrère, a French Calvinist possibly of Jewish origin, who had followers, perhaps Spinoza himself among them, for his 'pre-Adamite' theory, according to which the Bible was wrong and mankind had existed before Adam and was simply subject to the natural law.

In this crisis culture of the *marranos*, the name by which the Portuguese converts were known, Baruch Spinoza, a follower of Menasseh ben Israel, grew up. Expelled from the Jewish community for his philosophical ideas, he accepted the exclusion and went on to write up his thoughts in the *Tractatus theologico-politicus*, published in 1670. 'Divine law' was for him an innate 'law of nature', inscribed in men's minds, while everything else in religion, 'the ceremonies', had a merely political aim. It made no sense 'to subject reason, which is the greatest of gifts and a divine light, to certain writings – or Scripture – which are dead and may have been corrupted by human ill-will'. The proper foundations of politics would have to be sought outside the realm of theology. The basis of the state is the need men have to determine collectively – 'following the dictates of reason' – the use they should make of each individual's rights in order to avoid conflict between them. The aim of the state is 'to enable men to develop their mental and physical faculties in safety, to use their reason unrestrictedly, and to check dissension and mutual abuses to which hatred, anger, or deceit may lead them. The aim of the state is, in short, liberty.'

A course like this, from millenarianism to secularism, is the one that seems to have been followed among the Dutch Collegiants. Starting from a tradition which went back to radical strands of religious reform, particularly Anabaptism – Mennonite in its Dutch form, characterized by its rejection of violence – they undertook throughout the seventeenth century what has been described as 'a stormy spiritual journey from faith to reason'. If at the start they dedicated themselves particularly to discussing the Bible and singing hymns, they later received into their meetings men like Comenius, the Bishop of the Union of Brethren who had been forced to leave Moravia, and Spinoza – it was a bookseller of this group who published his *Tractatus*. They were influenced also by the Socinians, who had had to flee from Poland when persecuted by the Jesuit-King Jan Casimir, and who formed the only un-authorized Church in Holland, where on account of their extremism they were considered to be atheists (denying the Trinity, the divinity of Christ, and Providence). The evolution of the Collegiants towards a kind of religious rationalism is typical of this second Reformation of the seventeenth century. This was critical both of the alliance of the reformed Churches and of the established order: it caused the most diverse tendencies to flourish, and if, on one side, it led to the emergence of pietistic groups and various forms of millenarianism, it led also, on the other, to the development of the tolerant and rational attitudes that would encourage the birth of the first Enlightenment. It was not by chance that Holland became a refuge for the persecuted and a centre for the printing of works banned by all the inquisitions and censorships. It was in a climate of tolerance and freedom that Holland succeeded in creating its bourgeois republic, preventing Calvinism from influencing politics, and allowing the European Enlightenment to gestate there.

7

The Savage Mirror

Between 1664 and 1666 Jan van Kessel, a native of Antwerp, painted several allegories in which the four parts of the world appeared as women placed in scenes filled with objects, books, and groups of birds and insects representing each continent. Similar images were common in seventeenth-century European painting, their similarity deriving from a common source: the types created by Cesare Ripa in his *Iconologia*, published in 1593, a book in which many artists of the seventeenth and eighteenth centuries sought inspiration. In Ripa's text we find explanations of the attributes displayed by van Kessel's figures. Europe's crown represents her primacy over the other continents, 'for in Europe there reside the greatest and most powerful princes in the world', and her arms, books, and musical instruments 'show her perpetual and constant superiority ..., in arms as well as in letters and the liberal arts'.

Representations of 'the four parts of the world' begin in the middle of the sixteenth century and become common throughout the seventeenth and eighteenth centuries. The continents have ceased to be mere indications of geographical space, as they were earlier, and are now characterized by the diversity of flora and fauna that travellers have discovered in them, whose strangeness fascinated Europeans from 1500. The elephant presented by King Manuel I of Portugal to Pope Leo X – which, on its solemn entry into Rome in 1514, delighted the people present by spraying the prelates and cardinals with its trunk – was painted by Raphael. A rhinoceros followed two years later, but was drowned off Genoa when the vessel carrying it was wrecked: this was painted by Dürer, based on a sketch sent to him from Lisbon.

However, there is more than the exotic to van Kessel's depictions. The figures which symbolize the continents are not only abstract types, but representatives of human beings with distinctive physical characteristics. Europe has a white skin, Africa is black, while in America (in a scene the painter sets in Brazil) are both a red-skinned Indian woman and a black African. For Asia we have an Ottoman pair in the foreground, and behind them figures suggesting the more distant world of Mongols, Chinese, and Japanese. If the sixteenth century discovered that 'the parts of the world' had their own animals and plants, the seventeenth added to this the conviction that the human beings who peopled them were different and characteristic.

All people define themselves by looking in the mirror of 'the others', thus differentiating themselves from them. But this, so simple for communities that speak the same language and share lifestyle and customs, was not so simple for Europeans, especially after the sixteenth century, when religious unity had been broken and literary use of the various vernacular tongues was on the increase. The Treaty of Utrecht in 1714 was the last European document to be drawn up in terms of the *respublica Christiana*. This now plural people looked at itself from this moment in a more complex set of mirrors in order to make out what identifying marks it had within its diversity, and what distinguished it from the rest. The new way in which Europeans thought about themselves was born out of an awareness that no longer had to do with religion, but was based on a belief in moral and intellectual superiority. The new term of reference on which this image was elaborated was that of the inferior nature of the non-Europeans. Yet the mirror they looked into when seeking to define themselves had two surfaces. In one of them racial differences were seen and the savage showed his face; in the other, reflecting a Eurocentric view of history, the primitive was displayed. Out of the first there emerged genocide and the slave-trade; out of the second, imperialism.

Savage man, hairy as a bear and armed with a club, is a typical figure in medieval European mythology, found in pious tales of saints and penitents, or in popular legends about the bear-man who gave rise to festivities such as that shown in a famous engraving by Pieter Bruegel. Yet if in religion the savage represents a penitent, and if in popular lore he represents the force and simplicity of nature, in chivalresque literature he is generally a huge and evil giant, a symbol of dreaded peasant rusticity, like the ox-driver in Chrétien de Troyes' *Le Chevalier au Lion*, 'a creature who looked like a Moor, so ugly and so black and hideous'. In some late medieval representations he appears as a man who lives in harmony with nature and is even integrated into agricultural life. Those were times when the patrician view of society had still not finally imposed itself. But at the start of the seventeenth century Giovan Battista della Porta contrasts the savage, defined as a rustic, 'uncultured and melancholic', with the 'citizen', who is 'peaceful and human, gentle and sociable'.

The discovery of America and its inhabitants opened a scientific debate on this theme. The first news conveyed by Columbus spoke of naked, pacific people – 'they have no iron or steel or weapons, and have no inclination for them' – who lived in a state of innocence. As mentioned in the bull in which Alexander VI granted these lands to the Catholic Monarchs, they believed in a creative God and seemed ready for conversion to Catholicism. This idyllic image was not to last. In an intermediate phase it turned out that there were some 'good' natives and others who were 'evil' – cannibal Caribs who attacked the innocent Arawaks – but in the end they were all fierce barbarians, abounding in vices, particularly cannibalism (certain native tribes believed, on the other hand, that it was the Europeans who were the anthropophagi). By then deism had already turned into idolatry.

The theologian Juan Ginés de Sepúlveda maintained that it was lawful to subdue the natives by armed force because they were 'all barbarous in their customs and most of them by nature have no letters or good sense, and they are infected with many barbarous vices'. But Father Las Casas argued that they were not evil in their conduct – rather, 'this name "barbarians" applies to certain Spaniards who inflicted upon the Indians, in truth the most innocent and docile people of all, such horrendous cruelties, such terrible slaughter, and torments worse than those of hell' – nor were they evil on account of their intellectual and moral capacities.

Columbus's voyages had an undertone of religious inspiration, but also an economic motivation. This is proved by the agreements signed with the monarchs, for they would not have provided him with resources, of which they had few, had they not cherished hopes of profit. Since in the western Indies there were no spices to be bought, and since the Indians were no good for selling as slaves – it turned out that they died all too readily 'on account of the unwonted change of soil, air, and food' – it was essential to find gold and silver in sufficient quantity. On his second voyage, financed in good measure by money confiscated from the expelled Jews, Columbus had seventeen ships and one thousand three hundred fighting men, with the aim of 'discovering what is known about gold, and acquiring it for the King and Queen, either with the goodwill of the inhabitants, or by force'. It was to be by force, since the only way to get it was by obliging the natives to work to win precious metals.

Once settled on the continent the Spaniards found silver mines and, what was much more important, 'immense mines' of people living in organized societies whom they could put to forced labour. It was not that the veins of precious American metal were especially rich, rather that the labour used to work them was much cheaper than that of European miners. But this required that the natives should first be subjected to the conquerors' will, that is, that they should be converted, since the concept of conversion as the conquistadors understood it implied that the Indians should live 'as Christians, in submission, obedience, and polity, like the rest of the vassals their Majesties have and possess in their other realms'.

Societies accustomed to syncretic cults might have thought initially that it would suffice for them to add the Christian god and his rites to their culture, as the Mayas at first did. But the missionaries clarified matters for them in their inquisitorial visitation in 1562, torturing more than 4,500 Indians, of whom 158 died as a result of the treatment received. Something similar happened in the Andes during the 'extirpation of idolatries'.

It is not a question of opposing religious motivation and the lust for gain. As V. M. Godinho has said, there was in the discoverers a complicated overlap of motives 'in which crusade and commerce mingled, as did piracy and evangelization'. We find this mixture in Columbus, as in Vasco da Gama. In *The Lusiads*, the great poem of the discoveries, confusion between the two levels is constant. If the first cry of the Portuguese as they reached Calcutta was 'Now you have arrived, now you have before you a land abounding in riches', this was followed by a plea to the Christian monarchs of Europe to unite in a crusade against the Turks, in which Camoens speaks of Portuguese expansion beyond the seas as a series of crusading acts, of 'daring Christian ventures'.

Lust for gain and religious legitimation were present in the daily life of the Spanish conquistadors. One thing should not hide the other from us. It is certain that the governors concerned themselves with the fate of the natives and took steps to prevent their being abused. But the conversion and exploitation of the Indies was essentially a private enterprise, in which a share was reserved for the king, just as in the Middle Ages part of the booty was reserved for him. After studying the lives and careers of those controlling more than 500 Mexican *encomiendas*, a historian defines them as 'entrepreneurs who pursued economic motives'. It was natural enough that these 'businessmen' should ensure that the Indians were first enslaved and then exploited in the most diverse ways, direct and indirect.

It is hypocritical to be shocked about this, since the whole colonial development that made it possible for Europe to create, between 1650 and 1850, those mercantile empires on which modern economic growth would be based, has the same origin and was undertaken with the same methods. When other European peoples decided to instal themselves in the Caribbean and set up the first plantation economies, they used the same rhetoric about native cannibalism and vices, and harassed the natives until disease, suicide, and escape left them as no more than small residual groups.

In the English colonies to the north it was disease that began the task of depopulating the land of natives. But the settlers afterwards enthusiastically continued hunting down the savage. Such confrontation was not inevitable. There were instances of peaceful collaboration, such as that of the so-called Iroquois empire, born out of agreements signed by the five Iroquois tribes and the British colonies, which between 1677 and 1755 regulated relations and trade between the two peoples. However, the British Crown never accepted that treaties could be made with its subjects, and the Indians were subjects by the mere fact that the monarchy, like the American republic later, never recognized the Indian communities as nations.

However, collaboration was not widespread, nor did it suit the Puritan settlers who thought themselves superior to the unbelievers and knew they had heaven on their side. During the late seventeenth and early eighteenth centuries in the British colonies in America a tale with episodes of captivity at Indian hands, burdened with religious motifs, became popular. If the coming of the settlers to America could be explained as a flight from European depravity, tales of Indians and captives recalled the struggle of the sinner for the redemption of his soul: 'The captive, with God's help, battles Satan's agents.' Cotton Mather, a Puritan minister, adorned his *Magnalia Christi Americana* with spine-chilling tales of Indians who stopped the bawling of captive children by smashing their heads against tree-trunks. He forgot, however, to say that such acts were the result of warfare, and that the atrocities suffered by the Indians at the hands of Christian invaders of their lands were no less horrifying.

About 1685, when disease had already begun to destroy them, there were some 40,000 natives in Virginia and the two Carolinas. Pressures from the settlers to take from them lands they wished to devote to tobacco-growing, and the wars resulting from that despoilment, did the rest. A hundred years later the survivors of the native population numbered fewer than 1,000. The same process spread later towards the West, while new settlers were pressed to set themselves up in inland areas snatched from the Indians. In this way they became a living wall which defended the security of the landowners on the Atlantic coast. These settlers came from Europe on voyages like those of the slaves – in 1741 almost half the 106 passengers on a ship out of Belfast died of hunger on the crossing, and six were eaten by their companions – having paid for their passage with labour contracts which obliged them to stay subject to a master for from five to seven years, as if they were serfs. How can one be surprised that these, the most needy and the most exposed to confrontation with the Indians, should become their most bitter enemies?

In time the arguments that legitimized despoilment became secular. North American society in the nineteenth century went in for the schizophrenic game of celebrating the idealized Indian as the noble savage and considering the real Indians as barbarians who impeded the westward advance of civilization. That abstraction of an Indian never existed, since it was a matter of very diverse peoples, who included some sedentary farmers; but in order to be able to fight them as barbarians it was necessary to start by denying them their cultural identities. The Indian was inferior and had no right to impede 'the obvious designs of Providence'. He would survive while there remained corners of land on which he could take refuge from the advance of civilization, but his destiny in the long run was extinction.

From the middle of the nineteenth century, after the territorial annexations made at Mexico's cost, the white north Americans proclaimed their right to rule over the whole continent, and at the end of the Civil War they prepared to take over what they considered theirs. This is how the epic of the West came to be. In those lands the pioneer would establish a more equitable and a freer society, an agrarian Utopia based on the granting of lands free to all settlers. Out of this was to emerge a new civilization that would spread through the Pacific islands and regenerate the Orient. Walt Whitman expressed this dream forcefully:

I chant the new empire grander than any before, as in a
   vision it comes to me,
I chant America the mistress, I chant a greater supremacy,
I chant projected a thousand blooming cities yet in time on
   those groups of sea-islands,
My sail-ships and steam-ships threading the archipelagoes,
My stars and stripes fluttering in the wind,
Commerce opening, the sleep of ages having done its work,
   races reborn, refresh'd,
Lives, works resumed – the object I know not – but the
   old, the Asiatic renew'd as it must be

Beside this grandiose dream in which Columbus's unfinished search for the passage to India would be made a reality, what could the lives of a few bloodthirsty savages matter? Paradoxically, the exterminator presented himself as a victim too. In the literature of the West the redskin was assigned the role of the villain who killed settlers and scalped them (though the scalping business was a white man's invention to facilitate payment by heads to the Indian-hunters).

The series of campaigns against the Indians from 1860 up to the massacre of the Sioux at Wounded Knee in 1890 is not only a tale of crimes and deceits but, above all, a tale of the systematic annihilation of communities and cultures. There was the bitter addition of the fact that the egalitarian Utopia died at the hands of the railroad companies, the land speculators, and the demands of a mechanized agriculture which required considerable physical capital in order to work efficiently. Out of all this there remained only the urge to rule and the conviction of a racial and moral superiority that has gone on serving to legitimize the extermination of evil savages, from Wounded Knee up to Iraq and Somalia, taking in on the way the frequent lynching of blacks (at the rate of about one a week from 1882 to 1930).

The later case of Brazil is interesting because the arguments were then expressed in terms of science. The idyllic descriptions of Brazilian tribes who lived in a natural paradise and a social harmony undisturbed by either greed or war (they had served to inspire Rousseau) were forgotten at the start of the nineteenth century, when it was hoped to embrace these peoples and their lands in a civilizing process. In 1818 two Bavarian scientists, one a zoologist and the other a botanist, reached the conclusion that the Indians were incapable of assimilating the advanced culture of Europeans, for which reason they were destined to disappear – that is, to 'leave the ranks of the living' – as many other species in natural history had done. If the scientific quality of their analysis was debatable, their prophecy is turning out to be correct. The 3,500,000 tribal natives there were on Brazilian territory in the sixteenth century, and the 2,000,000 there were at the end of the eighteenth, had been reduced to fewer than 1,000,000 by 1910. Their extermination in the name of the demands of progress has continued and continues without pause.

Criticism of the arguments of those who try to justify conquest by the barbarity of those being brought into subjection was voiced by Montaigne in words that have lost none of their actuality. He not only relativized the concept itself – 'each of us calls whatever is not customary with him barbarity' – but confronted the great argument about cannibalism like this:

I think there is greater barbarity in eating a live man
than in eating him dead, in destroying with torture
a body that is still full of feeling, burning him slowly,
having him bitten and torn by dogs and pigs (we have
not only read about this but have seen it too, recently,
not among old enemies, but among neighbours and
fellow-citizens, and what is worse, under the pretext
of piety and religion), than in roasting and eating him
after he has died.

Those who took pleasure in the death of witches, heretics,
and Jews – worthy successors, then, of the inhabitants of
classical Greece who gathered to enjoy watching slaves
being tortured – had no right at all to feel themselves
superior to American cannibals.

What had become meanwhile of the noble savages?
For a long time explorers sought them in the Edens and
Eldorados they expected to find in some remote part of
the American interior. When they failed to appear there,
people thought they might be found on Pacific islands,
where Bacon had placed *The New Atlantis*.

It was in Oceania that the image of happy and innocent natives dwelling in paradisiacal lands was to survive
longest, which is to be explained by the fact that for a time
there was no interest in exploiting them. Voyagers, especially Bougainville and Cook, propagated an idyllic image
of the islands. When the missionaries finally got there in
the nineteenth century, things began to change. To them
the noble savages, with their natural lifestyle, were 'de-
praved beings under sentence of damnation'. Bougainville
had described Tahiti as the island of nakedness and love.
Cook found that things were not very different in Hawaii,
and the French who reached New Zealand in 1772 declared that the women were 'very amorous'. The result
was that European seamen rapidly spread syphilis and
other venereal diseases throughout the islands. In the late
nineteenth century, when Gauguin arrived on Tahiti, the
doctors considered that most of the women were sick with
'that complaint which civilized Europeans have brought

them as a reward for their generous hospitality'. Aside from their erotic yearning, the natives were also thieves (which meant mostly that they did not share their visitors' conception of private property). Joseph Banks, a young naturalist on Cook's expedition, spent a night of love with Queen Oberea, discovering next morning that his clothes had vanished.

All these were mere bagatelles, however. Literary folk and painters – Melville, Stevenson, Gauguin, Jack London – preserved the paradisiacal image for the broad public, and the cinema has kept it alive. In *Noa Noa* Gauguin describes an innocent world, inhabited by kindly benevolent people: 'These black people, these cannibals' teeth' – it didn't matter that there had never been any cannibalism in Tahiti, since we already know every savage is a cannibal by definition – 'brought the word "savage" to my lips. For them, on the other hand, the savage was I. Rightly so, perhaps.'

The truth is that the noble savage of fiction, whose essential characteristic was docility, never existed. The encounter with real natives was complex and contradictory. It was a confrontation between two cultural worlds which did not understand each other – the Europeans, for example, sought out kings in the image and likeness of those in their own world, not understanding that society might be organized differently – and were able to do little more than barter objects. At times the native leaders discovered that the new system of European civilization, less egalitarian, might prove personally beneficial for them, and they helped to europeanize their islands to their own profit.

In the sole case in which there was a sizeable European population from the start, Australia, the model of what had happened in North America was repeated. The natives were an obstacle. While their lands were being taken from them so that they could be better exploited, the black Australians were held to be a barbarous and ignorant race destined for an extinction which the European settlers speeded up by killing them without scruple. Afterwards, much reduced in numbers and defenceless, they were simply forgotten: they were not fierce cannibals, or noble savages, but merely 'aboriginals'.

The plantation economy, as it was organized in the Caribbean, Brazil, and the United States, had one problem: it required a huge number of workers at low cost. In these lands moreover there were no 'mines of men' ready to be subjected to labour, like those the Spaniards had found in Mexico and Peru. It was necessary to bring slaves from Africa. Slavery is an age-old fact to which all civilizations have grown accustomed, but nothing the human race had known earlier could be compared with the huge proportions assumed now by the trade in black slaves: between 1600 and 1800 8,000,000 slaves from Black Africa crossed the Atlantic.

Whenever there is an effort to legitimize overlordship, there appear theories which demonstrate that those overlorded are inferior. What the Castilian theologians did for the subjection of the native Americans, the French philosophers of the eighteenth century did for the subjection of the black slaves. Voltaire did not hesitate to say that 'the negro race is a kind of men as different from ours as the race of bloodhounds differs from that of the greyhounds'. He added: 'It may be said that, unless their intelligence is of a different kind from our understanding, it is very inferior.' Montesquieu was still more direct. This man who wrote that 'slavery goes against the natural law according to which all men are born free and independent' went on to defend the enslavement of negroes paradoxically with reasons such as the following: 'Nobody can get used to the idea that God, a most wise being, could have placed a soul, especially a good soul, in an entirely black body.' The apparent illogicality of this has a key provided by a practical argument: 'Sugar would be excessively dear, were it not that the plant producing it is made to work by slave labour.'

This is, in the last analysis, a good reason to explain the increase in slavery in the period of the Enlightenment. The development of the plantation economies which provided Europe with great quantities of tobacco, coffee, sugar, and cotton at prices within the reach of ordinary consumers – and which stimulated trade out of which modern economic growth has arisen – would not have been possible without the forced labour of 'the others'. To legitimize this it had to be maintained that the slaves were not properly human beings, or that they were barbarians and that their subjection was designed to civilize them. In the early nineteenth century, when the slave-trade was abolished, the Spanish government justified it retrospectively by saying it had been necessary in order to allow the christianization of the Africans to be undertaken.

Scorn for the cultures of 'the others' was based on the ignorance that Europeans maintained about them and on their inability to understand anything that deviated from their mental horizons. Despite the abundance of travellers' tales and descriptions of exotic lands and peoples, the ignorance of most Europeans in the period of the Enlightenment about the diversity of humankind was extraordinary. The amazement Montesquieu imagined being felt by a Frenchman faced with a Persian – 'So the gentleman is Persian? How very odd! How can one be a Persian?' – was confirmed some years later in a real incident; Bougainville took a Tahitian to Paris and had to listen to questions such as: 'How' – some said to me – 'in this man's country is it possible for French, English, or Spanish not to be spoken?' (remember, however, that there are still north Americans today convinced that Jesus Christ spoke English). When a Turkish ambassador arrived in Madrid in 1787, the public knew absolutely nothing about his religion: 'There I heard some say the Turks worshipped a horse as their god; others, the moon; others again, that they were atheists; and still others who held that they said their Mass at such-and-such an hour and went to confession at another.'

If this happened in relation to Islamic culture, the only one Dr Johnson was willing to take into consideration beside the European one, it can be imagined how bad the situation concerning others was. With regard to savage or primitive thought, study of it was handed over to anthropology, since its elementary, 'prelogical' nature made it unworthy of being analysed by methods and rules applied to civilized cultures.

In the eighteenth century the natural inferiority of savages was legitimized by European naturalists, who applied to the human race a view similar to that they used when classifying animals. Linnaeus, the great systematizer of nature, contented himself with enumerating four great human groups, one for each continent, and characterized each in an elementary way: Europeans were governed by laws, Americans by customs, and Asians by opinion, while Africans acted in arbitrary ways. Buffon, who knew and admired Montesquieu's work, maintained that differences between peoples derived from differences in the environment:

> Everything contributes to proving that the human race is not composed of species differing in essential ways among themselves, but that on the contrary there was originally only one species of mankind which, having multiplied and spread all over the earth's surface, has undergone various changes under the influence of climate, because of differences in food, of lifestyle, of epidemic diseases, and also by infinitely varied cross-breeding with more or less similar individuals.

This led him to conclude that, on account of the hostile environment in which they had developed, American natives were inferior to those of the Old World, as were, in general, all the animals of that continent. With this he finally ended up denying that equality he was supposed to be defending. In fact the first theorists of racism started from the enlightened tradition of Montesquieu, Buffon, and Voltaire, and received considerable help from medicine, which offered them several methods (Retzius's cephalic index, which distinguished between dolichocephalic and brachycephalic races, etc.) by which to objectivize the claim that the various races had each a different origin and nature. Later, this science helped to develop methods, ranging from eugenics to extermination, to ensure ethnic purity.

All this went on while the struggle to abolish slavery and suppress the slave-trade was developing. Beside the humanitarianism of the abolitionists a new racism with scientific pretensions was growing up; European governments were beginning a second and greater phase of imperial expansion and starting a new kind of trade in human beings, that involving the Coolies of east and south-east Asia, on a much larger scale than that of black slavery. Prejudice and political interests went hand in hand. The attitude of the Revolution to black slavery, Napoleon said, had been the outcome of its ignorance of reality. His, on the other hand, showed a strange mixture of rationalization and prejudice: 'How is it possible to grant freedom to Africans, to people who have no civilization? ... I am in favour of the whites because I am white; I have no other reason, and this is the right one.'

So convincing and useful was the racial myth that it was even applied within European societies. France, for example, saw itself as a nation made up of two peoples: the victorious one, Franks, nobles, and warriors; and the defeated one, Gauls, peasants, and plebeians. The Revolution had brought these peoples into confrontation and its paradoxical result had been a society in which 'the Franks' went on commanding but wealth stayed in the hands of the 'Gauls', from whom came the industrial and business bourgeoisie. Those who claimed descent from the Franks made speeches with aristocratic tendencies like that of Gobineau, who declared that everything of any note in human history was the work of the Aryans, and that the decadence of societies came from the mingling of their blood with that of inferior races – France's defeat by Prussia in 1870 seemed to him to be proof of this. Those who claimed a 'Gaulish' origin for France, having a more populist and democratic stance, elaborated myths about Celtic culture, based on the ancient warlike heroes who had faced Caesar, and on up to Asterix.

Racism has gone on firmly implanted in our societies, despite the fact that scientific research has removed all pretensions to legitimacy from it. We condemn it when it takes on an acute character and presents itself in all its crudity – arson attacks on immigrants' residences in Germany, the extermination of natives in Brazil, ethnic cleansing in the Balkans. But we pass over its daily reality in the forms of discrimination and prejudice, and we even remain unaware of how far it shapes our culture, and, with it, our set of mental tools. Indeed, it does not matter whether it has any foundation or not, since it is not based on reasoned ideas but on unconfessed fears. It is simply the face taken by irrational fear of 'the other'.

8

The Mirror of Progress

The great geographical discoveries forced people to compare the reality of what was being observed with what was said in the old books. This led to mistrust of the whole of traditional learning, once the falsity of much that had been generally accepted was noticed, and it promoted the replacement of bookish knowledge by a new kind based on direct observation. Galileo said: 'Philosophy is written in that enormous book which is continually open before our eyes: I mean the universe.' Descartes proposed we should learn in 'the great book of the world'. Europeans took a passionate interest in new reports about geography, flora, fauna and inhabitants and objects from the new lands, as is reflected in illustrated books, collections and the *Wunderkammer*. Above all, the very image of the planet was changed on new maps; after them, our knowledge of nature and finally our knowledge of mankind and its cultures were changed too.

This new learning about mankind was gathered up in orderly schemes. At first they were static, being merely classifications of diversities, without any suggestion that some peoples might be superior to others. 'The capacity to judge correctly and to distinguish truth from falsity, this being what is properly called good sense or reason, is, by its nature, the same in all men', said Descartes. Differences of opinion depended on custom: 'All those who have opinions contrary to our own are not thereby barbarians or

savages.' Montesquieu supplied an explanation for this diversity: 'Laws have a considerable relationship to the way
in which different peoples secure their subsistence.'

There was another way of classifying these data, by
placing them in a temporal scheme which presupposed an
evolutionary dynamic. 'The traveller-philosopher who sails
to the farthest corners of the globe' – wrote a traveller in
1800 – 'travels, in fact, along the road of time. He travels
in the past.' The peoples he found were living evidence of
the origins of human civilization. When a comparison was
made between the customs of the various peoples discovered and those of the European past – those of the
American redskins and the Germans, for example – it was
possible to classify them in accordance with the degree to
which each had evolved up the civilization scale.

In this way, starting from this historical focus, a group
of Scottish philosophers, historians, and economists gave
Montesquieu's statement a new dimension: laws and customs depended on the ways in which peoples secured
their subsistence, but the explanation to be sought for this
was not geographical (the influence of climate and natural
conditions) but historical. Each phase in human development corresponded to a concrete mode of subsistence,
and the differences to be observed among various peoples
at a given time reflected their position on the scale of
human progress. David Hume was the first to trace the
broad lines of this scheme, in which mankind passed from
hunting and fishing to agriculture, and thence to the pre-
dominance of commerce, this being the stage which only
Europe had reached, thanks mainly to the influence of the
discoveries. To each one of these stages there corresponded
certain forms of social organization and a cultural equip-
ment suited to the preoccupations and potentialities of
men.

This view, which was to be rounded off later by Adam
Smith with his theory of the four stages of human history
– hunting, pasturing, agriculture, and commerce – allowed
the diverse known societies to be situated in an evolutionary scheme. In this, the savage hunters and gatherers

of Black Africa and north America were at the first stage; the nomadic peoples of central Asia were at the second; the greater part of the Orient was in the agricultural stage (also called the 'feudal' one); while only western Europe had attained to full development in the fourth stage, the mercantile one, which ensured prosperity for its nations and, within them, of the whole of society, even of the lowest ranks of its people.

The reconversion of the savage to 'primitive' man, which implies that all men are potentially equal, allowed the exploitation of 'backward' peoples to be legitimized, in a period when slavery was beginning to be rejected. It is often said that the thinkers of the Scottish school 'invented progress'. It would be more exact to say they 'invented the backwardess' of the others so that, viewing themselves in this mirror, they could define their own progress.

The orderly model of the development of society by various stages that all peoples had to pass through had advantages which explain its formidable success. It allowed the whole of history to be reduced to a single universally valid pattern and placed European mercantile societies – very soon to be defined as industrial – at the topmost point of civilization (thus eventually converting world history into the history of Europe). It also gave a 'scientific' character both to European claims to superiority and to European interference in the lives and history of everybody else. The colonizer became a missionary of new times who proposed to teach primitive peoples the true path of intellectual and material progress.

Primitive peoples became 'child-peoples' who must be educated. Knowledge of world history qualified the colonizers to control the evolution of backward countries. The invention of a feudal history for the Orient, for example, made it lawful for the British to control the Indian past and, with it, its present. The fact that the British had left their own feudalism behind them allowed them to teach the Indians to do the same. 'The British were ... in a position through their own history to direct the future course for India.'

In the nineteenth century this scheme was reinforced by parallel discoveries in other realms of science – in some cases what it did was orientate them – and eventually it created a universally accepted paradigm. At its base lay Laplace's cosmic determinism, with its claim that, once the laws governing it had been discovered, it would be possible to attain to an exact knowledge of the universe and to predict the behaviour of each of its components, from particles to heavenly bodies. This certainty was transferred later to the human plane, when the use of social statistics led to the conviction that here too there were regular features which acted almost as laws. Du Bois-Reymond declared in 1872 that whoever was able to know for a few moments the position, direction, and speed of all the atoms in the universe would be able to predict future events in the history of mankind.

In that same year, 1872, Auguste Blanqui published his scientific speculations in Paris under the title *L'Éternité par les astres*. He maintained that, since nature made an infinite number of combinations out of a small number of elements, it could not avoid repeating the same combinations from time to time. From this he deduced that everything that happened at a given moment had happened many times before, and would happen again in an identical way throughout eternity. Coming as this did from a revolutionary who had striven during his whole lifetime to change society, this vision of 'everlasting return' was, as Walter Benjamin said, 'an unconditional surrender and, at the same time, the most terrible judgement that could be issued about a society that projects this cosmic vision of itself onto the sky'.

Still more important was the influence of the evolutionist view of the world elaborated by Darwin, Huxley, Wallace, and above all, Spencer, who, perceiving in the struggle for survival a special mechanism of progress, used it to legitimize the most predatory aspects of capitalism. Evolutionary theory took up the ordered scheme of living beings which the eighteenth-century naturalists had produced, and introduced an explanatory dynamic into it.

History – the theory of social evolution originally designed by the Scottish school – had provided the scientists with the key to set their predecessors' systems of nature in motion. On the other hand, the sciences now came along to confirm the intuitions of social philosophers and historians, and supplied a basis for the new social disciplines, such as anthropology and sociology, which aspired to become like them: for Radcliffe-Brown, social anthropology was 'a branch of the natural sciences'.

That this global paradigm, whose central element was a linear view of history – both natural and human – animated by a concept of progress, should have about it much that implied a projection of society onto science, does not mean that it was merely the legitimation of certain class interests at the heart of capitalist societies and of colonial domination by Europeans over other peoples all over the world. It was a broad framework of ideas, within which both legitimizing and critical stances could be developed at the same time. Social evolutionism has been defined as 'a kind of cosmic genealogy of bourgeois civilization', but it was also compatible with a critical view of this. In 1869 Alfred Russel Wallace ended his narrative of eight years of travels and research in the Malay archipelago with a comparison between the solidarity and justice he had known among its savage peoples and the evils of British society, leading him to maintain that 'in matters of true social science, we are still in a phase of barbarism'.

To use this theory critically it was enough to refuse to accept the present as 'the end of history', reducing the present instead to a transitory phase of human progress in which there remain negative features to be overcome as evolution is carried forward. This was Marx's initial view. Educated in the adoration of Greece so typical of the Germany of his times, he began to elaborate his interpretation of society and history as criticism of the Scottish school, transforming modes of subsistence, ranked according to command of technical skills, into 'modes of production' defined by the nature of relationships between people. With this he accepted the unique linear scheme of progress from which he was to free himself only towards the end of his life. The dramatic consequence of this was that his followers stayed with the more schematic formulations of his early years and were unable to correct these in the light of the doubts and rectifications of his mature years.

So-called 'scientific socialism' fell victim to its acceptance of the fundamentals of bourgeois social science, which led it to believe that capitalism could be overcome by means of 'superindustrialization'. In the same way non-European peoples who accepted these fundamentals were victims too, believing they were appropriating them when eliminating their legitimizing function from them.

World history built on the basis of this theory rests on a series of falsifications, starting with its way of conceiving the motor of progress. Our interpretations of European superiority are rooted in a skewed idea of technological advance, generally reduced to two key elements: energy and the machine. 'Only energy tamed by technology gives cultural progress.' The so-called industrial revolution has usually been defined in terms of steam and mechanization. When an effort has been made to analyse it in terms of ways of organizing human work, someone has always hastened to insist that the essential factor was passing from an economy depending on organic energy to another using mostly mineral energy. It was machines that gave the European decisive superiority in navigation and in warfare and facilitated his rapid imperial expansion in Africa and Asia, so it is not surprising he should see in them the reason for his primacy and should think that man's ability to make machines provided a safe yardstick by which to measure his degree of civilization.

Our histories of technology are usually little more than histories of mechanization, and they have little to say about all the rest. They additionally describe the contributions made by the Islamic world and those of Chinese technology – without accepting, however, that 'the great inventions that would allow modern times to arrive in the

West' were fundamentally legacies from Chinese expertise, as the Sinologists tell us – while the autochthonous civilizations of America and Black Africa, lacking machines, either are not mentioned or are relegated to prehistory.

In views of this type there is no room, for example, for artefacts that are modest but immensely important, such as the wheelbarrow which allows a man to transport great weights easily, a Chinese invention unknown in Europe until the late Middle Ages. But its most shocking distortion is that which concerns the relationship of man with his natural environment. The fact that machine-based civilization requires an enormous consumption of energy and raw materials has made us convert the pillaging of resources – also called 'domination over nature' – into a criterion of progress.

Our inability to perceive forms of technology as related to our use of the environment can thus be understood. When we speak of exchanges between America and Europe, for example, it is taken for granted that maize and potatoes are two natural products which the explorers discovered. We overlook the fact that they were developed by American peoples as the result of lengthy cultural action within a complex strategy of making use of the environment, which led them to a combined exploitation of the ecological strata in the Andes and to the agricultural system of the Mayas. The latter used the canals to breed fish which, beside serving for direct consumption, fertilized the crops with their excreta. This system, as has been said, also required a 'social technology', expressed in the invention of 'political symbols that transformed and coordinated such age-old institutions as the extended family, the village, the shaman and the patriarch into the stuff of civilized life'.

Basing ourselves on distorted criteria, we have formed false historical views, such as that which presents Europeans pulling south and south-east Asian countries out of their lethargy and drawing them into modernity. (I have not dealt with this concept, since it is merely the legitimation of everything we consider correct solely by reason of its position at the end of an evolutionary time-scale.) When we examine them in the light of these countries' own dynamic, things look very different. We might start with the fact that when Vasco da Gama reached Calcutta he found there a Tunisian who spoke Spanish, this being something more than a mere anecdote.

For the fact was that these lands had long been integrated into a world market extending from north Africa to the Indian subcontinent and from the cities on the caravan routes in central Asia to east Africa, having as their driving forces the Chinese economy and Islamic culture. At the end of the fifteenth century, when the Portuguese reached this part of the world, hundreds of traders from Arabia, Persia, India, Indonesia, and China came to the port of Melaka, perhaps the greatest commercial centre of the planet, where eighty-four languages could be heard. In an active Asian market which was expanding, the Europeans began as carriers above all, taking part in local traffic, since their coarse manufactured goods had little interest for the Asians. 'They intruded, brawled, and shoved the other merchants against whom they were competing and among whom they lived', ending up on top thanks, above all, to their military superiority which allowed them to destroy 'pre-existing Muslim and Indian trading arrangements'.

What happened next was much more complicated than is usually said. The threatening presence of the Europeans, combined with a local crisis and the decline in the availability of silver which financed international trade, led a good part of these peoples to withdraw into themselves, abandoning crops that had been destined for export. They thus ended their active participation in this first age of trade. Where they could, the Europeans opposed the withdrawal by force, imposing their rule (as the Dutch did in Indonesia, and as later the British were to do in India and the French in Cochin China). Alternatively, they imposed conditions for trade, as the British did in China in the middle of the nineteenth century with their forced introduction of opium as a commodity with which to pay for their purchases. The high Chinese functionaries were shocked by this: they had not known that opium was in use in Great Britain too, where working mothers used it in pharmaceutical preparations to help their children to sleep during the mothers' long days in the factories.)

In places where Europeans did not manage to impose themselves, as happened in Japan, the withdrawal prepared the conditions for a phase of internal economic growth, which led later to their renewed integration into the world market in a second age of trade, the one we are living in now. But this time they did it in an independent way, without subordinating themselves to foreign intermediaries. This process, begun in Japan at the end of the nineteenth century, has continued after the Second World War in the new Asian industrial countries, and seems now to have reached China. Viewed from the late twentieth century, after the collapse of colonial empires and the decline of the old industrial countries, these 200 years of reflux do not seem like the victory of Europe over the Orient that our history books tell us about, but instead a provisional withdrawal allowing those countries to adapt in their own way to the new conditions of the world economy.

Some of the errors of interpretation we make in this area proceed from the false images of others which, surprisingly, we have managed to get them to accept for themselves. In order to construct our idea of the European in the light of the diversity of peoples and cultures, we invented Asians, Africans, and native Americans, and credited them with a collective identity they did not possess. The preamble to a UNESCO declaration says that race is something that becomes obvious to the senses when one sees together 'an African, a European, an Asian, and an American Indian' (these being animals as unreal as a unicorn or a mermaid).

To these depictions unified on a continental scale there correspond equally stereotyped historical interpretations, such as that of a Black Africa that has not passed beyond the tribal stage, overlooking the importance cities have had in its history – in about 1600 there were some thirty with more than 20,000 inhabitants on the continent – and the fact that on its soil there were such important states as the kingdoms of Aksum and Mali.

The subtlest of these inventions was precisely that of Asia, which after being a merely geographical concept became a historical and cultural entity, the Orient. This allowed us to solve the problem of knowing where in our linear scheme to place those societies with an advanced culture that we could not consign to prehistory, as we had done with those of Africa, America and Oceania.

The concept of 'the Orient' was being forged at the same time as our conviction that Asian societies were inferior, and it was rounded off in the late eighteenth and early nineteenth centuries. That was when the Turks were 'orientalized', they having up to that time terrified Europe with their formidable administrative and military machine. (Lepanto had been just an incident; in 1622 Anthony Sherley declared that 'the two greatest powers there are in the world today are those of this monarchy – the Spanish – and the Turk'.)

The same was done with north Africa, traditionally associated with Barbary pirates and with unconfessed fear about the attractions of Islam: the great number of Christian renegades contrasted with the rarity of Muslims converted to Christianity. The French Bourbons declared war on Algiers on the pretext of avenging three taps with a fan which the French consul had received from the Dey (historians are still debating whether the taps were given with the handle or the feathers; what is sure is that the consul deserved them for his impertinence). It is usually held that the Bourbons acted in order to preen themselves on the military prestige of the conquest, but nothing is said about there figuring among their aims that of looting the Algerian treasure-chests, as they hastened to do.

China was orientalized too in the late eighteenth century. Up till then its culture was held in high esteem, since, even though it was supposed that the Chinese could not be compared with Europeans in the speculative sciences, it was thought the former were superior in other realms:

'I cannot say how greatly they excel in the study of politics and how marvellously they order their empire, keep it free from all rebellion, and how much attention they give to the administration of their republic.' The physiocrats went on thinking, on the eve of the French Revolution, that Chinese despotism was a political model worthy of imitation.

However, things were already beginning to change. For a start, the description of the skin colour of the Chinese and Japanese was changed, a simple and effective way of orientalizing them. Until the end of the eighteenth century travellers and naturalists considered them white. In the late eighteenth century, at the same time as the scornful image of a decadent China was being created, they began to be described as 'yellow', within the supposed division of humankind into five differently-coloured races.

This change of attitude can be observed in the *Encyclopédie*. Diderot agreed that the Chinese have an admirable culture, but he went on: 'In general, the spirit of the Orient is more serene, lazier, more enclosed in essential needs and limited to what it finds already established, less avid for novelty, than the spirit of the West.'

The matter of the spirit of the Orient was to cause havoc. It served on one side to spread a skewed view of those cultures. Chinoiserie had nothing to do with the great art of China, which became known in Europe only when works stolen by the military who had stormed and destroyed the Peking palace were put on show in a London exhibition of 1862 ('ownership was discreetly attributed to their wives'). In the same way the image of exotic Japan which one kind of European literature spread could convey no idea of the vigorous protean world of Hokusai, nourished by popular culture. (French painters discovered this thanks to engravings which arrived as fillings in crates of merchandise, and were sold cheaply in teashops.)

The caricaturing of the Oriental eventually blinded its creators and prevented them seeing the reality it masked. They failed to realize, for example, that if Japanese industrialization adopted European technology, it would not all the same repeat the supposedly universal model of British industry, since it was undertaken without urban growth and with an intelligent adaptation of imported technology to local conditions. The existence of industrialization gave the lie to the belief that primitive peoples could embark upon progress only under the tutelage of colonizers. When this industrializing process displayed itself in full strength after the Second World War, the problem of fitting it into previous patterns encouraged all manner of speculation about the Japanese spirit, but as was to be expected nobody said anything sensible about it.

Fascination with the Islamic Orient which inundated Europe in the Romantic period was an outcome of this same lack of understanding. That was when an impressive list of travellers set off to cover Turkey, the Holy Land, Egypt, Palmyra and the Caucasus (which was the Orient to the Russians). They were not explorers or researchers, but writers – Chateaubriand, Flaubert, Pushkin; painters athirst for exoticism who helped to build a new image of those lands – Lewis's harems, David Roberts's monuments, but also Delacroix; Saint-Simonian planners ('to each his Orient, according to his needs'); and a great number of women – Lady Hester Stanhope, Isabel Burton, Florence Nightingale, Jane Digby, Aimé Dubucq de Rivery, and Isabelle Eberhardt.

The Orient they were looking for was a European invention, a refuge from the wretched ugliness of the industrialized West which they themselves had fashioned in their dreams, adorning it with everything they missed in their surroundings. Hardly had she set foot in Alexandria in 1849 than Florence Nightingale was speaking of 'a new world of ancient poetry, images of the Bible, light, life, and beauty'. She had brought that world with her, and all she needed was a setting in which to make it flesh. What really existed and was happening in those lands mattered little to them. The Orient was an escape – Goethe wanted to flee away to 'the pure Orient' in order 'to mix with shepherds, cool myself at the oases, travelling with the caravans, trading in silks, coffee, and musk': a day-dream or a disguise.

The worst thing was that the non-European peoples ended up accepting, together with the false identities we had given them, the fiction for which they had been created: the linear view of history. They thus abandoned their own past, replacing it with a critical revision of the past the Europeans had foisted upon them, not realizing that this prevented them perceiving the true nature of their problems. It was not enough to transform the old epic of progress into the shameful history of exploitation. With it people's characterization changed, but the scenario and the most substantial part of the argument persisted.

The explanation for European growth could not be reduced to that based on colonial despoilment. It is certain that the construction of a world market was the stimulus which fed the modern growth of Europe, but once the process had been set in motion, it went on to depend upon a more complex driving-force, as is shown by the fact that from the late nineteenth century up to our time international trade has tended to be ever more an exchange between developed countries.

Nor should we overstate the profits made by colonialism. The notion that imperialism generated huge profits – an idea which those Europeans who made great sacrifices to conquer and keep colonial empires should have shared – turned out to be an unfounded illusion based on a mistaken estimate of the wealth of tropical colonies. The final balance-sheets of the two biggest empires, the British and the French, show similar results: the overall income was lower than the costs. The fact that certain special sectors in the mother-country's societies made huge profits at the cost of expenditure borne by the nation as a whole merely shows that the borderline of exploitation passes not so much between the mother-country and the colony as between a restricted group of profit-makers in the mother-country – and in the colony too, it should be remembered – and the great mass of the population of both.

This does not mean we should accept an image that is an apologia for colonization – the white man's burden, the white man being generously devoted to the welfare of the coloured man, from whom he would receive only in-gratitude. Rather it means that it is dangerous to retain an excessively elementary and simplistic image for some-thing so complicated, an image that has persuaded us to believe that all the ills of the underdeveloped world would end with independence.

To reduce the history of Africa, for example, to the tale of 'how Europe underdeveloped Africa', in which every-thing is explained by depredation and slavery, draws us away from reality. European slave-traders were warmly welcomed by local rulers who sold them slaves. Slavery was firmly rooted on the Atlantic coast of Africa, where it represented the commonest form of productive private property (it held the place occupied in Europe by property in land). When the slave-trade rose to huge proportions this was owed especially to the way in which African sup-pliers responded to the growing demands of the Atlantic market. Both sets of people were accomplices, with the same degree of guilt, though the Europeans were more cynical because they used the slavery argument to describe Africans as barbarians and to justify their conquest as a civilizing necessity. Once the moral aspect of the question has been aired, what matters is understanding how the slave-trade helped transform African societies and opened the way for forms of commercialized agriculture which have turned out to be perhaps more destructive than the traffic in slaves.

To interpret the history of non-European peoples in the light of our conceptions of them is to steal their own history from them and make the solution to their problems harder. The anthropologists made the Bushmen of the Kala-hari, a people of hunter-gatherers, an example of primitive society, one that was on the lowest rung of historical evo-lution. This made them a fascinating subject of study, but it condemned them to real isolation with regard to other neighbouring African peoples, with the result that a British commissioner could even say in 1936: 'I [see] no reason whatever for preserving Bushmen. I can conceive no use-ful object to the world in spending money and energy in preserving a decadent and dying race, which is perfectly useless from any point of view, merely to enable a few theorists to carry out anthropological investigations and make money by writing books which lead nowhere.' This denied them the history they in fact had: the Bushmen had not lived detached from the evolution of other peoples round about, as some imagined, and the situation they found themselves in when colonization happened was the outcome of recent developments. Consequently they were placed outside all possibilities of progress, as though they were specimens to be kept in a reserve or a zoo, thus allowing them to retain their traditional way of life, without anyone noticing that this tradition was in good measure an invention of European anthropologists. Much the same could be said about Australia and the construction of the concept of 'aboriginal' by anthropologists. This defines an elementary contrast between aboriginals and Europeans, and it was eventually shared by those who saw colonization as lawful and by those who condemned it, including a good part of the natives who were thus taught to accept a false solidarity with their brothers.

When we impose upon him the primitive version, we make perception by the non-European of the reality of his society and his culture more difficult, and we condemn him to a cultural colonization. The way in which the response to the quincentenary of the 'discovery' of America developed may illustrate this. To claim that in 1492 there were 'Americans' and to hide the complicity which the conquistadors found in the native societies themselves (collaboration by certain peoples against others, or by certain social groups within the same people) serves only to mask the truth and directs the natives towards a supposedly critical stance from which only rhetorical protests and public gatherings in support of them can come. They are in fact being invited to accept European civilization, and to correct defects in this by applying the virtues of an idealized ancient native society. Instead we ought to be helping them to reject the global image of the past which has been imposed on them and to analyse the present and plan the

future on the basis of the problematic situation they live
in. This is not the same thing as dreaming up mythical
pasts in which to take refuge from their powerlessness.
That was what happened when the Peruvian peasants
dreamed up a kindly and provident Inca empire which did
not represent the reality of the matter: this probably helped
them to preserve their identity, but it made the formulation
of a policy for facing up to their problems in a realistic
way harder, the first problem being that of the ownership
of land at the present time.

Let us finally glance at this 'triumph of Europe' which
we have used to reorganize, and to falsify, world history.
When Volney wrote his meditations on the ruins of Palmyra, he started from the generally accepted idea that in
the race for progress Asia had lagged behind – 'the ec-
lipsed splendour of Asia in modern Europe' – but he did
not hasten to deduce from this the usual conclusion about
the natural superiority of Europeans, preferring to go one
step further:

> I reflected on the fact that activity in the countries
> before me had been no less: who knows, I thought
> to myself, whether one day the dereliction of my own
> mother-country will not be the same? Who knows
> whether a traveller will sit, as I do here today, by
> silent ruins on the banks of the Seine, the Thames, or
> the Zuider Zee, and will not be alone in weeping over
> the ashes of peoples and the memories of their past
> greatness?

What, finally, is the sense of this kind of culmination of
history into which we have converted our modern times
with their Europeanization of the world? For the Sinologist
Jacques Gernet the rise of Europe can be explained by the
fact that the establishment of the Mongol Empire favoured
the transmission to it of technological inventions from a
China that was much more advanced.

What, in a world history which in effect is reduced to
the history of the West, we are wont to consider to be

the start of modern times, is no more than the repercussions of the spread of urban and mercantile civilizations whose range extended, before the Mongol invasion, from the Mediterranean to the China Sea. The West received part of that legacy and the leavening which would promote its development.

Five hundred years of borrowed boom – and with regard to industrialization, no more than 300 – which seems to be on the point of being replaced by a return of initiative to the focal points in eastern Asia in which it originated, are not a very long time. At least they do not amount to anything which might justify talk of the culmination, or even the end, of history. We might think we are going to witness a simple geographical displacement of the centre of the world, like those displacements that have happened in earlier phases of history, in accordance with the clichéd idea of the march of civilization following the course of the sun, from the Mediterranean to the Atlantic, first, and now from the Atlantic to the Pacific.

Matters are really much more complicated. To maintain such an interpretation would condemn us to keeping all the defects and limitations of unilinear views of history and of progress. The consequences and perspectives of five centuries of the European miracle must be looked at in another way. For a start some of its keys have to be sought inside European society itself.

9

The Mirror of the Mob

One of the fundamental mechanisms in the restructuring of Europe after the social crisis of the fifteenth and sixteenth centuries was the making of the modern state, to which the privileged classes handed part of their political and military functions in exchange for assurances about the maintenance of their social and economic privileges. As Locke said: 'The great and chief end therefore, of men's uniting into commonwealths, and putting themselves under government, is the preservation of their property.' However, the idea that the modern state arose suddenly, with all its trappings, and reinforced as it might be by the designation 'absolutist', is erroneous.

The modern state was born with little ability to draw together and control the mass of its citizens. Between the sovereign and the subjects was inserted an intermediate plane. An upper stratum consisted of an oligarchy of magnates close to the central power. Another, allied or subordinated to the latter, was formed by the class of wealthy property-owners, noble and non-noble, who controlled local power. (The Crown of Castile has thus been described as 'a federation of municipalities'.)

However much talk there is of centralization, local life, including tax-collecting, stayed out of central control until a very late stage, as is shown by the survival of forms of patronage, rule by regional bosses, and client status until well on in the nineteenth century. In France in the seventeenth century, for example, the absolute monarchy was unable to repair the bridge over the Rhône at Lyons – the only one across which troops and provisions for Italy could pass – because provincial taxes for its repair had not been paid, since preference was being given to claims from private persons.

Another error present in a good deal of the theorizing about the modern state is the supposition that it was based on coercion. No state possesses enough power to maintain itself over a long period without consensus. The essential thing was, as the British held in the seventeenth century, to have 'opinion' on one's side: 'Power rests always with the governed, and those governing have nothing to support them other than opinion. This is the reason why government is based solely upon opinion; and this maxim is valid for the most despotic and military governments as it is for the most free and popularly-based.'

To keep 'opinion' on the state's side it was necessary to make the underclass believe not only that the ordering of society was God's will, but that it was also rational and just. There existed certain rules designed to ensure the well-being of subjects; and when they were infringed, it meant that somebody had infringed them, not that the system in itself was bad. 'It does not concern us to know whether the people has any right to overthrow us' – Goethe wrote – 'for we try to be sure only that it is not tempted to do it.' Laws existed to stop abuses, and governments tried to apply them, but they lacked the means, and often the will, to enforce compliance.

To explain intrusions by private interests into the public sphere it is customary to resort to the argument that the state was still fragile and immature. This is a fallacy based on a comparison with the theoretical model of a state which monopolized power and social control, which never existed in the absolutist period, and has never existed. Recent Italian experience shows up to what point the state is still fragile. This situation is denounced as 'corruption' only when its excesses become a threat to the survival of the system, since it is well known that the same corruption in reasonable doses is part of the game, even though it is not written into the rules.

Among the functions taken on by the state the defence of its citizens figured prominently, and this justified, in societies organized by estates, the privileges of the knightly class. A necessary condition for this was having money, 'the sinews of war', according to an ancient commonplace going back to Cicero. The importance that war had for absolutist monarchies (in the eighteenth century direct and indirect military costs could represent more than seventy-five per cent of the total) explains why the Empress Maria Theresa said that the treasury was 'the only mainspring of the state'.

War cost ever more because on each occasion it demanded more men: in the greatest battles of the sixteenth century there were generally not more than 30,000 combatants, counting both sides; by the start of the eighteenth century there might be more than 150,000. It also came to occupy a larger place in the life of the European states, since conflicts were ever more frequent and generalized. This led to the need for permanent paid armies ('soldier' derives from *solidus*, originally a gold coin) and naval fleets which involved great cost, this rising in times of war.

This expense created serious problems for governments, which could bring in more direct taxes only by making the privileged pay or by deflecting resources in the hands of these people into state coffers. Since either of these measures would have endangered the alliance on which the *ancien régime* was based, states came to depend more and more on indirect taxation, particularly that generated by overseas trade. This tied the fate of the state to the interests of the groups of major traders, who received in exchange the political and military support needed for their conquest of world markets.

This was what happened in Holland, with the creation of the first system of public debt that could be placed in the open market at low rates of interest. This was made possible by the confidence of bond-holders in a government whose treasury was under public control. (Absolute monarchies, losing prestige owing to their suspensions of payments, had to get credit at usurious rates of interest, resorting to financiers and intermediaries.) England was later to follow the same course, and there the Glorious Revolution of 1688 consolidated the alliance of landowners with merchants who traded overseas. The system of parliamentary negotiation created a national culture shared by a broad segment of the moneyed classes, who 'learned to see their private interests in terms of public or national objectives'.

The British created the first great European nation-state with the joining of the English and Scottish crowns in 1603 and in the Act of Union of 1707. Despite the Scottish Jacobite rebellions of 1715 and 1745, Great Britain and later the United Kingdom were states towards which the different nationalities of Scottish, Welsh, English and even the Irish could feel some loyalty while retaining their regional cultures.

There was a sense of a new collective identity which James Thomson (a Scot, as were also Walter Scott and the royal painter Davis Wilkie, who elaborated the national myths dear to Romanticism) expressed in song:

> The nations not so blessed as thee
> Must in their turn to tyrants fall;
> Whilst thou dost flourish great and free,
> The dread and envy of them all.
> Rule Britannia, Britannia rule the waves!
> Britons never never shall be slaves!

It is likely that by the end of the eighteenth century the process of nation-making had gone further in Great Britain than in the rest of Europe, but the homogenization was much less than complete. British society threatened to break up in the early nineteenth century, subjected as it was to the harsh consequences of industrialization. Those were years in which Shelley 'believed that a clash between the two classes of society was inevitable', and Byron wrote a *Song for the Luddites*: 'We will die fighting, or will live

free,/And down with all kings but King Ludd!' In 1845
Disraeli declared that in Great Britain there were

> Two nations; between whom there is no intercourse
> and no sympathy; who are as ignorant of each other's
> habits, thoughts, and feelings, as if they were dwellers
> in different zones, or inhabitants of different planets;
> who are formed by a different breeding, are fed by a
> different food, are ordered by different manners, and
> are not governed by the same laws. The rich and the
> poor.

Nation and nation-state must not be confused. National
sentiment – the awareness of collectivity based on a shared
culture – has existed at all times and in all places, and has
acted as a liberating force in communities struggling to free
themselves from dependency or colonialism. The nation-
state, on the other hand, in the form in which it was
consolidated in the nineteenth century, is usually nothing
other than the old absolutist state rejuvenated.

In the seventeenth century the French and Spanish monarchies were already thinking of basing themselves on
national sentiment for support, but did not achieve satisfactory results. In Spain, Olivares's plan for the 'Union
of Arms' was adorned with a nationalistic rhetoric which
convinced nobody and could not prevent separatist wars
in Portugal and Catalonia. It was the French Revolution
which, forced to bring together an aggregate of nations
inherited from absolutism ('a colonial empire formed down
the centuries'), fashioned the model for a community in
which all were to be 'children of the fatherland'.

Once the ideological cohesion of the old monarchies
with their divine right had been eroded, an effort was made
to replace it by another, secular in nature, expressed in a
'civil religion' by the cult of the fatherland and a few invented symbols, such as flags. The greatest binding forces
here were the home market – with the broadening on a
national scale of the economic relationship of countryside
and town, which created interdependence among people

living under the same laws and the same economic policy – and the state school.

Schooling inculcated the new mythology of the nation: a self-justifying view of its own history: not the true history of conquerors and conquered, but another in which the motherland appeared as the parent all had in common. This was accompanied by the imposition of the ruling people's language; the propagation of specially prepared traditions and myths, with the fabrication of a folklore which selected and adapted elements of popular culture and made them national; maps which helped to build a new image of the nation's territory, these demanding the establishment of precise frontiers, which separated the inhabitants of neighbouring districts who had been accustomed up to that time to coexist; etc. At the same time schooling served to inculcate the rules and values of patrician morality and culture, starting with the imposition of a normative language. This was a bookish language which sought not only to combat local patois but also to eliminate the subversive spontaneity of vulgar speech, thus serving to mould ways of reasoning, banishing those of the common herd.

The franchise on the other hand had little unifying effect, since in most countries only four or five per cent of the population were entitled to vote. These were citizens having sufficient property for it to be assumed they would have an interest in maintaining the social order. (So-called universal suffrage was not established until it was sure it could be controlled in such a way that the 'nation of the poor' could not use its vote to remove the 'nation of the rich' from power.)

The justice system and imprisonment also had an educative function in that they reinforced respect for the new laws of property, which turned millions of European peasants into thieves of timber from woods they considered their own, and the laws taught discipline at work and submissiveness too. It is not clear, however, whether the civilizing process reduced levels of violence, as is claimed, since we can see still at the present time that the rate of criminal violence per 100,000 inhabitants is higher in the most civilized countries (in 1977 it was 18.8 per 100,000 in the United States, between 4 and 5 per 100,000 in Britain and Germany, and as low as 2.7 per 100,000 in Italy and 1.4 per 100,000 in Spain).

What reason lay behind this effort to forge a new collective consciousness around a programme which crossed the classes? The campaign to win back the lower orders had begun in the early sixteenth century and had achieved notable results. It attained some of its objectives in the realm of religious control and succeeded, above all, in lining up the bourgeois sectors alongside the old ruling classes, but this did not suffice to destroy the culture and communal dynamic of the lower orders. These factors still had life in them in the middle of the eighteenth century and people were able to refashion ways of grouping together independently on the basis of relationships established at work or connected with subsistence and festivities.

Schooling, imprisonment, and military service did a lot to unify culture, but autonomy did not disappear until ways of working and living around which the community consciousness was formed were destroyed. According to the legitimizing historical view of modernization, these changes are to be explained by the objective needs of economic growth, hindered by the insistence of peasants and craftsmen on sticking to their traditional ways and customs. On this view its outcome was the great leap forward of the agricultural and industrial revolutions. Today we can see the fallacy in this interpretation: we can see that there were various ways of achieving the same results, and that some of these could have ensured a similar economic growth without breaking communal links and with a more equitable distribution of wealth.

The history of the agricultural revolution is usually presented in such a way as to make it appear that the destruction of communal methods of cultivation was a necessary precondition for it. Today we know there was a logic about the peasant economy which was achieving growth by a means quite different from that postulated by the great landowners; what the latter were after was only an increase in sales of produce, not maximizing production in general and improving peasant welfare.

Studies of traditional agriculture show not only that this was perfectly capable of improvement, but also that most of the great advances were achieved in it. The progress made in Flanders, where it all started, was the outcome of ordinary developments in traditional agriculture. The association between crops and stock-raising which characterizes the first British agricultural revolution started in open fields and not in enclosures (Laxton, the last English village to keep its open-field system, adopted all the improvements that suited its inhabitants). France, with its largely peasant agriculture, adapted perfectly to the new techniques. Russian peasant communities in the nineteenth century were capable of introducing 'improvements which needed a considerable investment in work, capital, and intelligence'. All this is enough to make us think that the version which justifies the destruction of the old communal world by the need to increase production needs to be revised.

This 'productivist' view devalues the complex world of peasant culture. E. P. Thompson has shown the extraordinary vitality and independence of this culture and the way it ensured, up to the end of the eighteenth century, that the poor would not be complete losers. A recent study of English country people in the eighteenth century brings independent peasants back to life – a life denied by an orthodoxy which has them disappear from the scene by the middle years of that century – and allows us to understand the reality of a world of farmers, based on the exploitation of communal property, which was destroyed by the enclosures.

This was the world nostalgically recalled by John Clare, the great rural poet, when he remembered 'There was a time my bit of ground/Made freeman of the slave', this time lasting 'Till vile enclosure came and made/A parish slave of me' and made others dependent on welfare handed out to the poor. It had been a time in which labourers did not imitate gentlemen, but lived in their old houses, 'At whose oak table that was plainly spread/Each guest was welcomd and the poor was fed,/Where master son and serving man and clown/Without distinction daily sat them down.' By the early nineteenth century 'These all have vanished like a dream of good.'

Something rather similar has happened in the case of the industrial revolution, a subject which has been under most drastic revision for some years (from the moment when British economic decline discredited the myth of self-sustaining growth). Some of these revisions – which start from the conviction that industries are not 'reducible to simple economic systems and structures', but involve 'systems of human cooperation and of social as well as economic relationships' – maintain that there were possibilities of an alternative evolution, based on various forms of cooperation. They maintain that the factory did not arise for any reason of technical efficiency but to ensure the owner's control over his manpower and make it easier for him to get a larger surplus. Employers managed to get technology to develop in such a way that it favoured manufacturing concentration and ensured the superiority of this over small-scale production, which made it seem as though the factory was a requisite of technical progress. Today when large industry is beginning to suffer the consequences of its rigidity and the future seems to lie with more flexible productive structures, it may be proper to turn our glance back to that crossroads at which industrial growth might have followed a different path.

In the early nineteenth century there were many workers who believed industrial production could be organized in a socially more equitable way, without giving up technological advances. They thought too that machines could be made to serve workers instead of enslaving them, and that capital and labour did not have to be separated, 'but they will be indissolubly joined together in the hands of workmen and work-women'. These people rejected manufacturing industrialization, not only because it impoverished them, but also because it condemned them to degrading labour in the 'dark satanic mills'. Blake wrote:

The hour-glass contemnd because its simple workmanship
Was like the workmanship of the plowman, and the water
   wheel,
That raises water into cisterns: broke and burnd with fire:
Because its workmanship was like the workmanship of the
   shepherd.
And in their stead, intricate wheels invented, wheel without
   wheel:
To perplex youth in their outgoings, and to bind to labours
   in Albion
Of day and night the myriads of eternity that they may
   grind
And polish brass and iron hour after hour laborious task!
Kept ignorant of its use, that they might spend the days
   of wisdom
In sorrowful drudgery, to obtain a scanty pittance of bread:

The debate about whether or not standards of living improved for the workers with industrialization has not provided, and probably cannot provide, satisfactory answers
in the terms in which it has been conducted: there are no
objective criteria for measuring welfare, and this should
be defined in terms that are not only material but cultural
too. There is, however, something which speaks eloquently
of how the workers themselves perceived what the factory
meant to them: the way they desperately resisted going
into it, giving way only when overcome by hunger. The
British hand-weavers preferred earning less to joining a system which took away their independence and their dignity,
and broke the relationship of the family to its work.

   All the same, throughout the nineteenth century this
resistance was overcome and there was an advance towards national integration. Gradually the aristocracy and
the bourgeoisie became identified: the aristocracy sought
middle-class outlets for its wealth – transforming privilege
into property – and the bourgeoisie adopted the culture
and lifestyle of the nobles. There was no persistence of the
ancien régime and no triumph of the bourgeoisie: instead,
capitalism's logic imposed itself, forcing the ruling groups

to make a pact in order to defend themselves against the aspirations of those below.

There was also a process by which the lower orders were culturally assimilated. British workers abandoned their aspirations for radical change and signed up with middle-class culture. The French peasants were 'nationalized' in the course of the nineteenth century (which has been explained, implausibly, as the result of city-dwellers leading them to drink at the fountain of progress). The germanization of the German masses was the result of a long and meticulous educative process functioning through all the media: monuments (for which a 'Germanic' style was devised), public festivals, choral societies, gymnastic clubs, and the like.

This homogenization was not so complete as had been wished, however. The bourgeoisie could not be sure that the poor had been well enough tamed. Periods of panic among the ruling classes went on uninterruptedly after each movement of the common people, for they always thought the horrors of the French Revolution were going to be repeated. In 1819, for example, when a peaceful meeting in favour of electoral reform was bloodily dispersed in Manchester, a politician maintained that if such gatherings were to be tolerated 'there is an end of all existing law and government, and the population of this country must be set loose to frame a new order of society through the same bloody practices which have attended the French Revolution.' In 1830, again, the moderate Paris revolution, which achieved little more than changing the dynasty, brought the death of the terrified Niebuhr closer, he having seen the day coming when the people would rise and demand 'a revision of property'.

Each new event renewed these fears: the 1848 revolution, when the spectre of communism ran through Europe, but never had any chance of becoming more than a spectre; the founding of the first International; the Commune; in the twentieth century the new and more frightening spectre of Bolshevism; and the wave of social commotions which shook central and western Europe after the First World

War, when for the first and only time there was a general strike in Great Britain.

Panic among the upper classes always went very much further than revolutionary intentions did among the lower. When in 1932 the United States war veterans marched to Washington to ask for advance payment of compensation granted them by Congress, money they were not to receive till 1945, the army violently repressed them. General MacArthur, who directed operations together with Majors Eisenhower and Patton, declared that if the starving veterans' demonstration had been allowed to continue, 'our government's institutions would have been gravely threatened'.

Nazism had broad popular support when it began to act against internal enemies by taking in beggars and tramps, and by putting antisocial elements into preventive custody in concentration camps. Later it applied the same technique to Jews and antifascists and then proceeded to exterminate them. Yet when we are horrified by this, as if it were something exceptional, we forget that the Nazis were acting with the same logic that in other times had served to defend the European citizen against 'the others' – heretics, witches, rebellious peasants, revolutionaries – and which many would have liked to apply against the lower classes. It is as damaging to absolve them from their crimes as it is to present them as something unique and aberrant, ignoring how normal it was and how much it had in common with options considered respectable.

In the twentieth century the poor townsman has replaced the countryman as an example of barbarousness and also as a threat, the more frightening because it is closer at hand. Poverty, which European societies in the period of absolutism eyed distrustfully and began to repress, acquired a colouring of vice or inferiority in the eyes of liberal and competitive society with its wish to give equal opportunities to all. In this way there was formed the 'degeneration' theory, on foundations claimed to be scientific, but nourished from sources as diverse as the search for a physical basis on which to explain delinquency

(Lombroso's 'born criminal'); novels in which Zola traced the steady decline of the Rougon-Macquart family; and even the resurrection of the vampire myth, that is of cor-ruption transmitted in the blood. Out of this complex of ideas emerged scientific-political attempts to resolve the problem: eugenics which was to improve the race by se-lecting individuals suitable for reproduction, and which inspired sterilizing programmes in the United States; and emigration, conceived as a means of relieving large cities of unwanted inhabitants. Nothing seemed too much to counter the risk of a rebellion by the masses.

The word 'mass', Raymond Williams says, is a new word that we use in place of 'mob' or 'common herd'. It is found in Britain from the start of the eighteenth century. In Spain it was not taken up by the 1791 edition of the Academy dictionary, its place still being occupied by *vulgo* or *plebe*: 'the ordinary or common sort among the people'. But, asks Williams, who constitutes the mass? No ob-jective definition is possible: 'The mass consists of "the others".'

These masses had increased in number with the growth of the European population in the nineteenth century. Education, which had been put at their disposal with the idea of integrating them into national culture, gave a still more threatening aspect to the mob which had thought it was being invited to participate as an equal in the feast. Intellectuals and artists could accept a countryman who stayed in his own sphere, and could even praise him – as Lawrence did – as a depositary of primitive instincts, but they could not stomach the cultivated urban mob which had assimilated bourgeois values. Flaubert ridiculed their elegant notions, and Pierre Louys made fun of their morality ('human hypocrisy which is also called "virtue" ').

Even the quality of the senses differed among these diverse white races. Huysmans said that in colour percep-tion one must distinguish between that of 'the majority of men, whose coarse retinas perceive neither the cadences peculiar to different colours nor the mysterious charm of their gradation', and 'bourgeois optics that are insensible to the pomp and glory of the clear, bright colours', and, finally, 'people with delicate eyes that have undergone the education of libraries and art-galleries', these last being the only ones able to savour vibrant colours and their shades at the same time.

'Philistines' (a term which German students applied to the non-university person) were not to be allowed access to 'great' art. Artists in the late nineteenth and early twentieth centuries wrote, painted, and composed for cultivated minorities. Later, their agents and dealers discovered that the vanguard was something that would fetch a good price from bourgeois suckers. They described themselves as 'poètes maudits', thought themselves above the morality of the masses, and took refuge in esoteric cults reserved for select initiates.

'Intellectuals' despised the masses and at the same time feared them. Like Niebuhr, they thought that if one day the masses woke up to the deception on which their submissiveness was based, they would rebel and destroy the intellectuals' world. If not all of them felt, like Nietzsche, able to make publicly 'a declaration of war against the masses', there were many who abominated that democracy which placed political decisions in the hands of a majority of the least suitable people. 'The great game' – said Ernst Jünger – 'is the one played between the *demos* with its plebiscites and what remains of the aristocracy.'

This led the intellectuals to dream of new Caesars, and some thought they had found them in Mussolini and Hitler, who had many more admirers among the European intelligentsia than is often believed, since few remained consistent in their views after the defeat. Most of them managed to get their adhesion forgotten, like Jünger (who in any case thought Hitler too plebeian), or like Heidegger, who had demanded that research and teaching should be devoted to the service of the National Socialist revolution (but the Nazis found him too 'metaphysical').

This struggle against the plebeian masses is never open warfare. Enemies to be fought would be too numerous, and in any case they have to be kept alive and deceived so that they go on working to provide for the expensive needs of their 'betters'. Internal enemies are invented in order to segregate certain human groups as inferiors or even as enemies: Jews, tramps, strikers and foreign immigrants (when they have ceased to be needed). In this way a double aim is achieved: to strengthen the illusion that a community of interests exists between the unsegregated masses – the good citizens – and their rulers, and to have someone who can be loaded with blame for problems.

It is not enough to attack these facts because of their injustice, claiming equal treatment for those excluded. That would be a pointless undertaking, unless at the same time we were to dismantle the framework of ideas that justifies the exclusion. In this framework an essential component is the view of history which legitimizes the superiority of Europeans because of their role in fomenting universal progress, and which seeks to convert us all into born accomplices of all their abuses by hiding from us the fact that that progress has been achieved at a cost to the greater part of those same Europeans too. For it is not a case of this Eurocentric view depriving non-Europeans of their history (though it does this). Its most important aim is surely to snatch their history away from great parts of European peoples themselves, concealing from them the fact that there are pasts other than that which has been canonized as official history. It hides from them also the fact that they can find a wealth of hopes and unrealized possibilities in those pasts, and that much of what has been presented to them as progress is only a mask to cover various forms of economic appropriation and social control. When we take their history and their consciousness away from the lower classes, we reduce them to the role of savages in their own countries.

This happened in the past to the countryfolk who tried to look for progress within the framework of their communally-based agriculture, and to the craftsmen who wanted machines put to the service of mankind. Today it is the turn of the factory worker and the employee who see the minimal concessions of stability and welfare they won through the trade-union struggle threatened, concessions now being denounced as obstacles to a progress that hopes to go on vampire-like sucking their blood, this depredation being disguised as competitiveness.

10

Outside the Hall of Mirrors

To justify their superiority, Europeans have speculated about the miracle of their history and the reasons – that is to say, the merits – which might explain it. The first of the causes adduced is the one which associates their success with the qualities of a race of superior people. The Indo-European myth – the word 'Aryan' does not seem tasteful today, but it means the same – arose in Germany in the early nineteenth century. It was inspired by the progress made in comparative linguistics, and served to liberate European culture from its presumed Mediterranean origins. According to this myth, people with white skin, fair hair, and blue eyes came from the Himalayas or the plains of central Asia to create, as Rosenberg said, 'the dream of Nordic humanity in Hellas'.

Other explanations proceed more subtly, basing the success on some kind of virtue. In this category we find explanations which relate capitalistic development to the effects of religion, or those that base success on some characteristic peculiar to European families, which, by delaying marriage, kept the birthrate low, thus favouring thriftiness and, in consequence, investment. This idea possibly began with Malthus, for whom the lowering of the birthrate had to be associated with an act of voluntary abstention, that is, with an acceptance by the poor that they should resign themselves to that small share in the good things of this world that Providence had assigned to them. What is sure is that the decline in fertility – that peaceful revolution which for some represents, together with urbanization and industry, one of the pillars of modernization – has been owed above all to the use of contraceptives and not to any kind of virtuous abstention.

I spoke earlier of technology. Even if we accept the distortion of reducing this to energy and machines, European superiority is of such recent date that we are forced to ask ourselves why the industrial revolution happened in Europe and not, for example, in China, which in the middle of the seventeenth century was ahead in many respects. Attempts to explain this end up repeating all the clichés of traditional orientalism: 'in China the impulse towards change was small', in contrast with the Faustian spirit, innovative and creative, of the Europeans. Even the most ambitious and carefully nuanced interpretations, such as that of E. L. Jones, finish up resorting to the old standby about an Orient in which 'despotic Asian institutions suppressed creativity or diverted it into producing voluptuous luxuries'.

Can we seriously maintain that the Islamic world, the Chinese Empire, or the sultanates of Java were more despotic than European absolutist monarchies? From the sixteenth century to the eighteenth the effort to strengthen the presence of the state and obedience to the ruler took the form in Europe of an increase of repression which has led to talk of the 'period of tortures'. Also, ever more frequent and costly wars were the price paid to ensure conditions which would allow an evolution, more or less rapid, towards modernity. This period moreover is that of witchhunts, wars of religion, and inquisitorial persecutions which filled scientists with fear. This period of generalized violence encouraged Europe to perfect her weapons and fighting techniques which would produce her hegemony.

Aside from military reasons, however, European success was linked to factors which stimulated productive investment, and which do not seem to have existed in the countries of eastern Asia at the time. These included guarantees of property rights and low rates of interest, two features related to the development of forms of parliamentary democracy which brought aristocratic landowners and bourgeois businessmen together in the political control of the state ('a part of the winning class' – says Queneau, referring to revolutions in general – ' "establishes" itself and reaches an agreement with the defeated class'). Thanks to this they were able to ensure the stability of their property, fiercely defended – even with the gallows – at the same time as they were despoiling the countryfolk of theirs. This should lead us to take more cautious and nuanced views of the contrast between the despotic Orient and the free West.

This hall of distorting mirrors which have allowed the European to strengthen his supposed superiority over the savage, over primitive man, and over the Oriental, is the base on which is set the conception of 'his' civilization and 'his' progress and by which he explains his successes. Or rather, with which he tries to explain them, since it is obvious that it fails to account for something so important as the interpretation of the factors which have given rise to modern economic growth. This is shown by the fact that the recipes for growth which have been deduced from this historical interpretation failed when they were applied to the colonial world, and that they failed again when put into practice in colonies as they became independent. Both those which used the most orthodox set of recipes, based on a mythical and fallacious understanding of British industrialization, and those that tried the formulas of so-called centralized planning, which seemed better for countries with slender resources, discovered this.

The fall of communism, which has been celebrated as a triumph, is merely one more chapter in the story of the failure of European attempts to change the world. Now that the sterility of both sets of recipes has been proved, what alternative can we offer today to the Third World, or to the countries of Latin America that have been 'third-worlded'? These were countries which at one time hoped they were going to join the rich men's club but have awoken with a hangover of overwhelming debts, and other countries which lived under the old 'real socialism' and have passed from poverty into wretchedness with no horizon in sight other than that of regaining a certain decorous level of poverty.

Nothing is happening in the way predicted by interpretative models deduced from history. In the developed countries of the West what it was thought would be an uninterrupted increase of wealth has stopped. This was self-sustaining growth, according to the usual formula, as if an economy had a built-in evolutionary capacity which could keep going by itself, independently of any action by people. Also the welfare state, which shared out among members of society as a whole the profits from this enrichment, finds itself bankrupt. In countries of the old 'real socialism' the return to liberalism has been accompanied by a fall in rates of growth, giving the lie to all the prophecies. There is also the paradox that the most rapid upward rhythm is being recorded in China, which has gone in for a mixture of systems that does not fit into any of the available schemes.

The fact is that of the many models we use, the best ones, those that really explain something, are based on patterns deduced from past experiences, and this makes them useless for anticipating what is to come; while those that try to see into the future are often based on illusions and untrustworthy expectations. It is hard to understand, otherwise, that North America should be proposing to imitate the model of the unified European market without waiting to see whether there will be a credit balance to be shown between the benefits this is going to engender and the high unemployment rates it has caused as a logical outcome of rationalizing production on a continental scale. That is, unless we start from the principle that the progress and welfare being sought by such programmes are, above all, those of the ruling groups in these societies, without it mattering that they are being secured at everybody else's cost.

That the outburst of peasant anger in the south of Mexico should have happened at the very moment the country was entering the North American free trade area may have seemed paradoxical. The logic of the protest can be better understood if we know the history of Chiapas, for there the modernizing process of the nineteenth and twentieth centuries has led to the enrichment of a few at the cost of impoverishing and subordinating the many, revolutions and reforms being unable to change the course of this. Was it not reasonable to deduce from this experience that a new modernizing stage might bring about yet more wretchedness and degradation, unless 'the intimate nexus of power and interests that keeps people poor in a rich land' could be broken?

As Schumpeter said, the evolution of the economy cannot be explained only in terms of that economy. This equally helps us to understand that the break-up of the welfare state we are witnessing is not due solely to its costs but is also, and especially, due to a fundamental change in its social context. From 1789 up to the collapse of the Soviet system the European ruling classes have lived with ghosts that often tormented their sleep: Jacobins, *carbonari*, anarchists, Bolsheviks ..., revolutionaries capable of placing themselves at the head of the masses in order to destroy the established social order. This fear led them to make concessions which today, when there is no longer any threat to keep them awake, they do not need to maintain – the worst that can happen is small explosions of discontent, easy to control.

Many of the victims of this crisis can be persuaded, moreover, that the blame lies with 'the others', with Asian entrepreneurs who produce at low cost because they pay poverty wages – but a German car company is proposing to build a factory in some part of the United States where wages are naturally 'Asian' – or that the blame lies with African immigrants who are taking 'our' jobs away. This fabrication of an external enemy helps to cover up the fact that the interests of both groups, those of the immigrants and of European workers, are held in common, and it prevents a consciousness of solidarity emerging among them.

All this has become much easier in a society in which the old links of community have been almost completely destroyed. Frameworks created to replace them, such as political parties, have not managed to draw citizens to them, because they neither offer the autonomy there was in the old communities, nor express their interests. And universal culture which was to have absorbed popular culture does not satisfy everybody's needs. In a world theoretically 'scientifist', most people know nothing of science: in the United States 'twenty-one per cent of people think the sun goes round the earth' and forty-seven per cent can hardly read or write. Millions of people have daily recourse to the most varied kinds of magic and es- oteric learning: what is to be hoped for from people able to believe that a UFO had 'sucked up' twenty-six elephants from an African safari park near Lugo (Galicia, Spain)? To satisfy the demands of this public there has arisen a cultural industry whose products, from the cinema to videogames, spread the values of an aggressive individ- ualism which rewards winners and utterly overlooks the great mass of the defeated.

There are many who, feeling abandoned in a society lacking solidarity, try to escape from their loneliness by forming groups of tolerated kinds. The young take refuge in alternative subcultures (with dress, language, and be- haviour patterns that seek to express their own lifestyle), and many adults channel their needs into militant support of a sports club, into some leisure activity, or into reli- gious sects whose success is based on being able to offer solidarity to insecure and rootless urban masses. Nothing here represents a danger for the established social order.

We have a reflection of this loss of our collective illu- sions in the change which forward-looking literature has undergone. Until recently this assumed that an uninter- rupted process of technological innovation would bring in its train a positive transformation of our society – this explaining why danger and threats had to be sought by going to other galaxies – while today writers have returned to our planet to describe for us a future exhaustion of resources, with catastrophes and poverty, among which heroes struggle for mere survival. The terrors of the year 1000 never existed, but those of the year 2000 are right there, darkening our days.

Some time ago a few people realized the need to give up this view of history on which we have based false expectations of the future. In times of crisis for Europe and for their own lives, two men, of different origins and cultures, both dying at almost the same time in Catalonia, expressed this, and together left a message of warning but, in spite of everything, of hope too, for the survivors.

The first, in 1939, was Antonio Machado, who had written shortly before his death as he fled from Franquism: 'When we meditate on the past, in order to inform ourselves about what was going on inside it, we easily find in it a store of hopes – not fulfilled, but not failed ones either – in sum, a future, a legitimate object of prophecy.' The kind of history which might allow us to make such discoveries will have to be very different from the one written up in the last 200 years, from Gibbon to Douglas North, in which everything happens fatalistically, inevitably.

Another refugee from fascism, Walter Benjamin, who died the following year at a spot not far from that in which the Andalusian poet passed away, insisted on calling our attention to the harm which this linear and simplistic view caused. He mentioned it in the specific case of the stance being adopted in the face of fascism, which led people to see it as something aberrant and exceptional, incompatible with progress, and not as the logical and natural outcome of a time and of circumstances. (We can corroborate this today, now that fascism is being reborn among us without our being scandalized except by its excesses.) But he particularly warned us about another consequence of the same error, which explains the present confusion on the left and in the working-class movement: the belief that these had the forces of history on their side, and that this – sooner or later, but with total certainty – would hand victory to them.

Historians read these and other similar warnings – and even used them as decorative quotations in their work – without being willing to face up to the fundamental problems which they posed. And when the present has confirmed the warnings and has overturned their interpretative constructions, they have fled away from the confrontation with reality and have devoted themselves to making discourses about discourse, since it is easier to busy oneself with words than with people. The way in which most present-day historians avoid compromising problems, shutting themselves away in a bookish world where questions that matter only to the academic tribe itself are debated, shows to what degree Kant's words written in 1766 are still valid: 'The methodical babble of the universities is often no more than an agreement to avoid, by means of a shifting semantics, an issue that is hard to resolve.' Or whose resolution would be inconvenient.

We need to get out of the hall of distorting mirrors in which our culture is trapped. Only then shall we be able to start studying human societies in 'the great book of the world' – which in our case will be 'the great book of life' – and to tackle the task of dismantling that linear view of the course of history which mechanically interprets each change as an improvement, each new phase as progress. We shall then be able to replace it by another better suited to analysing the complicated structure of the various trajectories which link up, separate, and cross over each other, of forks in the road at which it was possible to choose between several possible paths. At such points the one which was best in terms of the wellbeing of the majority of men and women was not always chosen, but rather that which suited those groups that commanded persuasive powers and the necessary repressive force to do such persuading (as is still happening today, with the remedies for facing the crisis being proposed to us).

This multidimensional history will be able to aspire to being legitimately universal and will also restore to us the diversity of our own European culture. If, with regard to living beings, there is talk of the danger of losing the wealth stored up in the genetic treasure-house which may become very important in the future, why not apply a similar criterion to cultures? Modernization, with its programme of assimilation and uniformity, destroyed a great part of the wealth of popular communal cultures, in town and country. The little of them that managed to survive has been nearly extinguished by the levelling action of the mass communication media.

We must face up to the evidence that the modernizing programme begun some 250 years ago in the Age of Enlightenment is nearly exhausted, not only that part which concerned economic promises, but also as a civilizing project. This at least seems to be the case as we see it at the end of this 'century of dark shadows' which has seen more deaths in warfare, by persecution, and by genocide than any earlier period in human history (and which is still set upon the task).

To change our way of seeing and understanding things is not going to be easy. It is not likely that the guardians of our citadel will put up with changes which might mean their losing control over the feared plebeian masses. It can therefore be foreseen that they will defend themselves to the end, strengthening support for themselves by the ancient expedient of deflecting unrest towards the enemy, this enemy now seeming to be the non-European who has established himself in the citadel as an immigrant, or hopes to do so, and who is threatening our prosperity with his intolerable urge to achieve our standard of living.

Shortly before he died, Bruno Bettelheim reflected on the drama of those Jews who had promoted their own extermination by their ghetto mentality, and warned us: 'The Western world itself seems to embrace a ghetto philosophy by not wanting to know, not wanting to understand, what is happening in the rest of the world. If we are not careful the white world of the West, which is a minority of humankind, will wall itself up in its own ghetto.' To which I would add: 'and will thereby prepare its own extermination'.

The problem is not only that the wall oppresses and limits those who take refuge behind it, but also that its defensive usefulness is not great. The largest building work of mankind, the only one that can be made out by the eyes of an observer stationed on the moon, is the Great Wall of China. But it is well-known that this was merely one part of a system whose essential element was the agreements reached with settlers on the other side. One of the few lessons of history which seems to be universally valid is that no wall can permanently protect a collectivity from invaders who threaten it, unless it is accompanied by some kind of pact with them.

The first thing we need to learn is that our problems and those of the underdeveloped world must be solved jointly. If we persist in shutting ourselves away behind walls, we shall perish at the hands of attackers both inside and from outside. Europeans and their civilization will then disappear, as all communities which have lost their ability to adapt to a changing environment have disappeared. If this happens, a chapter in the history of mankind will have ended and another will begin.

Annotated Bibliography of Essential References

Note: Dates of original editions will be given in parentheses where appropriate, for example Routledge, 1993 (1990).

1 The Barbarian Mirror

What is said about the geographical image of the world is from James S. Romm, *The Edges of the Earth in Ancient Thought*, Princeton, Princeton U. P., 1992. The 'circumlatrator' ocean is in Avienus, *Ora maritima*, lines 390–1. On the origins of European man, Christopher Stringer and Clive Gamble, *In Search of the Neanderthals*, London, Thames & Hudson, 1991, and Luca & Francesco Cavalli-Sforza, 1991, *Chi siamo?*, Milan, Mondadori, 1993. The view of the origins of our civilization is based on Charles Keith Maisels, *The Emergence of Civilization*, London, Routledge, 1993 (1990). On domestication I follow Ian Hodder, *The Domestication of Europe*, Oxford, Blackwell, 1990, and on the genetic dating of agricultural expansion, A. J. Ammerman & L. L. Cavalli-Sforza, *The Neolithic Transition and the Genetics of Populations in Europe*, Princeton, Princeton U. P., 1984. The quotation about the Persian peril is from Giuseppe Nenci in *Historia y civilización de los griegos*, ed. by R. Bianchi Bandinelli, Barcelona, Icaria, 1981, III, pp. 41–5. The quotation from Thucydides is from *History of the Peloponnesian War*, I.3–3, and those from Herodotus from *Histories*, V.78 & 92 and VIII.77. On the theme of the barbarian and fifth-century literature I follow Edith Hall, *Inventing the Barbarian. Greek Self-definition through Tragedy*, Oxford, Clarendon, 1989. The following quotations are from Euripides, *The*

Bacchae, lines 1354–5, and Aristotle, *Politics*, I.ii.13. The quotation from Arnaldo Momigliano is from his *Filippo il Macedone*, Milan, Guerini, 1987 (1934), p. 170. The demythification of Greek liberty is based on Pierre Grimal, *Les Erreurs de la liberté*, Paris, Les Belles Lettres, 1990 (quotation from pp. 10–11). The text about Solon is from Plutarch, *Solon*, 19. There follows a quotation from Claude Mosse, *Historia de una democracia: Atenas*, Madrid, Akal, 1981, p. 140. The following paragraphs depend greatly on G. E. M. de Ste Croix, *The Class Struggle in the Ancient Greek World: From the Archaic Age to the Arab Conquests*, London, Duckworth, 1981, and on *Filippo il Macedone* of Momigliano (p. 199). There is also a quotation from Demosthenes, *Olynthiacs*, III.10. On the myth of Europe, Ovid, *Metamorphoses*, II.833–75 and VIII.23; Pierre Chuvin, *La Mythologie grecque. Du premier homme à l'apothéose d'Heraklès*, Paris, Fayard, 1992 (see p. 53). On the crisis of the twelfth century BC, W. A. Ward & M. S. Joukowsky (eds), *The Crisis Years: The 12th Century BC*, Dubuque (Iowa), Kendall/Hunt, 1992, particularly J. D. Muhly's synthesis (pp. 10–26). A recent interpretation of military matters is that of Robert Drews, *The End of the Bronze Age. Changes in Warfare and the Catastrophe ca. 1200 BC*, Princeton, Princeton U. P., 1993. On the origin of writing, Denise Schmandt-Besserat, *Before Writing*, Austin, University of Texas Press, 1992, 2 vols, and Hans J. Nissen, 'The Context of the Emergence of Writing in Mesopotamia and Iran', in John Curtis (ed.), *Early Mesopotamia and Iran. Contact and Conflict c. 3500–1600 BC*, London, British Museum Press, 1993, pp. 54–71. The phrase about Crete is from Y. V. Andreyev in I. M. Diakonoff (ed.), *Early Antiquity*, Chicago, University of Chicago Press, 1991 (p. 309). That about the Etruscans, from Massimo Pallottino in the collective volume *Les Étrusques et l'Europe*, Paris, Éditions de la Réunion des Musées Nationaux, 1992 (p. 33). On Carthaginian culture, M'hamed Hassine Fantar, *Carthage, approche d'une civilisation*, Tunis, Alif, 1993, I, pp. 263–5, and II, pp. 144–74 and 361–3. On Alexander and his successors I have used Peter Green, *Alexander of Macedon, 365–323 BC*, Berkeley, University of California Press, 1991, and especially *Alexander to Actium*, London, Thames & Hudson, 1990 (quotation from p. 156). The Plutarch text is from 'On the fortune or the virtue of Alexander' (*Moralia*), I.6 (329). On the political structure and the reality of the Empire I have used Fergus Millar, *The Emperor in the*

Roman World, London, Duckworth, 2nd edn, 1992, and especially *The Roman Near East, 31 BC – AD 337*, Cambridge (Mass.), Harvard U. P., 1993; Andrew Lintott, *Imperium Romanum: Politics and Administration*, London, Routledge, 1993 (a quotation from p. 54); David Braund (ed.), *The Administration of the Roman Empire*, Exeter, Exeter U. P., 2nd edn, 1993; and Benjamin Isaac, *The Limits of Empire. The Roman Army in the East*, Oxford, Clarendon, 1993 (quotation from p. 395). On religion I have taken much from the excellent book by Mary Beard & J. North (eds), *Pagan Priests*, London, Duckworth, 1990 (particularly from the paper by Richard Gordon, pp. 201–31). The quotation from Pliny is from his *Natural History*, III.i.3–5, and that from Ovid from *Epistulae ex Ponto*, I.iii.49. The paragraphs about the barbarians owe much to Malcolm Todd, *The Early Germans*, Oxford, Blackwell, 1992; John Matthews, *The Roman Empire of Ammianus*, London, Duckworth, 1989; W. Goffart, *Barbarians and Romans, AD 418–584. The Techniques of Accommodation*, Princeton, Princeton U. P., 1980; J. H. W. G. Liebeschuetz, *Barbarians and Bishops*, Oxford, Clarendon, 1992; Peter Heather, *Goths and Romans, 332–498*, Oxford, Clarendon, 1991, etc. There is a quotation from C. M. Wells, *The German Policy of Augustus. An Examination of the Archaeological Evidence*, Oxford, Clarendon, 1972, p. 31. Quotations from classical texts are from Livy, *History of Rome*, V.41; Polybius, *History*, II.17; Tacitus, *Germania*, IV. I have used Procopius in the French translation by D. Roques, *La Guerre contre les Vandales*, Paris, Les Belles Lettres, 1990, p. 30. The quotations from Cassiodorus – one explicit, the other implicit, about Attila's army – are from the synthesis which Jordanes made of his lost *Historia Gothorum*. On the fall of the Empire, P. S. Barnwell, *Emperors, Prefects and Kings. The Roman West, 395–565*, London, Duckworth, 1992; Averil Cameron, *The Mediterranean World in Late Antiquity, AD 395–600*, London, Routledge, 1993; Jean Durliat, *Les Finances publiques de Dioclétien aux Carolingiens, 284–889*, Sigmaringen, Jan Thorbecke, 1990; Joseph A. Tainter, *The Collapse of Complex Societies*, Cambridge, Cambridge U. P., 1988; Ramsay Macmullen, *Corruption and the Decline of Rome*, New Haven, Yale U. P., 1988; Georges Depeyrot, *Crises et inflation entre antiquité et Moyen Âge*, Paris, Armand Colin, 1991; and the lucid final pages by Santo Mazzarino, *L'impero romano*, Bari, Laterza,

174   *Annotated Bibliography*

1980, III, pp. 812–15. Mikhail Rostovtzeff is quoted from *The Social and Economic History of the Roman Empire*, Oxford, Oxford U. P., 2nd edn, 1957.

2 The Christian Mirror

The paragraphs on the origins of Christianity owe much to John Dominic Crossan, *The Historical Jesus. The Life of a Mediterranean Jewish Peasant*, San Francisco, Harper, 1991; also to the above-mentioned book by Millar, *The Roman Near East*, pp. 337–51; Marie-Françoise Baslez, *Saint Paul*, Paris, Fayard, 1991; Herbert Grundmann, 'Oportet et haereses esse. Il problema dell'eresia rispecchiato nell'esegesi biblica medievale', in Ovidio Capitani (ed.), *L'eresia medievale*, Bologna, Il Mulino, 1971, pp. 23–60; Peter Brown, *The Body and Society. Men, Women and Sexual Renunciation in Early Christianity*, London, Faber & Faber, 1990 (a quotation from p. 435). On the apocalyptic expectations of early Christians, see Norman Cohn, *Cosmos, Chaos and the World to Come*, New Haven, Yale U. P., 1993, pp. 194–219, and *Apocalissi apocrife*, ed. by A. M. di Nola, Parma, Guanda, 1978. The quotation from Minucius Felix is from *Octavius*, II. On Manichaeism, see S. N. C. Lieu, *Manichaeism in the Later Roman Empire and Medieval China*, Manchester, Manchester U. P., 1985. References to patristic writings about sex will be found in James A. Brundage, *Law, Sex and Christian Society in Medieval Europe*, Chicago, University of Chicago Press, 1987. On Constantine I follow Santo Mazzarino, *L'impero romano*, Bari, Laterza, 1980, III, pp. 651–751, with ideas also from A. H. M. Jones, *Constantine and the Conversion of Europe*, Toronto, Medieval Academy of America, 1978 (1948); Paul Keresztes, *Imperial Rome and the Christians from the Severi to Constantine the Great*, II, Lanham, University Press of America, 1989; Antonio Fontán, 'La revolución de Constantino', in J. M. Candau et al. (eds), *La conversión de Roma. Cristianismo y paganismo*, Madrid, Ediciones Clásicas, 1990, pp. 107–50; Garth Fowden, *Empire to Commonwealth. Consequences of Monotheism in Late Antiquity*, Princeton, Princeton U. P., 1993 (from whom elements for many other points are taken too), etc. On the emperors' gifts to the Church, Georges Depeyrot, *Crises et inflations entre antiquité et Moyen Âge*, Paris, Armand Colin, 1991, pp. 49–62. The quotation from Hobbes is from *Leviathan*, IV, ch. 47. On the way the image of heresy was formed, Norman Cohn, *Europe's Inner Demons. The Demonization of Christians in Medieval Europe*, London, Pimlico, 2nd edn, 1993, pp. 35–50 and passim. On dualist features in Jesus, Cohn's book mentioned earlier, *Cosmos, Chaos and the World to Come*. Malcolm Lambert, *Medieval Heresy*, London, Edward Arnold, 1977 (quotation from p. 7; second edition 1992, Oxford, Blackwell). For the history of the formation of Christianity, Judith Herrin, *The Formation of Christendom*, Oxford, Blackwell, 1987 (one literal quotation from p. 59); Robert Markus, *The End of Ancient Christianity*, Cambridge, Cambridge U. P., 1990; Pierre Chuvin, *Chroniques des derniers paiens*, Paris, Fayard/Les Belles Lettres, 1990; Peter Brown, *Power and Persuasion in Late Antiquity. Towards a Christian Empire*, Madison, University of Wisconsin Press, 1992 (especially pp. 102–17). The reference to Alexandria in the time of Julian is from Ammianus Marcellinus, *History of the Roman Empire*, XXII. On the flight of the pagan philosophers, Michel Tardieu, *Les Paysages reliques. Routes et haltes syriennes d'Isidore à Simplicius*, Louvain-Paris, Peeters, n.d. (about 1989). The note about the attempt to integrate Christianity into the religion of the Empire is from 'Alexander Severus' in the *Historia Augusta*, 43.6. On the Christian sense of time, Jacques Le Goff, *Time, Work and Culture in the Middle Ages*, tr. Arthur Goldhammer, Chicago, University of Chicago Press, 1980 (1977), and D. S. Milo, *Trahir le temps (histoire)*, Paris, Les Belles Lettres, 1991, pp. 101–27. On Priscillian, María Victoria Escribano, 'Herejía y poder en el siglo IV', in Candau et al., *La conversión de Roma*, pp. 151–89; Henry Chadwick, *Priscillian of Avila*, Oxford, Clarendon, 1976, and L. A. García Moreno, 'Disidencia religiosa y poder episcopal en la España tardoantigua', in F. J. Lomas & D. Devoes (eds), *De Constantino a Carlomagno. Disidentes, heterodoxos, marginados*, Cadiz, Universidad de Cádiz, 1992, pp. 135–58. I quote Martin of Braga from the bilingual edition of the *Sermón contra las supersticiones rurales*, Barcelona, El Albir, 1981 (p. 43). The sermon of St Caesarius of Arles is printed by Dag Norberg, *Manuel pratique de latin médiévale*, Paris, Picard, 1980, pp. 93–104. The interpretation of Christianity mentioned is that of Valerie I. J. Flint, *The Rise of Magic in Early Medieval Europe*, Oxford, Clarendon, 1991 (though this is not so new; see J. B. Russell, *Witchcraft in the Middle Ages*, Ithaca, Cornell U. P., 1988 (1972), pp. 45–62). Quotations from A. Gurevich come from *Categories of Medieval Culture*, tr. G. L. Campbell, London, Routledge, 1985. Those from Pletho, from his *Treatise on the Laws*, I.4. On the nomination of the patriarch by the sultan, Nicholas Iorga, *Byzance après Byzance*, Paris, Balland, 1992, pp. 84–6.

3 The Feudal Mirror

For definitions of the Middle Ages and the Renaissance, see Jacques Heers, *Le Moyen Âge*, Paris, Perrin, 1992; Alain de Libera, *Penser au Moyen Âge*, Paris, Seuil, 1991, pp. 33–8; Lucien Febvre, *Michelet et la Renaissance*, Paris, Flammarion, 1992; and Jacques Le Goff, 'The Several Middle Ages of Jules Michelet', in *Time, Work and Culture in the Middle Ages*, tr. Arthur Goldhammer, Chicago, Chicago University Press, 1980 (1977), pp. 3–28. For use of the word 'barbarian' in the Middle Ages, Arno Borst, *Medieval Worlds. Barbarians, Heretics and Artists*, Cambridge, Polity Press, 1991, pp. 3–13. On the continuity of the early post-Roman centuries and the evolution of barbarian Europe, Klaus Randsborg, *The First Millennium* AD *in Europe and the Mediterranean*, Cambridge, Cambridge U. P., 1991, passim; D. Austin & L. Alcock (eds), *From the Baltic to the Black Sea. Studies in Medieval Archaeology*, London, Unwin Hyman, 1990; one quotation from Richard Holt, *The Mills of Medieval England*, Oxford, Blackwell, 1988 (p. 2). Richard Hodges, *Dark Age Economics. The Origins of Towns and Trade*, AD 600–1000, London, Duckworth, 2nd edn, 1989, and *The Anglo-Saxon Achievement*, London, Duckworth, 1989. J. Haywood, *Dark Age Naval Power*, London, Routledge, 1991, etc. On the Trojan origins of France, Colette Beaume, *Naissance de la nation France*, Paris, Gallimard, 1993 (1985), pp. 25–74. There is a quotation from Bede, *Ecclesiastical History of the English Nation*, ch. 16. The collective volume *Les Vikings ... Les Scandinaves et l'Europe 800–1200*, Paris, AFAA, 1992; Lotte Hedeager, *Iron-age Societies*, Oxford, Blackwell, 1992; Helen Clarke & Björn Ambrosian, *Towns in the Viking Age*, Leicester, Leicester U. P., 1991; R. Boyer (ed.), *Les Vikings et leur civilisation: problèmes actuels*, Paris-The Hague, Mouton, 1976 (especially pp. 211–40). The acceptance of the consulship by Clovis is in Gregory of Tours, *Historiae Francorum*, II.38 (in English as *The History of the Franks*, tr. L. Thorpe, London, Penguin Classics, 1974). Snorri Sturluson, *The Prose*

Edda of Snorri Sturluson, tr. J. I. Young, Cambridge, Cambridge U. P., 2nd edn, 1965. 'Artorius is a Roman family name', John Morris, *The Age of Arthur. A History of the British Isles from 350 to 650*, London, Weidenfeld, 1993 (1973), p. 95. One quotation from the English version by Timothy Reuter, *The Annals of Fulda*, Manchester, Manchester U. P., 1992 (p. 37). On literate culture, Rosamond McKitterick (ed.), *The Uses of Literacy in Early Medieval Europe*, Cambridge, Cambridge U. P., 1992; M. T. Clanchy, *From Memory to Written Record. England, 1066–1307*, Oxford, Blackwell, 2nd edn, 1993; Pierre Riché, *Écoles et enseignement dans le haut Moyen Âge*, Paris, Aubier, 1979 (also Paris, Picard, 1989); Erich Auerbach, *Literary Language and its Public in Late Antiquity and in the Early Middle Ages*, Princeton, Princeton U. P., 1993 (1958) (quotation from p. 121); V. H. Galbraith, 'The Literacy of the Medieval English Kings', in *Kings and Chroniclers*, London, Hambledon Press, 1982. There is a quotation from Gregory of Tours, *Historiae Francorum*, V.44. On Carolingian culture, Rosamond McKitterick (ed.), *Carolingian Culture: Emulation and Innovation*, Cambridge, Cambridge U. P., 1994. References to Charlemagne from his life written by Egginhard, and that to St Boniface are from R. R. Bolgar, *The Classical Heritage and its Beneficiaries*, Cambridge, Cambridge U. P., 1977, p. 106. Mary Carruthers, *The Book of Memory. A Study of Memory in Medieval Culture*, Cambridge, Cambridge U. P., 1990. Joachim Bumke, *Courtly Culture. Literature and Society in the High Middle Ages*, Berkeley, University of California Press, 1991 (see especially pp. 14–16). What is said about the christianization of the Scandinavians is drawn from Olaf Olsen, 'Le Christianisme et les églises', in *Les Vikings*, pp. 152–61 (quotation from p. 155), and from Gwyn Jones, *A History of the Vikings*, Oxford, Oxford U. P., 1973, pp. 285–8; there is also a quotation from R. G. Poole, *Viking Poems on War and Peace*, Toronto, University of Toronto Press, 1991, p. 26. For the conversion of Clovis see Patrick J. Geary, *Before France and Germany. The Creation and Transformation of the Merovingian World*, New York & Oxford, Oxford U. P., 1988. The account of the christianization of the Baltic peoples is based on Eric Christiansen, *The Northern Crusades: The Baltic and the Catholic Frontier, 1100–1525*, London, Macmillan, 1980. Concerning Bulgars and Slavs, Francis Conte, *Gli slavi. La civiltà dell'Europa centrale e orientale*, Turin, Einaudi, 1991, passim;

John V. A. Fine, *The Early Medieval Balkans. A Critical Survey from the Sixth to the Late Twelfth Century*, Ann Arbor, University of Michigan Press, 1983, pp. 113–31; Ibn Fadlan, *Voyage chez les Bulgares de la Volga*, Paris, Sindbad, 1988 (quotation from p. 73); César E. Dubler, *Abu Hamid el granadino y su relación de viaje por tierras eurasiáticas*, Madrid, Maestre, 1953 (quotation from pp. 54–5). On Islamic cultural contributions, Franz Rosenthal, *The Classical Heritage in Islam*, London, Routledge, 1992; Bernard Lewis, 'Translation from Arabic', in *Islam and the West*, New York, Oxford U. P., 1993, pp. 61–71 (quotation from p. 61); Andrew M. Watson, *Agricultural Innovation in the Early Islamic World*, Cambridge, Cambridge U. P., 1983; Donald Hill, *A History of Engineering in Classical and Medieval Times*, London, Croom Helm, 1984; Ahmad Y. al-Hassan & D. R. Hill, *Islamic Technology. An Illustrated History, Cambridge*, Cambridge U. P., 1988; J. M. Millas Vallicrosa, *Assaig d'història de les idees físiques i matemàtiques a la Catalunya medieval*, Barcelona, Edicions Científiques Catalanes, 1983; Said al-Andalusi, *Science in the Medieval World. Book of the Categories of Nations*, Austin, University of Texas Press, 1991 (quotations from pp. 11, 32). The scientist mentioned is J. D. Barrow, *Pi in the Sky. Counting, Thinking and Being*, Oxford, Clarendon, 1992, p. 92. Population changes and their regional distribution are drawn from C. M. Evedy & R. Jones, *Atlas of World Population History*, London, Allen Lane, 1978; J. Cox Russell, *Medieval Regions and their Cities*, Newton Abbot, David & Charles, 1972, and Paul Bairoch, *De Jéricho à Mexico. Villes et économie dans l'histoire*, Paris, Gallimard, 1985 (table of comparative estimates on p. 668). On the increase in trade, Robert S. López, *The Commercial Revolution of the Middle Ages, 950–1350*, Cambridge, Cambridge U. P., 1971, and on technological change, Lynn White, Jr, *Medieval Religion and Technology*, Berkeley, University of California Press, 1986 (1978), and Arnold Pacey, *The Maze of Ingenuity. Ideas and Idealism in the Development of Technology*, Cambridge (Mass.), MIT Press, 2nd edn, 1992. The matter of the 'explosive' nature of economic growth comes from Alexander Murray, *Reason and Society in the Middle Ages*, Oxford, Clarendon, 1978; R. L. Benson et al. (eds), *Renaissance and Renewal in the Twelfth Century*, Toronto, University of Toronto Press, 1991. About invention, see the work of Lynn White Jr cited above, p. 219. The paragraphs about the birth of feudalism are based on Georges Duby, *The Three Orders: Feudal Society Imagined*, tr. Arthur Goldhammer, Chicago, University of Chicago Press, 1982 (1978), and *La Société aux XIe et XIIe siècles dans la région mâconnaise*, Paris, École Pratique des Hautes Études, 1971 (quotation from p. 481); Pierre Bonnassie et al., *Structures féodales et féodalisme dans l'Occident méditerranéen, Xe-XIIIe siècles*, Paris, Centre National de la Recherche Scientifique, 1980; Pierre Toubert, *Castillos, señores y campesinos en la Italia medieval*, Barcelona, Crítica, 1990; Paul Freedman, *The Origins of Peasant Servitude in Medieval Catalonia*, Cambridge, Cambridge U. P., 1991, etc. The 'binary' view of chess is that of Jacques de Cessoles, *Liber de moribus hominum* (*c*.1300), used in its fifteenth-century Catalan version printed in 1902. The 'revolutionary' view is that of Guy Bois, *The Transformation of the Year One Thousand: The Village of Lournand from Antiquity to Feudalism*, tr. Jean Birrell, Manchester, Manchester U. P., 1992 (1989). The more nuanced view examined later is that of Lluís To Figueras, *El monestir de Santa Maria de Cervià i la pagesia: una anàlisi del canvi feudal*, Barcelona, Fundació Vives i Casajuana, 1991. On chivalry, data and ideas have been taken from Jean Flori, *L'Essor de la chevalerie, XIe-XIIe siècles*, Geneva, Droz, 1986; Maurice Keen, *Chivalry*, New Haven, Yale U. P., 1984; papers by Bernard S. Bachrach and Rosemary Ascherl in H. Chickering & T. H. Seiler (eds), *The Study of Chivalry. Resources and Approaches*, Kalamazoo, Western Michigan Publications, 1988; Hans Delbruck, *Medieval Warfare (History of the Art of War*, III), Lincoln, University of Nebraska Press, 1990; Jim Bradbury, *The Medieval Siege*, Woodbridge, Boydell Press, 1992 (from p. 76 I take a text of William of Malmesbury's *Historia novella*, and there is a quotation from p. 71). On Gregory VII, the Gregorian reform and the consolidation of the papacy I have followed especially Gerd Tellenbach, *The Church in Western Europe from the Tenth to the Early Twelfth Century*, Cambridge, Cambridge U. P., 1993; I. S. Robinson, *The Papacy, 1073-1198. Continuity and Innovation*, Cambridge, Cambridge U. P., 1990, and Colin Morris, *The Papal Monarchy. The Western Church from 1050 to 1250*, Oxford, Clarendon, 1991. What is said about attitudes to sex and the family is from Georges Duby, *The Knight, the Lady and the Priest: the Making of Modern Marriage in Medieval France*, tr. Barbara Bray, London, Allen Lane, 1984 (1981); Jean-Louis Flandrin, *Un*

Temps pour embrasser. Aux origines de la morale sexuelle occidentale, VIe-XIe siècles, Paris, Seuil, 1983, etc. On the Peace of God, Thomas Head & Richard Landes (eds), *The Peace of God. Social Violence and Religious Response in France around the year 1000,* Ithaca, Cornell U. P., 1992. The innovative image I refer to is that conveyed, for example, by the above-mentioned book by Richard Hodges, *Dark Age Economics. The Origins of Towns and Trade,* AD *600–1000.* On agricultural growth in the early Middle Ages there is the collective volume *La Croissance agricole du haut Moyen Âge. Chronologie, modalité, géographie,* Auch, Centre Culturel de l'Abbaye de Flaran, 1990 (Flaran, 10). On new farming methods and their relationship to the peasants' collective organization, J. Guilaine (ed.), *Pour une archéologie agraire,* Paris, Armand Colin, 1991; John Langdon, *Horses, Oxen and Technological Innovation,* Cambridge, Cambridge U. P., 1986; Werner Rösener, *Peasants in the Middle Ages,* tr. Alexander Stützer, Cambridge, Polity, 1992 (1985); Richard C. Hoffmann, 'Medieval Origins of the Common Fields', in W. N. Parker & E. L. Jones (eds), *European Peasants and their Markets,* Princeton, Princeton U. P., 1975, pp. 23–71; Léopold Genicot, *Rural Communities in the Medieval West,* Baltimore, Johns Hopkins University Press, 1990; A. Guarducci (ed.), *Agricoltura e trasformazione dell'ambiente, secoli XIII–XVIII,* Prato, Istituto Datini, 1984, and *Forme ed evoluzione del lavoro in Europa: XII–XVIII seccoli,* Florence, Le Monnier, 1991, pp. 41–53. There is also the important (if debatable) book by Eric Kerridge, *The Common Fields of England,* Manchester, Manchester U. P., 1992; he believes the adoption of this system was 'one of the major events in the history of the western world' (p. 128). On towns in barbarian Europe, B. Cunliffe, *Greeks, Romans and Barbarians. Spheres of Interaction,* London, Batsford, 1988; Peter Sawyer, 'Early Fairs and Markets in England and Scandinavia', in B. L. Anderson & A. J. H. Latham (eds), *The Market in History,* London, Croom Helm, 1986, pp. 59–77; K. Randsborg, *The First Millennium AD,* pp. 82–119; Nikolai Todorov, *The Balkan City, 1400–1900,* Seattle, University of Washington Press, 1983. Views of European towns about the year 1000 have been arrived at using data of Paul Bairoch, J. Batou & P. Châvre, *La Population des villes européennes de 800 à 1850,* Geneva, Droz, 1988. See the table on p. 235 of the aforementioned book by Russell, *Medieval Regions and their Cities.*

Philip D. Curtin, *Cross-cultural Trade in World History*, Cambridge, Cambridge U. P., 1984 (pp. 8–9). For a comparative view of market towns in diverse periods and cultures see the posthumous book by Spiro Kostof, *The City Assembled. The Elements of Urban Form through History*, London, Thames & Hudson, 1992, pp. 92–102. On Asian 'port-towns', Frank Broeze (ed.), *Brides of the Sea. Port Cities of Asia from the 16th-20th Centuries*, Kensington, New South Wales University Press, 1989, and on Melaka in particular, Luis Filipe Ferreira Reis Thomaz, 'The Malay Sultanate of Melaka', in A. Reid (ed.), *Southeast Asia in the Early Modern Era*, Ithaca, Cornell U. P., 1993, pp. 69–90. Finally, A. D. van der Woude et al., *Urbanization in History. A Process of Dynamic Interactions*, Oxford, Clarendon, 1990.

4 The Devil's Mirror

A clear view of the way European society 'fell back upon itself' is provided by R. I. Moore, *The Formation of a Persecuting Society: Power and Deviance in Western Europe, 950-1250*, Oxford, Blackwell, 1987. On the origin of the crusades, Carl Erdmann, *The Origin of the Idea of Crusade*, Princeton, Princeton U. P., 1977; Jean Flori, 'Une ou plusieurs "première croisade"', in *Revue Historique*, 285:1 (1991), pp. 3–27. On the Inquisition, H. C. Lea, used in the recent French edition *Histoire de l'Inquisition au Moyen Âge*, Grenoble, Millon, 1986–90, 3 vols. The interpretation of the battle of Poitiers is from Bernard Lewis, *The Muslim Discovery of Europe*, London, Weidenfeld & Nicolson, 1982, pp. 18–20 (this book is widely used in this chapter). By the same author, *Islam and the West*, New York, Oxford U. P., 1993. How Muslims viewed Christians is drawn from William Montgomery Watt, *Muslim-Christian Encounters. Perceptions and Misperceptions*, London, Routledge, 1991. References to the Koran are: VI.85 (Jesus as prophet), XXI.91 (Mary's virginity), and IX.29 (payment of tribute by Christians and Jews). The Arabs' view of the world is in Dolors Bramon, *El mundo en el siglo XII: El tratado de al-Zuhri*, Sabadell, Ausa, 1991; Aziz al-Azmeh, 'Barbarians in Arab Eyes', *Past and Present*, 134 (1992), pp. 3–18, and the evaluation of various rulers' power is from André Wink, *Al-Hind. The Making of the Indo-Islamic World. I: Early Medieval India and the Expansion of Islam, 7th-11th Centuries*, Leyden, Brill, 1991,

182   Annotated Bibliography

p. 226. Evidence of Muslim travellers is from Ibn Jubayr, *A través del Oriente. El siglo XII ante los ojos*. *Rihla*, Barcelona, Serbal, 1988 (quotation from p. 376); Ibn Batuta, *A través del Islam*, Madrid, Editora Nacional, 1981 (quotation from p. 442; Ibn Batuta'a travels are published in English, tr. Sir Hamilton Gibb, by the Hakluyt Society, Cambridge, 1958–71, 3 vols), and Ibn Khaldun, *Le Voyage d'Occident et d'Orient*, ed. by Abdesselam Cheddadi, Paris, Sindbad, 1980. On the rarity of Muslim travellers to Europe, Lewis, *The Muslim Discovery of Europe*, pp. 89–133, and on the dirtiness of Europeans, ibid., pp. 280–1. There is a quotation from the *Histoire anonyme de la Première Croisade*, ed. by L. Brehier, Paris, Les Belles Lettres, 1964, pp. 216–17 (1924). The relationship between agricultural revolution, urbanization, and cultural development is from Andrew M. Watson, *Agricultural Innovation in the Early Islamic World*, Cambridge, Cambridge U. P., 1983. On the textile industry, the posthumous book by Maurice Lombard, *Les Textiles dans le monde musulman, VIIe-XIIe siècles*, Paris-The Hague, Mouton, 1978. On culture, M. J. L. Young, J. D. Latham, and R. B. Sergeant (eds), *Religion, Learning and Science in the Abbasid Period*, Cambridge, Cambridge U. P., 1990; A. A. Duri, *The Rise of Historical Writing among the Arabs*, Princeton, Princeton U. P., 1983. The quotation from Ibn Khaldun is from *Discours sur l'histoire universelle. Al-Muqaddima*, translated by V. Monteil, Paris, Sindbad, 1978, I, p. 69. On conquest and assimilation, Maurice Lombard, *The Golden Age of Islam*, tr. Joan Spencer, New York, Elsevier, 1975 (1971); Ira M. Lapidus, *A History of Islamic Societies*, Cambridge, Cambridge U. P., 1988 (a quotation from p. 251), and, especially, Speros Vryonis Jr, *The Decline of Medieval Hellenism in Asia Minor and the Process of Islamization from the Eleventh through the Fifteenth Century*, Berkeley, University of California Press, 1971, which has been widely used. The history of trade has been based particularly on Eliyahu Ashtor, *Levant Trade in the Later Middle Ages*, Princeton, Princeton U. P., 1983. The quotation from Ibn Jubayr is from *A través del Oriente*, p. 336. Reflexions on Byzantium are mostly based on A. P. Kazhdan & A. W. Epstein, *Change in Byzantine Culture in the Eleventh and Twelfth Centuries*, Berkeley, University of California Press, 1985. The quotation from Condorcet is from *Almanach anti-superstitieux*, Paris, CNRS, 1992, p. 98 (the text is of about 1774). There is also a quotation from

E. R. A. Sewter, in the introduction to his translation of M. Psellus, *Fourteen Byzantine Rulers*, Harmondsworth, Penguin, 1966, p. 9. On the ignorance of classical culture in the West, Ernst Robert Curtius, *European Literature and the Latin Middle Ages*, tr. Willard R. Trask, Princeton, Princeton U. P., 1973 (1948), pp. 405-6. On oriental Christianity, Denis Sinor (ed.), *The Cambridge History of Early Inner Asia*, Cambridge, Cambridge U. P., 1990, passim; René Grousset, *Histoire des croisades et du royaume de Jérusalem*, Paris, Perrin, 1991 (1934-6), III, pp. 562-727; Garth Fowden, *Empire to Commonwealth*, Princeton, Princeton U. P., 1993; and especially the fine book by Lev Gumilev, *Searches for the Imaginary Kingdom: The Legend of the Kingdom of Prester John*, tr. R. E. F. Smith, Cambridge, Cambridge U. P., 1987. I have used the *Secret History of the Mongols* in the English version by Urgunge Onon, Leyden, Brill, 1990, and a quotation from 103 (p. 33). On the entry of the Mongols into Damascus, Lewis, *Islam and the West*, p. 51. Following paragraphs contain quotations from Colin Morris, *The Papal Monarchy*, pp. 339-44, and Sophia Menache, *The Vox Dei. Communication in the Middle Ages*, New York, Oxford U. P., 1990. The quotation about the 'folkloric reaction' is from J. Le Goff's paper, 'Culture cléricale et traditions folkloriques dans la civilisation mérovingienne', *Annales*, 4 (1967), pp. 780-91 (English version in *Time, Work and Culture in the Middle Ages*, pp. 153-8). The next is from Heinrich Fichtenau, *Living in the Tenth Century. Mentalities and Social Orders*, Chicago, University of Chicago Press, 1991, p. 303. A good general view of medieval heresy can be found in Malcolm Lambert, *Medieval Heresy. Popular Movements from Bogomil to Hus*, 2nd edn, Oxford, Blackwell, 1992 (1977), but there is a large bibliography on the subject. On Joachim de Fiore and Joachimism I have used especially the works of Marjorie Reeves. On the millennium and the end of the world, Bernard McGinn, *Visions of the End. Apocalyptic Traditions in the Middle Ages*, New York, Columbia U. P., 1979. On the *humiliati* and the Waldensians, Lester K. Little, *Religious Poverty and the Profit Economy in Medieval Europe*, Ithaca, Cornell U. P., 1978; Brenda Bolton, 'Innocent III's Treatment of the *humiliati*', in *Popular Belief and Practice*, pp. 73-82; Euan Cameron, *The Reformation of the Heretics. The Waldenses of the Alps, 1480-1580*, Oxford, Clarendon, 1984; Norman Cohn, *Europe's Inner Demons*, London, Pimlico, 1993, pp. 51-61.

The quotations from Guibert de Nogent are from his memoirs
(III, ch. 17) in the version by John F. Benton, *Self and Society
in Medieval France*, Toronto, University of Toronto Press,
1989, pp. 212–13. On Bogomilism, Dimitar Angelov, *Il bogo-
milismo. Un'eresia medievale bulgara*, Rome, Bulzoni, 1979
(1947); Borislav Primov, *Les Bougres*, Paris, Payot, 1975; Jordan
Ivanov, *Livres et légendes bogomiles. Aux sources du catharisme*,
Paris, Maisonneuve et Larosse, 1976 (1925). For ideas on the
other world, Jacques Le Goff, *The Birth of Purgatory*, tr. Arthur
Goldhammer, London, Scolar, 1984 (1981). On Catharism I
have used particularly Jean Duvernoy's works, especially his two
fine volumes of synthesis, *La Religion des cathares* and *L'Histoire
des cathares*, Toulouse, Privat, 1986, also *Les Cathares en
Languedoc*, Toulouse, Privat, 1989 (1968) and *Inquisition à
Pamiers*, Toulouse, Privat, 1986, with quotations from pp. 36,
61, 107, and 126. Some elements have been taken from the bilingual anthology compiled by René Nelli, *Ecrivains anticon-
formistes du Moyen Âge occitan: Hérétiques et politiques*, Paris,
Phébus, 1977 (quotation from p. 40), and from various volumes
of the *Cahiers de Fanjeaux*, particularly from 20, *Effacement
du catharisme? (XIIIe-XIVe s.)*, Toulouse, Privat, 1985. I have
also used the reissue of Joseph R. Strayer, *The Albigensian
Crusade* (with a new epilogue by Carol Lansing), Ann Arbor,
University of Michigan Press, 1992 (1971), with a quotation
from p. 76, and I have made wide use of Lansing's excellent
text. The quotation from *La Chanson de la croisade albigeoise*,
Paris, Librairie Générale Française, 1989, is from p. 536. Martin
Aurell, *La Vielle et l'épée. Troubadours et politique en Prov-
ence au XIIIe siècle*, Paris, Aubier, 1989, pp. 51–8 and passim.
Quotations from Peire Cardenal, but not their interpretation,
are from Martín de Riquer, *Los trovadores. Historia literaria
y textos*, Barcelona, Ariel, 1983, III, pp. 1500–14. In the
large bibliography used about the Jews I quote from Steven B.
Bowman, *The Jews of Byzantium, 1204–1453*, Alabama, University of Alabama Press, 1985 (p. 177); Jean Delumeau, *La
Peur en Occident*, Paris, Hachette, 1988 (p. 359); Norman
Roth, 'Maimonides as Spaniard: National Consciousness of a
Medieval Jew', in *Maimonides. Essays and Texts, 850th Anni-
versary*, Madison, Seminary of Medieval Studies, 1985, pp.
139–53. Lawsuits by Jews against Christian usurers are in Luis
Rubio García, *Los judíos de Murcia en la baja Edad Media,
1350–1500*, Murcia, Universidad de Murcia, 1992, pp. 46–8.

On ritual crimes, R. Po-Chia-Hsia, *The Myth of Ritual Murder*, New Haven, Yale U. P., 1988, and *Trent 1475. Stories of a Ritual Murder*, New Haven, Yale U. P., 1992. Texts of the Middle Ages and early modern period have been used also from Selomoh ibn Verga, *La vara de Yehudah*, Barcelona, Riopiedras, 1991; Abraham ben David, *Sefer ha-Kabalah: Libro de la tradición*, Valencia, Anubar, 1972; St Vicens Ferrer, *Sermons*, Barcelona, Barcino, 1932–88 (a quotation from III, p. 14).

5 The Rural Mirror

Bibliography on the crisis of the later Middle Ages is almost inexhaustible. Guides are provided by Frantisek Graus, *Das Spätmittelalter als Krisenzeit*, Prague, Mediaevalia Bohemica, I, 1, 1969; Ferdinand Seibt & Winfried Ederhard (eds), *Europa 1400: die Krise des Spätmittelalters*, Stuttgart, Klett-Cotta, 1984; John Day, 'Crises and Trends in the Late Middle Ages', in *The Medieval Market Economy*, Oxford, Blackwell, 1987. The quotation from Ausiàs March is from 6, lines 33–6. On the plague there is the fundamental book by Jean Noël Biraben, *Les Hommes et la peste en France et dans les pays européens et méditerranéens*, Paris-The Hague, Mouton, 1975, but also an immense literature. Quotations of Villani are from *Cronica. Con le continuazioni di Matteo e Filippo*, ed. by G. Aquilecchia, Turin, Einaudi, 1979, pp. 287–8 (earthquakes) and 196–8 and 273–5 (the financial crisis). From the bibliography about the social crisis in Italy there are quotations from Lauro Martines (ed.), *Violence and Civil Disorder in Italian Cities, 1200–1500*, Berkeley, University of California Press, 1972 (pp. 351–3). What is said about the *potenze* is from Richard C. Trexler, *Public Life in Renaissance Florence*, Ithaca, Cornell U. P., 1991 (1980), and remarks about building and sumptuary spending from Richard A. Goldthwaite, *The Building of Renaissance Florence. An Economic and Social History*, Baltimore, The Johns Hopkins U. P., 1990 (1980), with a quotation from p. 425. The quotation from the Bible is of St Peter, Second Epistle 3.13; those from Machiavelli, from *Istorie fiorentine*, Book III, 1 and 13. I have used Savonarola's writings in the French version by J. L. Fournel & J. C. Zancarini, *Savonarola: Sermons, écrits politiques et pièces du procès*, Paris, Seuil, 1993 (the quotation is from the 'Treatise on the Manner of Ruling and Governing the City of Florence', III.1; in this edition, p. 172).

On England I owe much to Bruce M. S. Campbell (ed.), *Before the Black Death. Studies in the 'Crisis' of the Early Fourteenth Century*, Manchester, Manchester U. P., 1991; L. R. Poos, *A Rural Society after the Black Death. Essex, 1350–1525*, Cambridge, Cambridge U. P., 1991; Christopher Dyer, *Lords and Peasants in a Changing Society. The Estates of the Bishopric of Worcester 680–1540*, Cambridge, Cambridge U. P., 1980; also in general to R. H. Hilton, A. R. Bridbury, & N. Swanson, *Church and Society in Late Medieval England*, Oxford, Blackwell, 1989; Mavis Mate, 'The Economic and Social Roots of Medieval Popular Rebellion: Sussex in 1450–1451', *Economic History Review*, 45:4 (1992), pp. 661–76. On laws about hunting and their bearing upon rural revolts (the first was in 1389–90), R. B. Manning, *Hunters and Poachers*, Oxford, Clarendon, 1993, pp. 57–8. The quotation from *Piers Ploughman* is line 67 of the Prologue (which does not mean the poem had the intentions some attribute to it). On the Hussite revolution, works by Joseph Macek, F. M. Bartos, and Frantisek Smahel; also, of the last-named, 'The Idea of Nation in Hussite Bohemia', *Historica*, 17 (1969), 93–107; Stanislaw Byelina, 'Le Mouvement hussite devant les problèmes nationaux', in D. Loades & K. Walsh (eds), *Faith and Identity: Christian Political Experience*, Oxford, Blackwell, 1990, pp. 57–67. On the Peasants' War one might do well to start with the helpful survey by Tom Scott, 'The Peasants' War: A Historiographical Review', *Historical Journal*, 22 (1979), pp. 693–720 and 963–74, then on Hans Behem, Richard Wunderli, *Peasant Fires. The Drummer of Niklashausen*, Bloomington, Indiana U. P., 1992; and collective volumes compiled by Tom Scott & Bob Scribner, and by James M. Stayer. On the origins of the Reformation, R. Po-Chia Hsia (ed.), *The German People and the Reformation*, Ithaca, Cornell U. P., 1988; Andrew Pettegree, *The Early Reformation in Europe*, Cambridge, Cambridge U. P., 1992; Heiko A. Oberman, *The Dawn of the Reformation*, Edinburgh, T. & T. Clark, 1992; Josef Macek, *La riforma popolare*, Florence, Sansoni, 1973 (the text about the death of Hutter is from this); G. H. Williams, *The Radical Reformation*, Philadelphia, Westminster Press, 1962, and the anthology of texts by M. G. Baylor (ed.), *The Radical Reformation*, Cambridge, Cambridge U. P., 1991. The scheme for a monument to a dead peasant, sketched by Dürer, has been interpreted as a joke (Erwin Panofsky, *Life and Art of Albrecht Dürer*, Princeton,

Princeton U. P., 1955), but this shows unawareness of the artist's relationship to men involved in the war (Jane Campbell Hutchinson, *Albrecht Dürer. A Biography*, Princeton, Princeton U. P., 1990, pp. 181-2). The Luis Vives texts used are *Tratado del socorro de los pobres*, ed. by Pedro Carasa, Madrid, Ministerio de Asuntos Sociales, 1992, and *De la comunidad de los bienes*, in W. González-Oliveros, *Humanismo frente a comunismo*, Valladolid, Calderón, 1937. On satirical and popular images in medieval art I have used Michael Camille, *Images on the Edge. The Margins of Medieval Art*, London, Reaktion Books, 1992, and Claude Gaignebet & J. Dominique Lajoux, *Art profane et religion populaire au Moyen Âge*, Paris, P.U.F., 1985. On literature, R. Howard Bloch, *The Scandal of the Fabliaux*, Chicago, University of Chicago Press, 1986; Lucia Lazzerini, *Il testo trasgressivo. Testi marginali, provocatori, irregolari del medioevo al cinquecento*, Milan, Franco Angeli, 1988; R. Wolf-Bonvin, *La Chevalerie des sots*, Paris, Stock, 1990. On festivities, Jacques Heers, *Fêtes des fous et carnavals*, Paris, Fayard, 1983. On popular culture in general, the aforementioned book by Heinrich Fichtenau; Mikhail Bakhtin, *Popular Culture of the Middle Ages and the Renaissance: Rabelais and his World*, Bloomington, Indiana U. P., 1984; Aron Gurevich, *Categories of Medieval Culture*, tr. G. L. Campbell, Routledge & Kegan Paul, 1985; *Medieval Popular Culture. Problems of Belief and Perception*, Cambridge, Cambridge U. P., 1988, and *Historical Anthropology of the Middle Ages*, Cambridge, Polity Press, 1992; Pieter Spierenburg, *The Broken Spell. A Cultural and Anthropological History of Preindustrial Europe*, New Brunswick, Rutgers U. P., 1991; also the collective volumes ed. by C. J. Cuming & Derek Baker and by Steven L. Kaplan. The interpretation of Bruegel (that of M. Mullett is criticized) rests on Ross H. Frank, 'An Interpretation of *Land of Cockaigne* (1567) by Pieter Bruegel the Elder', *The Sixteenth Century Journal*, 22 (1991), pp. 299-329. On Rabelais, in addition to Lucien Febvre and Bakhtin, Madeleine Lezard, *Rabelais: L'humaniste*, Paris, Hachette, 1993. I have used the *fabliaux* in the edition by Luciano Rossi & William Straub (1992), *Trubert* in the edition by R. Wolf-Bonvin, *Les Evangiles des quenouilles* in that by Jacques Lacarrière, Paris, Imago, 1987, and the selection of *Farces du Moyen Âge* ed. by André Tissier, Paris, Flammarion, 1984. The quotation from the *Roman de Renart* is from Branch IX, 311-17. That from Machiavelli is from *Dell'asino d'oro*, 139–41. For Rabelais I used the edition by Boulenger & Scheler in La Pléiade; the quotations are from *Pantagruel*, VIII, and the *Third Book*, VI. Ronsard's lines are from *Continuation du discours des misères de ce temps*, 7–8.

6 The Courtly Mirror

The first paragraphs owe much to Heikki Ylikangas, 'The Historical Connection of European Peasant Revolts', *Scandinavian Journal of History*, 16:2 (1991), pp. 85–104, and to Jean Jacquart, 'L'Echec des résistances paysannes', in G. Duby & A. Wallon (eds), *Histoire de la France rurale*, Paris, Seuil, 1992 (1975), II, pp. 312–41. Figures are taken from Peter Blickle, *Unruhen in der ständischen Gesellschaft 1300–1800*, Munich, Oldenbourg, 1988, p. 13. Francis Rapp, *Les Origines médiévales de l'Allemagne moderne*, Paris, Aubier, 1989 (quotation from p. 332). From the large bibliography used about witchcraft and witchhunts, textual quotations have been made from Jean Bodin, *De la démonomanie des sorciers*, Paris, 1587 (facsimile edn, 1979; pp. 1, 355, 219v); W. Andersen, 'Os vulvae in *Proverbs* and in the *Malleus Maleficarum*', *History of European Ideas*, 14:5 (1992), pp. 715–22; Robert Muchembled, *Société et mentalités dans la France moderne, XVIe–XVIIIe siècles*, Paris, Armand Colin, 1990 (pp. 110–11). The quotation about the Bishop of Nîmes is from E.-G. Leonard, *Mon village sous Louis XV*, Paris, P.U.F., 2nd ed., 1984, p. 236; Francisco Bethencourt, *O imaginário da magia. Feticeiras, saludadores e nigromantes no século XVI*, Lisbon, Universidade Aberta, 1987 (pp. 258–60); A. Th. van Deursen, *Plain Lives in a Golden Age*, Cambridge, Cambridge U. P., 1991, pp. 241–53. The quotation from Father Francisco Garau is from *La fe triunfante*, ed. by L. Muntaner, Palma de Mallorca, 1984, p. 51. Concerning the Moriscos I mention only the Inquisition's condemnation taken from L. Pérez, L. Muntaner & M. Colom, *El tribunal de la Inquisición en Mallorca. Relación de causas de fe, 1758–1806*, I, Mallorca, M. Font, 1986, p. 4. For the context of this, M. Colom, *La Inquisició a Mallorca, 1488–1578*, Barcelona, Curial, 1992. On the ease with which Granadine *mudéjares* were enslaved after the conquest, Angel Galán, *Los mudéjares del Reino de Granada*, Granada, Universidad de Granada, 1991, pp. 322–8. The Cervantes text is from *El coloquio de los perros* in the *Novelas ejemplares* (available in

English as *Exemplary Stories*, tr. C. A. Jones, Penguin Classics, London, Viking Penguin, 1986). For a general view of European Jewry's golden age, Jonathan I. Israel, *European Jewry in the Age of Mercantilism, 1550–1750*, Oxford, Clarendon, 1985. I have kept away from repetitive recent writing on the Inquisition. Figures for those tried are from Michèle Escamilla-Colin, *Crimes et châtiments dans l'Espagne inquisitoriale*, Paris, Berg International, 1992, 2 vols. On the diaspora, there is the personal testimony of Yosef Ha-Kohen, *El valle del llanto*, Barcelona, Riopiedras, 1989, and R. Barnett & W. Schwab, *The Western Sephardim*, Grendon, Gibraltar Books, 1989; on Sabatai Zevi, books by Gershom Sholem. On the 'religious reconquest' of Germany, R. Po-Chia Hsia, *Social Discipline in the Reformation. Central Europe 1550–1750*, London, Routledge, 1992, but especially the excellent book by Thomas Robisheaux, *Rural Society and the Search for Order in Early Modern Germany*, Cambridge, Cambridge U. P., 1989 (quotation from p. 90, and many ideas adopted from him); also David Warren Sabean, *Power in the Blood. Popular Culture and Village Discourse in Early Modern Germany*, Cambridge, Cambridge U. P., 1987. For England, G. R. Elton, *Policy and Police. The Enforcement of the Reformation in the Age of Thomas Cromwell*, Cambridge, Cambridge U. P., 1985; S. Doran & C. Durston, *Princes, Pastors and People. The Church and Religion in England, 1529–1689*, London, Routledge, 1991; Robert Whiting, *The Blind Devotion of the People. Popular Religion and the English Reformation*, Cambridge, Cambridge U. P., 1984, and other works by Margaret Spufford, Anthony Fletcher, and John Stevenson. For France, Robin Griggs, *Communities of Belief. Cultural and Social Tension in Early Modern France*, Oxford, Clarendon, 1989 (quotation from p. 381); Denis Crouzet, *Les Guerriers de Dieu. La violence au temps des troubles de religion*, Seyssel, Champ Vallon, 1990, 2 vols (quotation from I, p. 114); Louis Châtellier, *La Religion des pauvres. Les sources du christianisme moderne, XVIe-XIXe siècles*, Paris, Aubier, 1993; and various works by Muchembled. On Spain, especially Henry Kamen, *The Phoenix and the Flame. Catalonia and the Counter-reformation*, New Haven, Yale U. P., 1993; Sara T. Nalle, *God in La Mancha. Religious Reform and the People of Cuenca, 1500–1650*, Baltimore, The Johns Hopkins U. P., 1992; William A. Christian Jr, *Local religion in Sixteenth-century Spain*, Princeton, Princeton U. P., 1989; etc.

The exorcism of fifteen million demons comes from Barrio-
nuevo, but I take it from Fernando Ortiz, *Historia de una pelea
cubana contra los demonios*, Havana, Editorial de Ciencias
Sociales, 1975, p. 129. On the 'inflation of the cult of the
dead', Ana Guerrero Mayllo, *Familia y vida cotidiana de una
élite de poder. Los regidores madrileños en tiempos de Felipe II*,
Madrid, Siglo XXI, 1993, pp. 375–89, and Fernando Martínez
Gil, *Muerte y sociedad en la España de los Austrias*, Madrid,
Siglo XXI, 1993, pp. 57–65, 471–9, and 640–50. On blasphemy in France, Elizabeth Belmas, 'La Montée des blasphèmes
à l'Âge Moderne du Moyen Âge au XVIIe siècle', in J. Delumeau (ed.), *Injures et blasphèmes*, Paris, Imago, 1989, pp.
13–33 (for Spain, Nalle, p. 62). The history of confession is
in Jean Delumeau, *Sin and Fear: The Emergence of a Western
Guilt Culture, 13th-18th Centuries*, New York, St Martin's
Press, 1991 (1983), and *L'Aveu et le pardon. Les difficultés de
la confession, XIIIe-XVIIIe siècles*, Paris, Fayard, 1990; J. T.
McNeill & H. M. Gamer, *Medieval Handbooks of Penance*,
New York, Columbia U. P., 1990 (1938); Gérard Sivery, *Ter-
roirs et communautés rurales dans l'Europe occidentale au Mo-
yen Âge*, Lille, Presses Universitaires de Lille, 1990 (quotation
from pp. 206–7); Albert R. Jonsen & Stephen Toulmin, *The
Abuse of Casuistry. A History of Moral Reasoning*, Berkeley,
University of California Press, 1988. Martín de Azpilcueta,
Manual de confesores y penitentes, Barcelona, Claudio Bornat,
1567; Jaime de Corella, *Práctica del confesionario*, Madrid,
Herederos de Juan García, 1743 (1687); Antoine Arnauld,
Oeuvres, vol. XXIII, Paris-Lausanne, Sigismond d'Arnay, 1779,
pp. i-v; and especially José Gavarri, *Noticias singularísimas [...]
de las preguntas necesarias que deven hazer los padres con-
fesores con las personas que oyen de confesión*, Barcelona, Pedro
Pablo Matheu, 1677, from which various quotations are taken.
Sainte-Beuve, *Port-Royal*, Paris, Gallimard, 1952 (quotation
from I, pp. 634–5). Remarks about Galicia are from Pegerto
Saavedra, *A vida cotiá en Galicia de 1550-1850*, Santiago,
Universidad de Santiago, 1992 (p. 179). On the sacralization
of the family and the criminalization of sexuality, Arlette Farge
& Michel Foucault, *Le Désordre des familles*, Paris, Gallimard,
1982; P. Laslett, K. Oosterveen & R. M. Smith (eds), *Bastardy
and its Comparative History*, London, Edward Arnold, 1980;
Richard Davenport-Hines, *Sex, Death and Punishment*, London,
Collins, 1990; R. P. Maccubin (ed.), *'Tis Nature's Fault. Un-*

authorized Sexuality during the Enlightenment, New York, Cambridge U. P., 1987; Lynn Hunt (ed.), *The Invention of Pornography*, New York, Zone Books, 1993; etc. On peasant sexuality, Jean-Louis Flandrin, *Les Amours paysannes*, Paris, Gallimard, 1975; G. R. Quaife, *Wanton Wenches and Wayward Wives. Peasants and Illicit Sex in Early Seventeenth-century England*, London, Croom Helm, 1979; J. Michael Phayer, *Sexual Liberation and Religion in Nineteenth-century Europe*, London, Croom Helm, 1977; J. Liliequist, 'Peasants against Nature; Crossing the Boundaries between Man and Animal in Seventeenth- and Eighteenth-century Sweden', in J. C. Fout (ed.), *Forbidden History. The State, Society and the Regulation of Sexuality in Modern Europe*, Chicago, University of Chicago Press, 1992, pp. 57–87, and E. P. Thompson, 'The Sale of Wives', in *Customs in Common*, London, Merlin Press, 1991, pp. 404–66. Also Romano Canosa, *La restaurazione sessuale*, Milan, Feltrinelli, 1993. On the 'moralizing' function of medicine, Alex Comfort, *The Anxiety Makers*, London, Panther, 1968; J. Stengers & A. van Neck, *Histoire d'une grande peur: la masturbation*, Brussels, Université de Bruxelles, 1984; Frank Mort, *Dangerous Sexualities. Medico-moral Politics in England since 1830*, London, Routledge & Kegan Paul, 1987. Remarks about prostitution in Paris are based on E.-M. Benabou, *La Prostitution et la police des moeurs au XVIIIe siècle*, Paris, Perrin, 1987. Hans Peter Duerr, *Nackheit und Scham. Der Mythos vom Zivilisationsprozess*, Frankfurt am Main, Suhrkamp, 1988, criticizes Elias's interpretations. For the Middle Ages there is the splendid book by Joachim Bumke, *Courtly Culture. Literature and Society in the High Middle Ages*, Berkeley, University of California Press, 1991 (quotation from p. 307). On the step from the Middle Ages to the Renaissance, Aldo Scaglione, *Knights at Court. Courtliness, Chivalry and Courtesy from Ottonian Germany to the Italian Renaissance*, Berkeley, University of California Press, 1991. Gregory Hanlon, *L'Univers des gens de bien*, Bordeaux, Presses Universitaires de Bordeaux, 1989. On the struggle against popular culture there is the fundamental book by Peter Burke, *Popular Culture in Early Modern Europe*, London, Temple Smith, 1978, to which I owe more than this passing quotation might lead the reader to think. On the appropriation and 'grammatization' of vernacular languages I have used for the general framework the second volume, 'Le Développement de la grammaire occidentale', of the collective work directed by Sylvain Auroux, *Histoire des idées linguistiques*, Liège, Mardaga, 1992, and Peter Burke & Roy Porter (eds), *The Social History of Language*, Cambridge, Cambridge U. P., 1987. On the survival of Latin in modern Europe, Peter Burke, *The Art of Conversation*, Cambridge, Polity Press, 1993, pp. 34–65. Statements about the Spanish Academy come from Juan Sempere y Guarinos, *Reflexiones sobre el buen gusto en las ciencias y en las artes*, Madrid, Sancha, 1782 (I use the facsimile ed. issued in Madrid, Marcial Pons, 1992), with quotations from pp. 207, 227, and 228. For France, Danielle Trudeau, *Les Inventeurs du bon usage, 1529–1647*, Paris, Éditions de Minuit, 1992, reflections by Marcel Schwob, *Etude sur l'argot français*, Paris, Allia, 1989, and especially Raymond Queneau, *Bâtons, chiffres et lettres*, Paris, Gallimard, 1965 (a quotation from 'Langage académique', p. 50). The Malherbe reference is to 'A la reine sur les heureux succez de sa regence', line 147. I use *Le Moyen de parvenir* in the edition by Iliana Zinguer, Nice, CMMC, 1985. The quotation about the Renaissance is the last sentence in Burckhardt's *The Civilization of the Renaissance in Italy*. From the large literature about renewal I specially mention the work of Eugenio Garin, from *Scienza e vita civile nel Rinascimento italiano* (in English as *Science and Civic Life in the Italian Renaissance*, Magnolia, MA, Peter Smith, 1993) to *Umanisti artisti scienzati*. On medieval magic there are the above-mentioned book by Valerie I. J. Flint, works by Frances A. Yates, and Brian Easlea, *Witch-hunting, Magic and the New Philosophy*, Brighton, Harvester Press, 1980; also Patrick Curry, *Prophecy and Power. Astrology in Early Modern England*, Cambridge, Polity Press, 1989. The text about magi as men of science is from E. M. Butler, *The Myth of the Magus*, Cambridge, Cambridge U. P., 1993 (1948), p. 161. Paolo Rossi, *Francis Bacon: From Magic to Science*, tr. Sacha Rabinovitch, London, Routledge & Kegan Paul, 1968. The quotation from Agrippa is from *De occulta philosophia libri tres* (1529) (translated in 1651 and again by W. F. Whitehead, Chicago, Hahn & Whitehead, 1898). That about Galileo is from A. Banfi, *Galileo e suor Maria Celeste*, Milan, All'insegna del pesce d'oro, p. 37, and that from Galileo himself from his letter of 1 January 1611 to Giuliano de' Medici (in *Lettere*, Turin, Einaudi, 1978, p. 20). The text about the 'scholastic' university is from Juan Millé, *El horóscopo de Lope de Vega*, Buenos Aires, Coni, 1927, p. 12. On the importance

of theology and alchemy in Newton's life and thought, Richard
S. Westfall, *Never at Rest. A Biography of Isaac Newton*,
Cambridge, Cambridge U. P., 1980, pp. 281–334, and A.
Rupert Hall, *Isaac Newton, Adventurer in Thought*, Oxford,
Blackwell, 1992, pp. 239–42, 372–4, and 381–6 (quotation
from p. 381). The other quotation about him is from Keynes's
Essays in Biography. One could well include here a good part
of the bibliography of Christopher Hill and Margaret C. Jacob.
For the study of alternative ways forward, Eugenio Garin, *Dal
Rinascimento all'Illuminismo*, Pisa, Nistri-Lischi, 1970; J. G. A.
Pocock, *The Machiavellian Moment. Florentine Political Thought
and the Atlantic Republican Tradition*, Princeton, Princeton
U. P., 1975, etc. For Holland I have used, besides the above-
mentioned book by A. Th. van Deursen, Yirmiyahu Yovel,
Spinoza and Other Heretics, Princeton, Princeton U. P., 1989,
2 vols (taking indirect quotations of Prado from I, p. 72), and
especially Andrew C. Fix, *Prophecy and Reason. The Dutch
Collegiants in the Early Enlightenment*, Princeton, Princeton
U. P., 1991 (one quotation from p. 23, also many ideas taken
from this fine book). Spinoza's *Tractatus theologico-politicus*
(1670) is used in the edition by Shirley & Gregory, Leyden,
Brill, 1989 (quotations from ch. XV, p. 230; XVI, p. 239;
and XX, p. 293), his *Correspondence* in the edition by J. D.
Sánchez Estop, Madrid, Hiperión, 1988, and Menasseh ben
Israel's *Esperanza de Israel* in the edition by H. Méchoulan &
G. Hanon, Madrid, Hiperión, 1987 (quotation from p. 111;
an English version was published in London, 1650).

7 The Savage Mirror

On representations of the four parts of the world in the 16th
and 17th centuries, A. Pigler, *Barockthemen. Eine Auswahl von
Verzeichnissen zur Ikonographie des 17. und 18. Jahrhunderts*,
Budapest, Akadémiai Kiadó, 1974, II, pp. 521–3; Roelof van
Straten, *Einfürung in die Ikonographie*, Berlin, Dietrich Reimer
Verlag, 1989, pp. 41–8. Texts of Cesare Ripa are taken from
Iconología, Madrid, Akal, 1987 (1593), pp. 102–3. Details
about the elephant and the rhinoceros presented to the pope
are in Donald F. Lach, *Asia in the Making of Europe* (II, 'A
Century of Wonder', 1), Chicago, University of Chicago Press,
1970, pp. 135–72, and M. Massing, 'The Quest for the Exotic:
Albrecht Dürer in the Netherlands', in J. A. Levenson (ed.),

Circa 1492. Art in the Age of Exploration, New Haven, Yale U. P., 1991, pp. 115–19. On the change in the perception of Christianity in Europe from the late eighteenth century, M. E. Yapp, 'Europe in the Turkish Mirror', *Past and Present*, 137 (November 1992), pp. 134–55.

On the savage, C. Gaignebet & J.-D. Lajoux, *Art profane et religion populaire au Moyen Âge*, Paris, P.U.F., 1985, pp. 90–136; Roger Bartra, *El salvaje en el espejo*, Mexico, Era, 1992; G. H. Gossen et al., *De palabra y obra en el Nuevo Mundo. 3: La formación del otro*, Madrid, Siglo XXI, 1993; Ronald L. Meek, *Social Science and the Ignoble Savage*, Cambridge, Cambridge U. P., 1976, etc. The quotation from Chrétien de Troyes is from *Le Chevalier au lion*, lines 288–9. That from Giovan Battista Della Porta, from *Della fisonomia dell'uomo*, Parma, Ugo Guanda, 1988 (1610), p. 102. (The Latin original of 1586 was reprinted at Paris, Aux Amateurs de Livres, 1990.) I omit bibliography about the discoveries, especially about the Quincentenary. There is a quotation from Robert Himmerich y Valencia, *The Encomendero of New Spain, 1521–1555*, Austin, University of Texas Press, 1991 (p. 104). What is said about religion owes much to the books of Nancy M. Farris, Inga Glendinen, and G. D. Jones about the Mayas, Jan de Vos on the Lacandones, and Pierre Duviols on the Andes. On native slavery there is impressive evidence in Ricardo Rodríguez Molas, *Los sometidos de la conquista. Argentina, Bolivia, Paraguay*, Buenos Aires, Centro Editor de América Latina, 1985. On demographic consequences, N. D. Cook & W. G. Lovell (eds), *'Secret Judgments of God': Old World Disease in Colonial Spanish America*, Norman, University of Oklahoma Press, 1991. Textual quotations are from Columbus's letter announcing the discovery; from Juan Ginés de Sepúlveda and Fray Bartolomé de Las Casas, *Apología*, ed. by Angel Losada, Madrid, Editora Nacional, 1975, pp. 61 and 142; from Pietro Martire d'Anghiera, *De orbe novo decades*, book II (Englished by Richard Eden as *The Decades of the Newe Worlde or West India*, 1555); from Andrés Bernáldez, *Memorias del reinado de los Reyes Católicos*, Madrid, Academia de la Historia, 1962, p. 301 (available as *History of Two Catholic Sovereigns, Don Ferdinand and Doña Isabella* in *The Voyages of Christopher Columbus*, tr. Cecil Jane, London, Argonaut Press, 1930); from Juan de Villagutierre, *History of the Conquest of the Province of Itzá*, Culver City, CA, Labyrinthos, 1983; from

V. M. Godinho, *Mito e mercadoria*, p. 95; from Camoens, *The Lusiads*, canto VII, lines 7-8, and XIV, lines 3 and 7. On the activities of the English, French, and Dutch in the West Indies, Philip P. Boucher, *Cannibal Encounters. Europeans and Island Caribs, 1492-1763*, Baltimore, The Johns Hopkins U. P., 1992. Very useful have been Alden T. Vaughan & E. W. Clark (eds), *Puritans among the Indians. Accounts of Captivity and Redemption, 1676-1724*, Cambridge (Mass.), Belknap Press, 1981 (quotation from p. 5; Cotton Mather's accounts on pp. 136-44); Timothy Silver, *A New Face on the Countryside. Indians, Colonists, and Slaves in South Atlantic Forests, 1500-1800*, Cambridge, Cambridge U. P., 1990; T. G. Jordan & M. Kaups, *The American Backwoods Frontier. An Ethnic and Ecological Interpretation*, Baltimore, The Johns Hopkins U. P., 1992; Richard White, *The Middle Ground. Indians, Empires, and Republics in the Great Lakes Region, 1650-1815*, Cambridge, Cambridge U. P., 1991; Francis Jennings, *The Ambiguous Iroquois Empire*, New York, W. W. Norton, 1984; and R. A. Bartlett, *The New Country. A Social History of the American Frontier, 1776-1890*, New York, Oxford U. P., 1974. Figures for lynchings are from E. M. Beck & S. E. Tolnay, 'A Season for Violence. The Lynching of Blacks and Labor Demand in the Agricultural Production Cycle in the American South', *International Review of Social History*, 37 (1992), pp. 1-24. The Whitman quotation is from *A Broadway Pageant*, 2, lines 38-44. On Brazil, John Hemming, *Amazon Frontier. The Defeat of the Brazilian Indians*, London, Macmillan, 1987. M. de Montaigne, *Essays*, I.xxxi ('Des cannibales'). On the 'oceanic paradises', O. H. K. Spate, *The Pacific since Magellan*, London, Croom Helm & Routledge, 1979-88, 3 vols (a quotation from III, p. 211), and the books by Alan Moorehead, Ernest S. Dodge, Marshall Sahlins (*Islands of History*, and, with P. V. Kirch, *Anahulu. The Anthropology of History in the Kingdom of Hawaii*), Anne Salmond (*Two Worlds. First Meetings between Maori and Europeans, 1642-1772*); B. Attwood, Aletta Biersack, Lynne Withey, N. Thomas, etc. Quotations from Paul Gauguin, *Noa Noa*, Paris, Pauvert, 1988, pp. 41 and 47. I also omit references to numerous studies of the slave-trade. Texts are those of Voltaire, *Essai sur les moeurs et l'esprit des nations*, ch. 141, 'Des découvertes des Portugais', and Montesquieu, *Mes pensées*, 1935, and *De l'esprit des lois*, XV, 5. Dr Johnson's opinion about Islamic culture is in James

Boswell, *Life of Johnson*, Oxford, Oxford U. P., 1970, p. 1218
(10 April 1783). The quotation from Buffon, *Histoire naturelle*,
V, 'Histoire naturelle de l'homme', 'Variétés dans l'espèce
humaine' (Paris, 1769, pp. 285–6). On this text see J. Roger,
Buffon, Paris, Fayard, 1989, pp. 236–47, and on the 'natural
inferiority' of America, Antonello Gerbi, *La disputa del Nuevo
Mundo*, Mexico, Fondo de Cultura Económica, 2nd ed., 1982
(about this, pp. 7–13). On racism and its genesis, Franz Boas,
and books by Bowler and Stocking cited in the next chapter;
Robert Miles, *Racism*, London, Routledge, 1989 (with good
bibliography); Yves Benot, *La Démence coloniale sous Napoléon*,
Paris, La Découverte, 1992 (from which Napoleon's words are
taken, p. 89). On the coolies, J. Breman & E. V. Daniel,
'Conclusion: The Making of a Coolie', *Journal of Peasant
Studies*, 19 (1992), pp. 268–95.

8   The Mirror of Progress

On the intellectual consequences of the discoveries, one must
cite especially the monumental study by Donald F. Lach, *Asia
in the Making of Europe*, particularly the third book of the
second volume ('The Scholarly Disciplines'), Chicago, University
of Chicago Press, 1977. Also Anthony Grafton et al., *New
Worlds, Ancient Texts. The Power of Tradition and the Shock
of Discovery*, Cambridge (Mass.), Belknap Press, 1992. There
are quotations from Descartes, *Discours de la méthode* (several
English translations are available), and Montesquieu, *L'Esprit
des lois*, XVIII, 8. The quotation about Degerando I take from
Anthony Pagden, *European Encounters with the New World*,
New Haven, Yale U. P., 1993, p. 118. In the abundant writings
about the 'invention of progress' – Bury, Pollard, Van Doren,
Nisbet, etc. – I have used especially David Spadafora, *The Idea
of Progress in Eighteenth-century Britain*, New Haven, Yale
U. P., 1990, and Peter J. Bowler, *The Invention of Progress.
The Victorians and the Past*, Oxford, Blackwell, 1989. For the
history of anthropology, George W. Stocking Jr, *Victorian
Anthropology*, New York, Free Press, 1987. On the appropria-
tion of Indian history by the British, Bernard S. Cohn, 'Cloth,
Clothes and Colonialism. India in the Nineteenth Century', in
A. B. Weinwer & J. Schneider (eds), *Cloth and Human
Experience*, Washington, Smithsonian Institution Press, 1989,
pp. 303–53 (quotation from p. 321). On scientific mechanism,

Michel Serres in M. Serres (ed.), *Éléments d'histoire des sciences*, Paris, Bordas, 1989, pp. 346-8; on its application to social sciences, Ian Hacking, *The Taming of Chance*, Cambridge, Cambridge U. P., 1990. Remarks about Blanqui are from Walter Benjamin, *Paris, capitale du XIXe siècle. Le Livre des passages*, Paris, Cerf, 1989, pp. 137-40 (quotation from p. 137). There is a quotation from Peter J. Bowler, *The Eclipse of Darwinism*, Baltimore, The Johns Hopkins U. P., 1983, p. 34. Alfred Russel Wallace, *The Malay Archipelago*, New York, Dover, 1962 (reprint of 1869 edn). The paragraphs on the machine and progress owe much to Michael Adas, *Machines as the Measure of Men. Science, Technology, and Ideologies of Western Dominance*, Ithaca, Cornell U. P., 1989. On industrialization as an energy revolution, E. A. Wrigley, *Continuity, Chance and Change. The Character of the Industrial Revolution in England*, Cambridge, Cambridge U. P., 1988. For a model view of the history of techniques which includes cultural elements from various contexts, B. Cotterell & J. Kamminga, *Mechanics of Pre-industrial Technology. An Introduction to the Mechanics of Ancient and Traditional Material Culture*, Cambridge, Cambridge U. P., 1990 (the example of the wheelbarrow is taken from pp. 214-16). Unfortunately, books such as this or those by Arnold Pacey, *Technology in World Civilization*, Oxford, Blackwell, 1990, and *The Maze of Ingenuity*, Cambridge (Mass.), MIT Press, 1992, are exceptional. From Jacques Gernet, *El mundo chino*, Barcelona, Crítica, 1991, there is a quotation from p. 304. On the European concept of the exploitation of nature, Clarence J. Glacken, *Traces on the Rhodian Shore*, Berkeley, University of California Press, 1990 (1967). I have used a large bibliography on agricultural technology and food production in pre-Columbine America: Angel Palerm, Bernard R. Ortiz de Montellano, Arturo Warman, Víctor Manuel Patiño, Eduardo Estrella, D. M. Pearsall, H. Lechtman & A. M. Soldi (quotation from p. 237), John Murra, Linda Schele, and David Freidel (*A Forest of Kings. The Untold Story of the Ancient Maya*, quotations from pp. 96 and 97), and Norman Hammond. On the Asian south and south-east, V. Magalhaes Godinho (*Mito e mercadoria, utopia e prática de navegar, séculos XIII-XVIII*, quotation from p. 339), K. N. Chaudhuri (*Asia before Europe. Trade and Civilization in the Indian Ocean*, etc.), Niels Steensgaard, J. C. van Leur; M. A. P. Meiling-Roelofsz (*Asian Trade and European Influence in the Indonesian*

Archipelago between 1500 and about 1630), Sanjay Subrah-
manyam (*The Political Economy of Commerce: Southern India,
1500–1650* (p. 366, among others), Anthony Reid (*Southeast
Asia in the Age of Commerce, 1450–1680*, I: *The Lands below
the Winds*, with the criticism by Clifford Geertz in *New York
Review of Books*, 16 February 1989, pp. 28–9, and the volume
compiled by him, *Southeast Asia in the Early Modern Era*),
James D. Tracy, Denys Lombard (*Le Carrefour javanais. Essai
d'histoire globale*, quotation from III, p. 152); Peter W. Klein,
'The China Seas and the World Economy between the Six-
teenth and Nineteenth Centuries: The Changing Structures of
Trade', in Carl-Ludwig Holftrerich (ed.), *Interactions in the
World Economy. Perspectives from International Economic
History*, Hemel Hempstead, Harvester Wheatsheaf, 1989, pp.
61–89; William S. Atwell, 'International Bullion Flows and the
Chinese Economy circa 1530–1650', *Past and Present*, 95 (May
1982), pp. 68–90. On the use of opium in Great Britain, Virginia
Berridge & Griffith Edwards, *Opium and the People. Opiate
Use in Nineteenth-century England*, New Haven, Yale U. P.,
1987. The ideas about Asian withdrawal owe much to the fine
book by Anthony Reid, *Southeast Asia in the Age of Com-
merce, 1450–1680*. II: *Expansion and Crisis*, New Haven, Yale
U. P., 1993. About how Europeans built up their concept of
Asia, Chaudhuri, *Asia before Europe. Economy and Civilization
of the Indian Ocean from the Rise of Islam to 1750*, Cambridge,
Cambridge U. P., 1990, pp. 22–3. The UNESCO quotation is
taken from Claude Lévi-Strauss (who does not appear to be
shocked by it), *Race et histoire*, Paris, Denoel, 1987, pp. 22–3.
On the invention of the Orient, Edward W. Said, *Orientalism*,
London, Routledge & Kegan Paul, 1978; see the critique by
Bernard Lewis, 'The Question of Orientalism', in the book next
mentioned, pp. 99–118; Bernard Lewis, *Islam and the West*,
New York, Oxford U. P., 1993; Thierry Hentsch, *L'Orient
imaginaire. La vision politique occidentale de l'Est méditerranéen*, Paris, Éditions de Minuit, 1988; Brandon H. Beck,
*From the Rising Sun. English Images of the Ottoman Empire to
1715*, New York, Peter Lang, 1987 (with full bibliography).
The text by Anthony Sherley is in *Peso político de todo el mundo
del conde D. Antonio Xerley*, Madrid, CSIC, 1961, pp. 51–60
(correcting obvious errors of transcription). On renegades, books
by the Bennassars, by Anita González-Raymond, and, especially,
by Lucetta Scaraffia, *Rinnegati. Per una storia dell'identità*

occidentale, Rome, Laterza, 1993. On the skin colour of Chinese and Japanese, Walter Demel, 'Wie die Chinesen gelb wurden. Ein Beitrag zur Frühgeschichte der Rassentheorien', *Historische Zeitschrift*, 255:3 (December 1992), 625–66; Hiroshi Wagatsuma, 'The Social Perception of Skin Color in Japan', *Daedalus* (Spring 1967), 'Colour and Race', pp. 407–43. On cultural aspects, Derek Massarella, *A World Elsewhere. Europe's Encounter with Japan in the Sixteenth and Seventeenth Centuries*, New Haven, Yale U. P., 1990; Masayoshi Sugimoto & D. L. Swain, *Science and Culture in Traditional Japan*, Tokyo, Tuttle, 1989; Thomas C. Smith, *Native Sources of Japanese Industrialization, 1750–1920*, Berkeley, University of California Press, 1988; Hiroyuki Odagiri & Akira Goto, 'The Japanese System of Innovation: Past, Present and Future', in Richard R. Nelson (ed.), *National Innovation Systems. A Comparative Analysis*, New York, Oxford U. P., 1993, pp. 76–114. Remarks about Chinese art are based on Walter Benjamin, *Paris, capitale du XIXe siècle*, Paris, Cerf, 1989, pp. 205–6. Quotations are from Athanasius Kircher, *China illustrata*, translated and ed. by Charles van Tuyl, Bloomington, Indiana U. P., 1987 (preface to the fifth part, p. 203); Montesquieu, *Lettres persanes*, 30; L. A. de Bougainville, *Viaje alrededor del mundo*, Barcelona, Adiax, 1982, p. 175. Essential texts by Quesnay about Chinese despotism will be found in *François Quesnay et la physiocratie*, Paris, Institut National d'Études Démographiques, 1958, II, pp. 913–16 and 917–34. Diderot, 'Chinois, philosophie des', in *Encyclopédie*, III (Paris, 1753), pp. 341–8. Magali Morsy (ed.), *Les Saint-Simoniens et l'Orient. Vers la modernité*, Aix-en-Provence, Edisud, 1990 (quotation from Philippe Regnier, 'Le Mythe oriental des saint-simoniens', p. 35); Florence Nightingale, *Letters from Egypt. A Journey on the Nile, 1849–1850*, New York, Weidenfeld & Nicolson, *c.*1987. The Goethe quotation is from 'Hegire', in *West-östlicher Diwan*. On empires and the colonial question, P. J. Cain & A. G. Hopkins, *British Imperialism*, London, Longman, 1993, 2 vols; Lance E. Davis & R. A. Huttenback, *Mammon and the Pursuit of Empire. The Economics of British Imperialism*, Cambridge, Cambridge U. P., 1988; Jacques Marseille, *Empire colonial et capitalisme français. Histoire d'un divorce*, Paris, Albin Michel, 1984; Michael Havinden & David Meredith, *Colonialism and Development. Britain and its Tropical Colonies, 1850–1960*, London, Routledge, 1993, etc. On the clichéd view of the history of

Africa, Walter Rodney, *How Europe Underdeveloped Africa*, Washington DC, Howard U. P., 1981. New ways of looking at this are in George E. Brooks, *Landlords and Strangers. Ecology, Society, and Trade in Western Africa, 1000–1630*, Boulder, Westview, 1993, and John Thornton, *Africa and Africans in the Making of the Atlantic World, 1400–1680*, Cambridge, Cambridge U. P., 1992; Cathérine Coquery-Vidrovitch, *Histoire des villes d'Afrique noire. Des origines à la colonisation*, Paris, Albin Michel, 1993; Steven Feierman, 'African Histories and the Dissolution of World History', in Robert H. Bates et al. (eds), *Africa and the Disciplines*, Chicago, University of Chicago Press, 1993, pp. 167–212. For a revision of points of view about African external trade, David Eltis & L. Jennings, 'Trade between Western Africa and the Atlantic World in the Pre-colonial Era', *American Historical Review*, 93 (1988), pp. 936–59; David Eltis, 'Trade between Western Africa and the Atlantic World before 1870: Estimates of Trends in Value, Composition and Direction', *Research in Economic History*, 12 (1989), pp. 197–239 (with good bibliography); Ernst van de Boogaart, 'The Trade between Western Africa and the Atlantic World, 1600–90: Estimates of Trends in Composition and Value', *Journal of African History*, 33 (1992), pp. 369–85, and interesting observations by J. F. Searing, *West African Slavery and Atlantic Commerce*, Cambridge, Cambridge U. P., 1993. Thoughts about the Bushmen are from Edwin N. Wilmsen, *Land Filled with Flies. A Political Economy of the Kalahari*, Chicago, University of Chicago Press, 1989 (quotation from p. 272). The invention of the Australian aboriginal is in Bain Attwood, *The Making of the Aborigines*, Sydney, Allen & Unwin, 1989. Out of much written about the 'Andean Utopia', Alberto Flores Galindo, *Buscando un inca: identidad y utopía en los Andes*, Havana, Casa de las Américas, 1986. Closing quotations are from Volney, in the old translation by Abate Marchena, Bordeaux, Beaume, 1820, p. 9, with a small modification (English versions are: *A Survey of the Revolutions of Empires*, London, Joyce Gold, 1807, and *The Ruins of Empires: Or Meditation on the Revolution of Empires and the Law of Nature*, Baltimore, Black Classic, 1990), and Jacques Gernet, *El mundo chino*, Barcelona, Crítica, 1991, p. 304.

9 The Mirror of the Mob

I forbear to mention the mass of writing about the modern State and nationalism which I have used. There is a quotation from Locke, from the second of the *Two Treatises on Civil Government*, IX, 124; see also Jeremy Black, *A Military Revolution? Military Change and European Society, 1550-1800*, London, Macmillan, 1991, p. 73. On the fragility of the State and corruption, Jean-Claude Waquet, *Corruption: Ethics and Power in Florence, 1600-1770*, tr. Linda McCall, Cambridge, Polity Press, 1991 (1984); Linda Levy Peck, *Court Patronage and Corruption in Early Stuart England*, Boston, Unwin Hyman, 1990. The matter of the Lyons bridge is told in a 1648 letter from the treasurers of France to chancellor Séguier, reproduced by A. D. Lublinskaya, [*The Internal Politics of French Absolutism, 1633-49*] (in Russian, but the texts of the letters in French), Moscow, 1966, pp. 251-2. The 'federation of municipalities' is from Guy Lemunier, 'Centralisme et autonomie locale: la guerre privée dans l'Espagne moderne', in M. Lambert-Gorges (ed.), *Les Élites locales et l'état dans l'Espagne moderne, XVIe-XIXe siècles*, Paris, CNRS, 1993, pp. 313-25, with a quotation from p. 323. I avoid also citing bibliography about war (Geoffrey Parker, Hans Delbrück, William H. McNeill, Michael Howard, J. A. Lynn, D. B. Ralston, Brian M. Downing, Frank Tallet, etc.). The same regarding the constitution of modern state treasuries (P. G. M. Dickson, J. F. Bosher, Gabriel Ardant, J. Berenger, J. C. Riley, Peter-Christian Witt, John Brewer, etc.). On Holland, James D. Tracy, *Holland under Habsburg Rule, 1506-1566. The Formation of a Body Politic*, Berkeley, University of California Press, 1990, and *A Financial Revolution in the Habsburg Netherlands. 'Renten' and 'Renteniers' in the County of Holland*, Berkeley, University of California Press, 1985; Martin van Gelderen, *The Political Thought of the Dutch Revolt, 1555-1590*, Cambridge, Cambridge U. P., 1992; Marjolein C. 't Hart, *The Making of a Bourgeois State. War, Politics and Finance during the Dutch Revolt*, Manchester, Manchester U. P., 1993. On England I have followed suggestions by Robert Brenner, *Merchants and Revolution. Commercial Change, Political Conflict, and London's Overseas Traders, 1550-1653*, Cambridge, Cambridge U. P., 1993; also D. W. Jones, *War and Economy in the Age of William III and Marlborough*, Oxford, Blackwell, 1988, and

books by Dickson and Brewer on the Treasury. On national-
ism, Linda Colley, *Britons. Forging the Nation, 1707-1837*,
New Haven, Yale U. P., 1992 (and the review by E. P. Thompson, reprinted in *Debats*, 46, September 1993, pp. 119-23).
The lines of *Rule Britannia* are from James Thomson, *Poetical
Works*, Ward, Lock & Co., n.d., p. 498. The mention of
Shelley comes from his wife Mary, in her note to the poems
composed in 1819 in the 1839 edition of his work. Byron's
Song for the Luddites was composed in December 1816. The
quotation by Disraeli is from *Sybil, or The Two Nations*, II,
ch. 5. The idea about France as a colonial empire is from the
end of the book by Eugen Weber detailed below. For the re-
modelling of the French absolutist state as a nation, Alan Forrest
& Peter Jones (eds), *Reshaping France. Towns, Country and
Region during the French Revolution*, Manchester, Manchester
U. P., 1991. Denis Wood, *The Power of Maps*, London, Rout-
ledge, 1993. Peter Sahlins, *Boundaries: The Making of France
and Spain in the Pyrenees*, Berkeley, University of California
Press, 1989. On the imposition of an official language, Susan
Scott Watkins, *From Provinces into Nations. Demographic In-
tegration in Western Europe, 1870-1960*, Princeton, Princeton
U. P., 1991, and Martyn Lyons, 'Regionalism and Linguistic
Conformity in the French Revolution', in Forrest & Jones,
Reshaping France, pp. 179-92; for uses of normative language,
Penelope J. Corfield, *Language, History and Class*, Oxford,
Blackwell, 1991. For the history of law and crime I have used
Howard Zehr, *Crime and the Development of Modern Society*,
London, Croom Helm, 1976 (and the critical revision of his
statements about Germany by Eric A. Johnson, 'The Crime
Rate: Longitudinal and Periodic Trends in Nineteenth- and
Twentieth-century German Criminality, from "Vormärz" to late
Weimar', in R. J. Evans (ed.), *The German Underworld. De-
viants and Outcasts in German History*, London, Routledge,
1988, pp. 159-88); Michael Ignatieff, P. C. Spierenburg, C. V.
Johansen, and H. Stevnsborg (*Annales*, 3, [1986], pp. 601-24),
R. P. Weiss (*Social History*, 12:3 [1987], pp. 331-50), Jean-
Claude Chesnais, M. J. Wiener (*Reconstructing the Criminal*),
J. S. Cockburn (*Past and Present*, 130 [February 1991], pp.
70-106), Robert Muchembled (*Les Temps des supplices. De
l'obéissance sous les rois absolus, XVe-XVIIIe siècles*), Piers
Beirne (*Inventing Criminology*). On the continuity of community
culture, see the chapter on 'Community' in E. P. Thompson's

The Making of the English Working Class, London, Gollancz, 1980 (1963) and the early pages of his *Customs in Common*, London, Merlin Press, 1991 (see especially pp. 38, 50, 54, and 57 for details used). On craft associations and the working-class movement, C. R. Dobson, *Masters and Journeymen. A Prehistory of Industrial Relations, 1717–1800*, London, Croom Helm, 1980; I. J. Prothero, *Artisans and Politics in Early Nineteenth-century London*, London, Methuen, 1979, and books by J. P. Bayard and Pierre Barret on 'compagnonage'. For a revision of clichés concerning the agricultural revolution, Marie Jeanne Tits-Dieuaide, 'Les Campagnes flammandes du XIIIe siècle au XVIIIe siècle ou les succès d'une agriculture traditionelle', *Annales*, 39:3 (1984), pp. 590–610; E. L. Jones, *Agriculture and the Industrial Revolution*, Oxford, Blackwell, 1974; Jacques Mulliez, 'Du blé, "mal nécessaire". Réflexions sur les progrès de l'agriculture de 1750 à 1850', *Revue d'Histoire Moderne et Contemporaine*, 26 (1979), pp. 3–47; Robert C. Allen & Cormac Grada, 'On the Road again with Arthur Young: English, Irish, and French Agriculture during the Industrial Revolution', *Journal of Economic History*, 48 (1988), pp. 93–116; W. Henry Newell, *Population Change and Agricultural Development in Nineteenth-century France*, New York, Arno Press, 1977; E. Kingston-Mann, 'Peasant Communes and Economic Innovation. A Preliminary Inquiry', in E. Kingston-Mann & T. Mixter (eds), *Peasant Economy, Culture, and Politics of European Russia, 1800–1921*, Princeton, Princeton U. P., 1991, pp. 23–51; J. M. Neeson, *Commoners: Common Right, Enclosure and Social Change in England, 1700–1820*, Cambridge, Cambridge U. P., 1993; J. V. Beckett, *A History of Laxton. England's Last Open-field Village*, Oxford, Blackwell, 1989, etc. Quotations from John Clare are from *The Parish* and *The Lament of Swordy Well* (ed. by Eric Robinson & David Powell in *The Oxford Authors*, 1984, in which the lines will be found on pp. 98, 99, and 152). On alternative views of industrialization, Stephen A. Marglin, 'A che servono i padroni? Origini e funzioni della gerarchia nella produzione capitalistica', and 'Conoscenza e potere', in D. S. Landes (ed.), *A che servono i padroni? Le alternative storiche dell'industrializzazione*, Turin, Bollati Beringhieri, 1987; C. Sabel & J. Zeitlin, 'Historical Alternatives to Mass Production: Politics, Markets and Technology in Nineteenth-century Industrialization', *Past and Present*, 108 (1985), pp. 133–76; Adrian Randall, *Before the Luddites*.

Custom, Community and Machinery in the English Woollen Industry, 1776–1809, Cambridge, Cambridge U. P., 1991 (quotation from p. 285). The most objective attempt to gauge living standards of the workers is perhaps that of Roderick Floud, Kenneth Wachter, and Annabel Gregory, *Height, Health and History. Nutritional Status in the United Kingdom, 1750–1980*, Cambridge, Cambridge U. P., 1990. On hand-weavers, Geoffrey Timmins, *The Last Shift. The Decline of Handloom Weaving in Nineteenth-century Lancashire*, Manchester, Manchester U. P., 1993. The Blake quotation is from *Jerusalem*, III, 65, lines 16–26. The treatment of the alternative industrialization from below is based especially on Thompson, *The Making of the English Working Class* (quotation of an 1833 text reproduced by Thompson on p. 912). For the integration of British culture, including behavioural norms, Raymond Williams, *Culture and Society, 1780–1950*, Harmondsworth, Penguin, 1963; F. M. L. Thompson, *The Rise of Respectable Society. A Social History of Victorian Britain, 1830–1900*, Cambridge (Mass.), Harvard U. P., 1988; Martin Wiener, *English Culture and the Decline of the Industrial Spirit, 1850–1980*, Cambridge, Cambridge U. P., 1981; W. D. Rubinstein, *Capitalism, Culture, and Decline in Britain*, London, Routledge, 1993; on the assimilation of the workers, John Foster, *Class Struggle and the Industrial Revolution*, London, Weidenfeld & Nicolson, 1974. On France, and the hypothesis about the late 'nationalization' of the French peasants, Eugen Weber, *Peasants into Frenchmen: The Modernization of Rural France, 1870–1914*, Stanford, Stanford U. P., 1976 (criticized, for what it says about the politicization of the peasants, by Peter McPhee, *The Politics of Rural Life. Political Mobilization in the French Countryside, 1846–1852*, Oxford, Clarendon, 1992). For the formation of a shared bourgeois culture, Anne Martin-Fugier, *La Vie élégante ou la formation du tout-Paris, 1815–1848*, Paris, Fayard, 1990; Walter Benjamin, *Paris capitale du XIXe siècle*, Paris, Cerf, 1989 (German original, *Das Passagenwerk. Supplement zur Werkausgabe*, 2 vols, Frankfurt am Main, Suhrkamp, 1983). For Germany I have used especially George L. Mosse, *The Nationalization of the Masses. Political Symbolism and Mass Movements in Germany from the Napoleonic Wars through the Third Reich*, Ithaca, Cornell U. P., 1991 (1975); T. Ziolkowski, *German Romanticism and its Institutions*, Princeton, Princeton U. P., 1990; Woodruff D. Smith, *Politics and the Sciences of*

Culture in Germany, 1840–1920, New York, Oxford U. P., 1991; Eric Dorn Brose, *The Politics of Technological Change in Prussia. Out of the Shadow of Antiquity, 1809–1848*, Princeton, Princeton U. P., 1993, etc. The reaction to the Manchester gathering is from a letter of Thomas Grenville's reproduced in J. E. Cookson, *Lord Liverpool's Administration, 1815–1822*, Edinburgh, Scottish Academic Press, 1975, p. 181. Niebuhr's fear, in Barthold C. Witte, *Barthold Georg Niebuhr. Una vida entre la política y la ciencia*, Barcelona, Alfa, 1987, pp. 205–8. On fears in the period following the First World War, Chris Wrigley (ed.), *Challenges of Labour. Central and Western Europe, 1917–1920*, London, Routledge, 1993; Wolfgang Ayass, 'Vagrants and Beggars in Hitler's Reich', in Richard J. Evans (ed.), *The German Underworld*, pp. 210–37; Michael Burleigh & W. Wippermann, *The Racial State. Germany 1933–1945*, Cambridge, Cambridge U. P., 1991. For the 'dangerous classes', Louis Chevalier, *Labouring Classes and Dangerous Classes in Paris during the First Half of the 19th Century*, New York, Howard Fertig Inc., 1973; Rob Sindall, *Street Violence in the Nineteenth Century*, Leicester, Leicester U. P., 1990; Daniel Pick, *Faces of Degeneration. A European Disorder, c. 1848–1918*, Cambridge, Cambridge U. P., 1989; José Luis Peset, *Ciencia y marginación. Sobre negros, locos y criminales*, Barcelona, Crítica, 1983; John Carey, *The Intellectuals and the Masses*, London, Faber & Faber, 1992. I omit as obvious references to texts by Flaubert, Pierre Louys, Huysmans (on the colours, ch. 1 of *A rebours*), Verlaine, etc. Political texts from Heidegger have been taken from Richard Wolin (ed.), *The Heidegger Controversy. A Critical Reader*, New York, Columbia U. P., 1991.

10 Outside the Hall of Mirrors

On European 'race', Léon Poliakov, *Le Mythe aryen*, Brussels, Complexe, 2nd ed., 1987; Alfred Rosenberg, *Race and Race History*, New York, Harper & Row, 1970 (quotation from p. 47); J. P. Mallory, *In Search of the Indo-Europeans. Language, Archaeology and Myth*, London, Thames & Hudson, 1989; Colin Renfrew, *Archaeology and Language. The Puzzle of Indo-European Origins*, London, Jonathan Cape, 1987. The subject of religion is analysed in the collective volume ed. by S. N. Eisenstadt, *The Protestant Ethic and Modernization. A*

Comparative View, New York, Basic Books, 1968. On the family and marriage, D. V. Glass & D. E. C. Eversley (eds), *Population in History*, London, Edward Arnold, 1965 (on pp. 101–43, Hajnal's fundamental study of European family and marriage patterns); Jack Goody, *The Development of the Family and Marriage in Europe*, Cambridge, Cambridge U. P., 1983, and *The Oriental, the Ancient and the Primitive. Systems of Marriage and the Family in the Pre-industrial Societies of Eurasia*, Cambridge, Cambridge U. P., 1990; A. J. Coale & S. C. Watkins (eds), *The Decline of Fertility in Europe*, Princeton, Princeton U. P., 1986; J. R. Gillis et al. (eds), *The European Experience of Declining Fertility*, Cambridge (Mass.), Blackwell, 1992. The reflection about non-industrialization in China is in Lloyd E. Eastman, *Family, Fields, and Ancestors. Constancy and Change in China's Social and Economic History*, New York, Oxford U. P., 1988, pp. 149–57. E. L. Jones, *The European Miracle. Environments, Economies and Geopolitics in the History of Europe and Asia*, Cambridge, Cambridge U. P., 1981 (quotation from p. 231). On the myth of Oriental despotism, in addition to works cited in the previous chapter, Brendan O'Leary, *The Asiatic Mode of Production. Oriental Despotism, Historical Materialism and Indian History*, Oxford, Blackwell, 1989, and Patricia Springborg, *Western Republicanism and the Oriental Prince*, Cambridge, Polity Press, 1992. On violence in modern Europe, Robert Muchembled, *Le Temps des supplices. De l'obéissance sous les rois absolus, XVe-XVIIIe siècles*, Paris, Armand Colin, 1992; S. T. Christiensen (ed.), *Violence and the Absolutist State*, Copenhagen, Akademisk Forlag, 1990 (particularly V. G. Kiernan, 'Why was Early Modern Europe always at War?', pp. 17–46).

On the reasons for backwardness in east Asia, Anthony Reid, *Southeast Asia in the Age of Commerce, 1450–1680. II: Expansion and Crisis*, passim. The Raymond Queneau quotation is from *Traité des vertus démocratiques*, Paris, Gallimard, 1993, p. 84. On the failure of policies for colonial development, the aforementioned book by Havinden & Meredith, *Colonialism and Development*. On the history of Chiapas, Thomas Benjamin, *A Rich Land, a Poor People. Politics and Society in Modern Chiapas*, Albuquerque, University of New Mexico Press, 1989 (quotation from p. 242). What is said about scientific knowledge in the United States is from Timothy Ferris, 'The Case against Science', *New York Review of Books*, 13 May 1993, p. 17, and from a press report of late 1993. News about elephants 'sucked up' by a UFO came in *Weekly World News* of 26 July 1988 as reproduced by Hillel Schwartz, *Century's End*, New York, Doubleday, 1990, p. 211. On science-fiction, Karl S. Guthke, *The Last Frontier. Imagining Other Worlds from the Copernican Revolution to Modern Science Fiction*, Ithaca, Cornell U. P., 1990. If Huxley had anticipated a pessimistic view in *Brave New World* (1931), he later declared that when he wrote the book 'I was convinced that there was still plenty of time' (A. Huxley, Brave New World Revisited, 1959, p. 11). The quotation from Antonio Machado, attributed to Juan de Mairena, is from *Obras. Poesía y prosa,* Buenos Aires, Losada, 1964, p. 428. References to Benjamin are to his *Tesis de filosofía de la historia*; on his death, Ingrid Scheurmann, *Neue Dokumente zum Tode Walter Benjamins*, Bonn, AsKI, 1992. The quotation from Kant, *Träume eines Geistehers*, I, ch. 1, is from the bilingual edition by Cinta Canterla, Cadiz, Universidad de Cádiz, 1989 (English version, *Dreams of a Spirit Seer*, tr. John Manolesco, New York, Vantage Press, 1969). That from Bruno Bettelheim is from *El peso de una vida*, Barcelona, Crítica, 1991, p. 234 (in 'liberarse de la mentalidad de gueto'). On the Great Wall of China and relations with the barbarians to the north there is a large bibliography (Arthur Waldon, Thomas J. Barfield, Sechin Jagchid, V. J. Symons, etc.).

Index

abacus, 46
aboriginals, 122–3, 142
Abu Hamid, 43
Act of Union, 148
Aeneas, 11
agora, 11
airesis, 21
Aksum, 137
al-Farabi, 44
al-Tabari, 56
Alans, 15
Alaric, 17
Albigensian crusade, 70
alchemy, 106, 107
Alexander, 6, 11, 13
Alexander Severus, 28
Alexander VI, 114
Alexandria, 7, 27, 28, 139
Alexius I, 58
Alfred, 36, 38
Algiers, 137
alphabet, 9, 41
Ammianus Marcellinus, 14
Amsterdam, 86
Anabaptism, Anabaptists,
    11, 85, 86, 108
Anatolia, 8, 57
Andes, 116, 134

Anglo-Saxon coins, 36
anthropology, 132, 141,
    142
apocryphal Gospels, 31
Apollinarians, 27
Apollo, 10, 23
Arab coins, 36
Arabia, 9, 135
Arabic, 9, 57
Arabic numerals, 45, 46
Arabs, 44
Aramaic language, 20
Arawaks, 114
Arian clergy, Arianism,
    Arians 15, 21, 26, 27
Aristotle, 4, 5, 7, 11, 108
Armenia, 59
Armenians, 67
Arnauld, Angélique, 100
Arnauld, Antoine, 100
Arthur, 36
Aryans, 126, 161
Asiatic Christianity, 58–62
astrology, 31, 106, 107
astronomy, 9
atheism, 110, 111
Athenian democracy, 5, 11
Athenian tragedies, 4

Athenians, 5, 6
Athens, 5
Attila, 15
Aucassin et Nicolette, 88
Audigier, 88
Augustus, 25, 35, 37, 52
Australia, 122, 142
Australians, black, 122
Azerbaijan, 60

Baal-Hammon, 13
Babylonian language, 9
Bacchae, The, 4
Bacon, 121
Baghdad, 37, 43, 56, 60, 61
Bakhtin, 89
Baldwin of Flanders, 54
Balkans, 8, 15, 68, 127
Ball, John, 80
Baltic, 42
Baltic peoples, 42
Barbary pirates, 137
Barrow, Isaac, 108
Basque language, 2
Bede, 36, 39
Behem, Hans, 84
Benjamin, Walter, 131, 167
Bettelheim, Bruno, 169
Bible, 26, 64, 65, 81, 91, 93, 109, 110, 111, 139
Birka, 36
Black Africa, 123, 130, 134, 136
Black Death, 75, 78
Black Forest, 84
Black Sea, 9, 14, 43
Blake, 153
Blanqui, Auguste, 131
blasphemy, 99

Bodin, 94
Bogomil, Bogomils, 67, 68
Bohemia, 82–4
Bolsheviks, Bolshevism, 155, 165
Bonaccorsi company, 76
Boniface, St, 39
Bosphorus, 1
Bougainville, 121, 124
Bourbons, 137
Boyars, 43
Brazil, 113, 120, 123, 127
Brethren (in Bohemia), 82
British, 130, 135, 146, 148
British Empire, 140
British Isles, 37
Bruegel, Pieter, 90, 114
Buddhism, 60
Buffon, 125
Bukhara, 37
Bulgaria, 43, 52, 67, 68
Bulgarians, Bulgars, 42
Bundschuh, 84
Bushmen, 141, 142
byblos, 9
Byron, 148
Byzantine Empire, 67, 68
Byzantines, 40, 43, 58
Byzantium, 24, 37, 41, 55, 58, 60

Cade, Jack, 81
Caesar, 14, 126
Caesarius of Arles, St, 33
Calcutta, 116, 135
calendar, 29
Caliph, 55
Caliphate, 37, 43
Calvinism, Calvinists, 86, 111
Campanella, 107
Canaan, 8

cannibalism, 114, 117,
120-3
Canti carnascialeschi, 90
Cappadocia, 22
Cardenal, Peire, 71
Caribbean, the, 117, 123
Caribs, 114
Carmina Burana, 88
Carnival, 88
Carolinas, the, 118
Carolingian empire, 38, 41
Carolingian renaissance, 39
Carthage, Carthaginians, 8,
10, 13
Caspian Sea, 37
Cassiodorus, 15
Castile, 65, 73, 75, 104,
123, 145
Catalan, 105
Catalans, 58
Catalaunian Fields, 15
Catalonia, 45, 48, 61,
149, 167
Cathar Church, Catharism,
Cathars, 67-9, 71
Caucasus, the, 59, 139
celibacy, 49, 67
Celtic art, 10
Celts, 8, 15, 32, 44, 126
Cervantes, Miguel de, 97
Chalicist Church, 82, 83
Charlemagne, 24, 38, 39,
42, 45
Chateaubriand, 139
Chevalier au Lion, Le, 114
Chiapas, 165
Chilperic, 39
China, 36, 52, 59, 60-2,
133-8, 143, 162, 164
China Sea, 59, 144
Chinese (people), 113,
137-8

Chinese Empire, 59, 162
chinoiserie, 138
chivalry, 47, 48, 88, 114
Chrétien de Troyes, 105,
114
Christian era, 29
Civil War (in USA), 119
Clare, John, 152
Clovis, 37, 41
coenobites, 25
coins, coinage, 36, 37
Collegiants, 108, 111
Colonna, Cardinal, 75
Columbus, 114, 115, 116,
119
Comenius, 83, 111
Commune, 155
communism, 163
concubinage, 64
Condorcet, 59
confession, 96, 99, 100,
101
Constantine, 20, 21, 23,
26, 29, 34, 35, 59
Constantine (St Cyril), 41
Constantine VI, 24
Constantinople, 26, 27,
34, 41, 55, 58, 59
Constitutio Antoniniana,
12
conversion (religious), 23,
27, 28, 32, 40, 42,
56, 57, 59, 60, 96,
97, 115, 137
Cook, 121, 122
Coolies, 126
Cordova, 56
Cornelius Agrippa, 107
Cosmas, 68
Costa, Uriel da, 110
Council of Constance, 82
Council of Elvira, 32

Council of Nicaea, 26
Council of Trent, 100
Counter-Reformation, 94,
    106
Cretan writing, 8
Crete, 7-9
Croats, 42
crusades, 42, 54, 55, 58,
    61, 65, 68, 70, 71,
    72, 83, 116
cuneiform script, 9
Cyril, St, 28, 41, 43
Cyrillic, 9, 41, 42
Czech, 82

Damascus, 61
Danegeld, 36
Danes, 41, 42
Dante, 104
Danube, 15, 17, 42
Dark Ages, concept of,
    35-8, 45
Darwin, 131
De communione rerum, 86
De correctione rusticorum,
    33
Decameron, 76
deism, 34, 110, 114
Delacroix, 139
Dell'asino d'oro, 90
Delumeau, Jean, 100
Demosthenes, 5
Denmark, 41
Descartes, 107, 128
devotio moderna, 85
Dey of Algiers, 137
Diálogo de las lenguas,
    104
Dictatus Papae, 49
Diderot, 138
*Discours des misères de ce
    temps*, 91

Disraeli, 149
Dolcino, Fra, 65
Dominicans, 70, 95
Don, River, 1, 43
Donation of Constantine,
    24
Donatists, 24
Du Bois-Reymond, 131
dualism, 25, 26, 67, 68
Dublin, 37, 51
Duby, 47
Dürer, 85, 113
Dutch (people), 135

Eastern Roman Empire,
    17, 24, 35
Ebstorf monastery, 30
Egypt, 8, 21, 36, 57, 59,
    139
Egyptian ascetics, 22
Egyptians, 1
Elias, Norbert, 103
Emir of Babylonia, 55
encomiendas, 116
Encyclopédie, 138
England, 38, 47, 80, 98,
    148, 152
English (language), 81, 124
English (people), 148
Enlightenment, the, 108,
    111, 123, 124, 169
Erasmus, 85, 86, 91
Esperança de Israel, 109
Essex, 80
Etruscans, 8, 10
Euripedes, 4
exorcism, 97

fabliaux, 88
fascism, 6, 167
Fathers of the Church, 30
Feast of the Donkey, 88

fertility, decline in, 162
First Crusade, 72
First International, 155
First World War, 156
Flagellants, 76
Flanders, 77, 152
Flaubert, 139, 157
Florence, 76, 78, 79, 107
Fontevraud, 64
Fournier, Jacques, 68, 71
Fourth Crusade, 58
Fourth Lateran Council, 72, 100
France, 39, 52, 70, 77, 82, 91, 94, 95, 98, 101, 105, 126, 138, 145, 149, 152, 155
Francis I de' Medici, 107
Francis of Sales, St, 100
Franciscans, 64, 65, 70
Frankish coins, 36
Frankish kingdom, 36
Franks, 38, 41, 43, 61, 126
Franquism, 167
French (language), 105, 124
French (people), 135
French Academy, 105
French Empire, 140
French Revolution, 126, 138, 149, 155
Froissart, 75

Galatians, 15
Galicia, 32, 33, 46, 99
Galileo, 107, 128
Garau, Father, 96
Gargantua, 91
Gauguin, 121-2
Gaul, 14, 15, 28, 33
Gauls, 15, 126

Gavarri, Father José, 101-2
Gélis, Arnaud, 68-9
Genghis Khan, 60
Genoa, 113
Genoese, 58, 74
geography of the world, concepts of, 1, 14, 112
geometry, 9
Georgia, 2
Georgius Gemistus, 34
Germania, 14
Germans, 14, 15, 32, 36, 129
Germany, 52, 84, 86, 93-5, 98, 101, 127, 132, 151, 155, 158, 161, 165
Gernet, Jacques, 143
Gherard, 65
Gibbon, 167
Glagolitic, 41
Glaris (Switzerland), 95
Glorious Revolution, 148
Gnosticism, 21, 31
Gobineau, 126
Godinho, V. M., 116
Goethe, 139, 146
Goliards, 88
Gospels of the Distaff, 88
Gothic language, 15
Goths, 15-17
Granada, 43, 67, 96, 104
Great Britain, 3, 136, 148-9, 151-7, 163
Great Wall of China, 170
Greece, 3, 5, 9, 13, 121, 132
Greek (language), 7, 8, 11, 20, 42, 60, 105
Greek polis, 5, 8, 11

Greeks, 1, 3, 4, 6–12, 14
Greenland, 36
Gregorian reform, 49, 63
Gregory Nazianzen, 27
Gregory of Tours, 35, 39
Gregory VII, 49, 62
Griggs, Robin, 99
Guibert of Nogent, 66
guilds, 45, 50, 78, 79, 88
Guinefort, St, 33
Gurevich, Aron, 33

Hadrian II, 41
Harald, King of Denmark, 41
Harran, 28
Hawaii, 121
Hebrew, 9, 42
Heidegger, 158
Helgö, 36
Helios-Mithras, 13
Hellenistic kingdoms, 11
Hellenists, 21
Henry VIII, 98
heretics, heresy, 21, 24–7, 34, 50, 54, 59–71, 81–4, 91, 94, 95, 109, 121, 156
Herod of Judaea, 13
Herodotus, 4, 5, 12, 57
Hispania, 23
Histoire anonyme de la Première Croisade, 55
Historia del futuro, 109
Hitler, 158
Hittite empire, Hittites, 8
Hobbes, 24
Hokusai, 138
Holland, 85, 95, 109–11, 147
Holy Child of La Guardia, 73

Holy Innocents' Day, 88
Holy Land, 109, 139
Holy Roman Empire, 77
Homer, 3, 11, 58
Hume, David, 129
humiliati, 65
humiliores, 23
Hunayn ibn Ishaq, 60
Huns, 14, 15, 60
Huss, John, 82, 84, 92
Hussites, 82–3, 108
Hutter, Jakob, 86
Huxley, T. H., 131
Huysmans, 157
Hypatia, 28

Iberian Peninsula, 52, 56, 100, 105
Ibn Batuta, 55
Ibn Fadlan, 37
Ibn Jubayr, 55, 57, 58
Ibn Khaldun, 56
Iceland, 36, 37, 40
iconography, 39
Iconologia, 112
Ilkhan Abagha, 61
illegitimacy, 101
Inca empire, 143
India, 36, 56, 119, 130, 135
Indian numerical system, 44
Indians, 130
Indians (of America), 113–20, 129
Indies (America), 116
Indonesia, 135
Indus, 9
Innocent III, 65
Inquisition, 54, 62, 65, 70, 86, 92, 96–7, 99, 101, 104, 116

Iranian Christians, 61
Iraq, 120
Ireland, 37
Irish (people), 148
Islam, 28, 40, 43, 44,
    52–62, 96, 109, 124,
    133, 135, 137, 139,
    162
Islamic science, 44
Israel, 109
Italian humanists, 106
Italy, 15, 17, 52, 68, 76,
    77, 78, 79, 80, 95,
    146, 151

Jacobins, 165
Jacobite rebellions, 148
Jacquerie, 83
James, St, 32
Jansenism, 100
Japan, 62, 136, 138
Japanese, 113, 138
Java, 52, 162
Jeling, 41
Jerusalem, 11, 61
Jerusalem, Kingdom of, 61
Jesuits, 99, 100, 105
Jesus Christ, 20, 25, 30,
    40, 55, 60, 71, 76,
    83, 86, 111, 124
Jewish priests, 11
Jewish religion, 43
Jewish sects, 21
Jews, 55, 72–3, 75, 94,
    97, 104, 109–10, 115,
    121, 156, 159
Joachim de Fiore, 64–5
John the Baptist, St, 21
Jones, E. L., 162
Joufre, Jean, 71
Judaism, 21, 32, 57, 60,
    97, 109

Judaizers, 96, 97
Julian, 13, 26, 27
Jünger, 158
Justinian, 27, 45

Kalahari, 141
Kama, 42
Kant, 168
Kent, 80
Keraits, 60
Khazars, 37, 43
Khundishapur, 60
Kiev, 51
Kingdom of the New Zion,
    86
Knossos, 8
Konrad, 84
Koran, 55
Kublai Khan, 61

L'Éternité par les astres,
    131
La mandragola, 90
La Peyrère, Isaac de, 110
Laplace, 131
Las Casas, Father
    Bartolomé de, 115
Latin, 10, 11, 13, 38–9,
    42, 57, 104–5
Lawrence, 157
Laxton, 152
Le Moyen de parvenir, 105
Lea, 65
Lepanto, 137
lepers, 67
Letts, 42
Lewis, 139
libraries, 7, 10
Lietard, 89
linear A, 8
linear B, 9
Linnaeus, 125

literacy, 6, 10, 39, 166
Lithuanians, 42
Livy, 90
Locke, 145
Lollards, 81, 84, 98, 108
Lombardy, 65
Lombroso, 157
London, 80, 81, 138
London, Jack, 122
Louys, Pierre, 157
Low Countries, 94
Lusiads, The, 116
Luther, 85

Macedonian empire, 5
Macedonians, 6
Machado, Antonio, 167
Machiavelli, 78, 90, 108
Madrid, 97, 100, 124
magic, 94, 106, 107, 108,
    166
Magnus Maximus, 31
Mago, 10
Majorca, 96
Malay archipelago, 132
Malaysia, 52
Malherbe, 105
Mali, 137
Malleus maleficarum, 95
Malthus, 161
Manchester, 155
Mani, 60
Manichaeans, Manichaeism,
    26, 31, 59, 67
mapamundi, 30
maps, 1, 12, 30, 128, 150
March, Ausiàs, 74
Marco Polo, 61
marranos, 110
Martin of Braga, St, 33
Martin, Bishop of
    Tours, 28

Marx, 132
Master Pierre Pathelin,
    farce of, 88
Maximilian, 22
Mayas, 116, 134
Mazdeism, Mazdeists, 55,
    60
medical science, 7, 9, 10,
    60, 75, 102
Melaka, 135
Melanchthon, 85
Melville, 122
Memmingen constitution,
    85
Menasseh ben Israel,
    109–10
Mennonites, 111
Mesopotamia, 28, 31, 59
Mesopotamian writing, 8
Mesopotamians, 1
Messiah, the, 109
Messina, 55, 75
Methodius, 41, 43
Mexico, 116, 119, 123,
    164
Middle Ages, concept of,
    35, 40, 44, 74, 106
Milan, 75
millenarianism, 64, 109,
    111
Minoan Crete, 7
Minos, 7
Minucius Felix., 22
missionaries, 32, 41, 43,
    60, 61, 99, 101, 116,
    121
Mithras, 13
Momigliano, 4, 6
Mongol Empire, 143
Mongolia, 61
Mongols, 58–62, 74, 113,
    144

Montaigne, 120
Montaillou, 71
Montanism, 21
Montesquieu, 123, 124,
    125, 129
Montpellier, 75
Moors, 72, 96-7, 114
Moravia, 82, 86, 111
Moriscos, 96-7
Muhammad, 55
Mülhausen, 85
Münster, 85, 86, 93
Müntzer, Thomas, 85
Murcia, 73
Muslims, 54-8, 61, 96,
    104, 135, 137
Mussolini, 158
Mycenaean culture, 9
Mycenaeans, 8

Napoleon, 126
Nathan of Gaza, 109
National Socialism, 158
Nazism, Nazis, 156, 158
Neo-Platonism, 28
Nestorian Christians, 44,
    60
Nestorian Church, 60
Nestorianism, 31, 60, 62
New Atlantis, The, 121
New Testament, 26
New Zealand, 121
Newton, 106, 108
Nicaea, 57
Nicaean doctrine, 27
Niebuhr, 155, 158
Nietzsche, 158
Nightingale, Florence,
    139
Niklashausen, 84
Nîmes, Bishop of, 95
Noa Noa, 122

North American free trade
    area, 165
North Sea, 36
North, Douglas, 167
Northumbria, 36
Norwich, Bishop of, 62
Nostradamus, 98
Noticias singularísimas,
    101
Novatians, 27
numerology, 31

Occitania, 68, 70
Oceania, 121, 137
Odin, 38
Olaf, King of Norway, 41
Olivares, 149
Ongut people, 60
opium, 135, 136
oral culture, 6, 13, 39,
    40
Ostrogoths, 15
Otto III, 40
Ottomans, 113
Ovid, 14
Oxford, 81, 82

paganism (Graeco-Roman),
    21, 23, 26, 27, 28,
    30
paganism (in general), 32,
    34, 38, 40, 42, 44,
    54, 94, 109
Palazzo Vecchio (Florence),
    79
Palestine, 20-1, 61
Palmyra, 139, 143
papacy, 24, 41, 50, 82,
    106
paper, 44
papyrus, 9, 44
parchment, 44

Paris, 38, 49, 103, 124, 155
Pascal, Blaise, 100
Paschal cycle, 29
Paul, St, 20–1
Paulicianism, Paulicians, 67, 68
Pauline Christianity, 26
pax romana, 25
Payne, Peter, 82
Peace of God, 47, 50
Pegu, 52
Peking, 138
Persia, 3, 28, 31, 60, 135
Persian Church, 60
Persian Empire, 4, 6
Persian Gulf, 57
Peru, 123, 143
Petrarch, 75–6
Philadelphia, 95
Philip II, 100, 107
Philip IV, 100
Philip of Macedon, 6
Philistines, 8
Phoenicia, 7, 9
Phoenicians, 9
Picard heretics, 82
pictograms, 9
Piers Ploughman, 80
plague, 74–7, 82, 87
Pletho, 34
Pliny, 14
Plutarch, 11
Poitiers, battle of, 55
Poland, 37, 111
Poles, 42
Polo brothers, 61
Polybius, 11, 15
Pontus, 21–2
population statistics, 45, 52, 74, 76, 96, 118, 120, 123, 157

Port-Royal, 100
Porta, Giovan Battista della, 114
Portugal, 95, 109, 112, 149
Portuguese, 116, 135
potatoes, 134
Prague, 83
Prester John, 61
Priam, 38
Priscillian, 31, 32
Priscillianism, Priscillianists, 31, 33
Procopius, 15
prostitution, 103
Prussia, 3, 126
Prussians, 42
Punic books, 10
Pushkin, 139

Queneau, 163

Rabban Çauma, 61
Rabelais, 91, 105
racism, 125, 126
Radcliffe-Brown, 132
Ramirdus, 64
Recared, 40
Reformation, 94, 98, 102, 104, 106, 111
reign of the Holy Spirit, 65
Renaissance, 35, 106, 108
Renaissance magi, 106
respublica Christiana, 113
Retzius, 125
Revolution of 1830, 155
Revolution of 1848, 155
Rhône, 46, 146
Ripa, Cesare, 112
Robert d'Arbrissel, 64
Roberts, David, 139
Roman de Renart, 89

Roman Empire, 9–17, 28, 52, 58
Romans, 6, 11–15, 35, 43, 58
Rome, 10, 11, 13, 15, 17, 24, 41, 52
Romulus, 11
Romulus Augustulus, 17
Ronsard, 91
Rosary, Brotherhoods of the, 99
Rosenberg, 161
Rostislav, Prince of Moravia, 41
Rostovtseff, 17, 18
Royal Spanish Academy, 105
Rule Britannia, 148
Rus, 43
Rus traders, 37
Russia, 37, 52, 58, 152
Russians, 42, 139

Sabatai Zevi, Sabateism, 109
Saint Victor, library of, 91
Samarkand, 37, 59
Santiago de Compostela, 32
Saturn, 13
Savonarola, 79, 92
Saxons, 42
Scandinavia, 9, 15, 37
Scandinavians, 36–7, 58
schismatics, 24
Schumpeter, 165
Scott, Sir Walter, 148
Scottish people, 148
Scottish school, 129, 130, 132
Scythians, 58

Second World War, 136, 139
Secret History of the Mongols, 60
Semitic languages, 9
Sephardim, 72, 109
Sepúlveda, Juan Ginés de, 115
Serapeion, 28
Serbs, 42
serfdom, 48–9, 80–4, 118
sermo humilis, 39
Servet, 86, 92, 109
sexuality, 22, 30, 50, 65, 66, 95, 99, 101, 103
Shelley, 148
Sherley, Anthony, 137
Siam, 52
Simeon, 25
Simon of Trent, 73
simony, 49, 63, 64
Sioux, 119
Slav language, 41, 43
Slav liturgy, 41
slave-trade, 114, 124, 126, 141
slavery, 4–5, 17, 48, 96, 115, 123–4, 126, 141
Slavs, 41–2, 58, 67, 72
Smith, Adam, 129
Snorri Sturluson, 38
social anthropology, 132
Socinian Church of Poland, 109
Socinians, 111
sociology, 132
Sol-Mithras, 26
Solon, 5
Somalia, 120
Somerset, 101
Song for the Luddites, 148
Sorbonne, 91

Soviet revolution, 17
Spain, 72, 95–7, 99, 109,
    124, 137, 149, 151,
    157
Spaniards, 115, 123
Spanish, 72, 109, 124, 135
Spartans, 6
Spencer, 131
Spinoza, 110–11
St Blasien, abbey of, 84
St Martin's in Tours, 37,
    38
Stevenson, 122
Sumatra, 60
Sumerians, 9
Sussex, 81
Sweden, 36, 101
syphilis, 121
Syria, 21, 22, 28, 56, 57,
    59
Syriac, 44
Syrians, 56

Tabor, 82–4
Tacitus, 14, 15
Tahiti, 121–2, 124
Templars, 25, 61, 66
Temple (Jewish), 20, 21
Temuchin, 60
Teutonic Order, 42
Thélème, abbey of, 91
Theodosius I, 27
Theophilus, 28
Thomas Aquinas, St, 108
Thompson, E. P., 152
Thomson, James, 148
Thucydides, 3
Tractatus theologico-
    politicus, 110
trade routes, 7, 43, 51,
    52, 57, 60
Trier, 31, 32

Trojan War, 3, 57
Troy, 8, 38
Trubert, 88
Turkey, 139
Turkic peoples, 59
Turkish, 43
Turks, 34, 59, 68, 109,
    116, 124, 137
Tyler, Wat, 80–1, 84
Tyre, 13

Uighur people, 59
Uighuria, 62
Unam sanctam bull, 62
UNESCO, 136
Union of the Brethren, 83
United Kingdom, 148
United States, 123, 151,
    156, 157, 165, 166
usury, 73
Utraquist Church, 82
Utrecht, Treaty of, 113

Valdés, Juan de, 104
van Kessel, Jan, 112, 113
Vasco da Gama, 116, 135
Venetians, 58
Venice, 79
vernacular languages, 38,
    39, 41, 104, 113
Verville, Béroalde de, 105
Vieira, António, 109
Vikings, 36–8, 44
Villani, Giovanni, 75–6
Villon, François, 58, 105
Vinland, 37
Virgil, 11
Virginia, 118
Visigothic kings, 40
Visigoths, 16
Vives, Luis, 86
Volga, 37, 42, 43

Volney, 143
Voltaire, 104, 123, 125

Waldensians, 64, 66, 82
Wallace, Alfred Russel,
    131-2
Wedding Banquet, the, 90
welfare state, 164
Welsh (people), 148
West Indies, 115
Whitman, Walt, 119
Wilkie, Davis, 148
Williams, Raymond, 157
witchcraft, 25, 31, 94, 95,
    99, 106, 121

women (in religious life),
    20, 26, 31, 64, 94,
    95
Wounded Knee, 119, 120
writing, 6, 8, 9, 39, 40,
    42, 43
Wycliffe, John, 81, 82,
    84

xenophobic myths, 4

Zeus, 7
Zola, 157
Zürich, 94
Zwingli, 85